SCIENCE AND LITERATURE

SCIENCE
AND
LITERATURE
a reader

JOHN J. CADDEN
PATRICK R. BROSTOWIN
Nassau Community College

D. C. HEATH AND COMPANY   BOSTON

PREFACE

The selections contained in this text are designed to show the impact of scientific thought upon English and American literature. At the outset the student is confronted with a series of general essays devoted to an inquiry into the "two cultures" of science and literature. This inquiry has been brought into sharp focus by Sir Charles Snow's famous diagnosis of Western culture, *The Two Cultures and the Scientific Revolution*, in which Snow describes a wide gap, "a gulf of mutual incomprehension," between literary intellectuals and scientists. The writers in the first section are seriously concerned about a cultural conflict in man and about the ultimate survival of his heritage.

The second section contains a selection of critical essays that allows students to carry the general inquiry into specific areas of English and American Literature. These studies of periods and authors explore some important shifts in our cultural heritage, some of the interaction between the worlds of science and literature, and some reactions of particular writers to the rising influence of scientific thought.

The third section, largely intended as a supplement to the second, is a short and highly selected anthology of poetry, fiction, and essays by principal authors discussed in the second section. The literature of each author has been presented in brief units without comment (beyond the thematic titles intended to suggest its relevance to the general inquiry), and although the representation of literature is necessarily very selective, it is hoped that students will find each unit worthwhile for study on its own merits.

Editorial apparatus in this collection has been kept to a minimum. There are footnotes in the essays and literature whenever special allusions cannot be explained through a reading of other selections in the collection. Study aids, including questions on selections, suggested topics for long themes, and a selected bibliography, are all placed at the back of the book.

❖　　❖　　❖

Science tends to be ignored by humanists or literary intellectuals, except defensively, as a discipline altogether outside the pale of

v

belles lettres. But the increasingly broad impact of science threatens to make deliberate ignorance indefensible and even "an act of literary cowardice," as Aldous Huxley has claimed in a recent book.[1]

The achievements of modern science are indeed increasingly awsome: nuclear fission, space exploration, and the discovery of molecular structure in genes are some of the most widely publicized. That these successes are intended to ameliorate man's condition, ultimately freeing him from disease, injury, hunger, and the thousand ills that flesh is heir to, is surely the devout hope of scientists engaged in these tremendous efforts. Hence it is felt that scientific thought, bulking large as it does in English and American letters, deserves more than passing consideration in the English curriculum.

An increasing concern, however, an uneasy feeling that science no longer exists for man, but man for science, has generated doubt and fear among many people. Just as God has slipped away from the epicenter of Western society, with the rise of humanism, giving place to man, so now the feeling exists that man himself is beginning to yield before the pure materiality of things. Finding himself propelled away from the center to the periphery, (where perhaps he will again find God) man leaves behind a vast scientific Pandora box issuing forth evils uncontrollable.

All these considerations have an implication for literature. Superficially they relate to the growing body of science fiction; more importantly they relate to the literary expression of man in a new environment, whether hostile or beneficial, an environment created in part by science, in part by man's political use of his new knowledge. At any rate, its impact upon the literature of the twentieth century is even more striking than that of Galileo on Milton or Newton on Pope and Swift in earlier times.

The editors sincerely hope that through a careful reading of the selections contained herein, followed by lively discussion, students will be better able, as Grimaldi says, to affirm the dignity of the human person against the frightening loss of self, engendered by that vision which Teilhard de Chardin says, "makes human wills founder daily under the crushing number of living things and of stars." [2]

The editors wish to express their gratitude to the Nassau Community College office staff, under the able direction of Miss Esther Wolsky, for typing the original draft of this book. Special thanks are also owed to Dean Thomas T. Johnston for his unfailing cooperation.   J. J. C.—P. R. B.

[1] Aldous Huxley, *Literature and Science* (New York: Harper, Row, 1963).
[2] Canon Teilhard de Chardin, *The Phenomenon of Man* (tr. by Bernard Wall), Harper, 1961.

CONTENTS

Part One THE TWO CULTURES

SCIENCE AND CULTURE thomas henry huxley   3
LITERATURE AND SCIENCE mathew arnold   15
SCIENCE, POETRY, AND POLITICS eric larrabee   24
WHY DO WE TEACH POETRY? archibald macleish   33
THE TWO CULTURES c. p. snow   45

Part Two SCIENCE AND LITERATURE SINCE THE RENAISSANCE

THE ELIZABETHANS: THE MEDIEVAL HERITAGE douglas bush   61
THE SEVENTEENTH CENTURY BACKGROUND basil willey   69
THE BREAKING OF THE CIRCLE marjorie hope nicholson   79
POETRY SOLEMNLY SURVEYS THE NEWTONIAN WORLD
  MACHINE ralph crum   99
THE INTERPLAY OF LITERATURE AND SCIENCE
  ernest de selincourt   114
WORDSWORTH AND SCIENCE b. ifor evans   126
DOUBT AND FAITH IN TENNYSON'S "IN MEMORIAM"
  jerome buckley   137
HAWTHORNE'S "THE BIRTHMARK": SCIENCE AS RELIGION
  r. b. heilman   148

CONTENTS

POE: A CRITICAL STUDY **edward h. davidson** 156

ROBERT FROST: THE STRATEGIC RETREAT
hyatt howe wagonner 168

Part Three ANTHOLOGY OF SELECTED
LITERATURE

TRADITION AND THE NEW PHILOSOPHY

john donne FROM "An Anatomy of the World" 183
FROM *Holy Sonnets*, v 188
"A Valediction: of Weeping" 188

SCIENTIFIC KNOWLEDGE
IN A BIBLICAL SCHEME

john milton *Paradise Lost*—FROM Book I 190
FROM Book VII 194
FROM Book VIII 196

THE WORLD AS AN ORDERED MACHINE

alexander pope *An Essay on Man*—FROM Epistle 1 201
FROM Epistle 2 203

MECHANISTIC THINKING
REDUCED TO ABSURDITY

jonathan swift *Gullivers Travels*—
FROM "A Voyage to Laputa" 206

A MYSTIC'S DENIAL OF
A MECHANICAL WORLD

william blake FROM *Auguries of Innocence* 219
FROM *Songs of Experience* 219
"Mock on, Mock on, Voltaire, Rousseau" 220
FROM *Milton* 220

FACT AND FEELING
IN POETIC IMAGINATION

william wordsworth "The Tables Turned" 222
"Lines . . . Tintern Abbey . . ." 223

FROM *The Prelude*   227
FROM The Preface, *Lyrical Ballads*   229

THE POET AND A DARWINIAN UNIVERSE

alfred tennyson   FROM *In Memoriam*   236

AN AMERICAN ROMANTIC
AND PSYCHOLOGICAL REALITY

edgar allan poe   "Annabel Lee"   250
"The City in the Sea"   251
FROM *Eureka*   252

AN ANALYSIS OF A SCIENTIST'S MORALITY

nathaniel hawthorne   "The Birthmark"   257

DEMOCRACY IN AN EXPANDING UNIVERSE

walt whitman   "Grand Is the Seen"   272
"On the Beach at Night Alone"   272

AN AMERICAN SATIRE ON SCIENCE-WORSHIP

mark twain   "Some Learned Fables for Good Old Boys
and Girls"   274

A MODERN POET'S SKEPTICISM
TOWARD FAITH AND SCIENCE

robert frost   "Astrometaphysical"   291
"Skeptic"   291
"Why Wait for Science"   292
"Sitting by a Bush in Broad Sunlight"   292
"The Armful"   293
"Riders"   293
"The Bear"   293
"Innate Helium"   294

STUDY AIDS

ANALYSIS AND DISCUSSION   297
THEME TOPICS   302
BIBLIOGRAPHIES   305

PART ONE

The Two Cultures

thomas henry huxley

SCIENCE AND CULTURE

. . . From the time that the first suggestion to introduce physical science into ordinary education was timidly whis-
pered, until now, the advocates of scientific education have met
with opposition of two kinds. On the one hand, they have been
pooh-poohed by the men of business who pride themselves on
being the representatives of practicality; while, on the other hand,
they have been excommunicated by the classical scholars, in their
capacity of Levites[1] in charge of the ark of culture and monopolists
of liberal education.

The practical men believed that the idol whom they worship—
rule of thumb—has been the source of the past prosperity, and
will suffice for the future welfare of the arts and manufactures.
They are of opinion that science is speculative rubbish; that theory
and practice have nothing to do with one another; and that the
scientific habit of mind is an impediment, rather than an aid, in
the conduct of ordinary affairs.

I have used the past tense in speaking of the practical men—for
although they were very formidable thirty years ago, I am not sure
that the pure species has not been extirpated. In fact, so far as
mere argument goes, they have been subjected to such a *feu
d'enfer* that it is a miracle if any have escaped. But I have remarked that your typical practical man has an unexpected resem-
blance to one of Milton's angels. His spiritual wounds, such as are
inflicted by logical weapons, may be as deep as a well and as wide
as a church door, but beyond shedding a few drops of ichor, celestial or otherwise, he is no whit the worse. So, if any of these
opponents be left, I will not waste time in vain repetition of the

From *Science and Culture and Other Essays*, 1881.
[1] *Levites:* Sect of privileged priests of the ancient Israelites [Ed.]

3

THOMAS HENRY HUXLEY

demonstrative evidence of the practical value of science; but knowing that a parable will sometimes penetrate where syllogisms fail to effect an entrance, I will offer a story for their consideration.

Once upon a time, a boy, with nothing to depend upon but his own vigorous nature, was thrown into the thick of the struggle for existence in the midst of a great manufacturing population. He seems to have had a hard fight, inasmuch as, by the time he was thirty years of age, his total disposable funds amounted to twenty pounds. Nevertheless, middle life found him giving proof of his comprehension of the practical problems he had been roughly called upon to solve, by a career of remarkable prosperity.

Finally, having reached old age with its well-earned surroundings of "honour, troops of friends," the hero of my story bethought himself of those who were making a like start in life, and how he could stretch out a helping hand to them.

After long and anxious reflection this successful practical man of business could devise nothing better than to provide them with the means of obtaining "sound, extensive, and practical scientific knowledge." And he devoted a large part of his wealth and five years of incessant work to this end.

I need not point the moral of a tale which, as the solid and spacious fabric of the Scientific College assures us, is no fable, nor can anything which I could say intensify the force of this practical answer to practical objections.

We may take it for granted then, that, in the opinion of those best qualified to judge, the diffusion of thorough scientific education is an absolutely essential condition of industrial progress; and that the College which has been opened today will confer an inestimable boon upon those whose livelihood is to be gained by the practise of the arts and manufactures of the district.

The only question worth discussion is, whether the conditions, under which the work of the College is to be carried out, are such as to give it the best possible chance of achieving permanent success.

Sir Josiah Mason, without doubt most wisely, has left very large freedom of action to the trustees, to whom he proposes ultimately to commit the administration of the College, so that they may be able to adjust its arrangements in accordance with the changing conditions of the future. But, with respect to three points, he has laid most explicit injunctions upon both administrators and teachers.

Party politics are forbidden to enter into the minds of either, so far as the work of the College is concerned; theology is as sternly banished from its precincts; and finally, it is especially declared

4

that the College shall make no provision for "mere literary instruction and education."

It does not concern me at present to dwell upon the first two injunctions any longer than may be needful to express my full conviction of their wisdom. But the third prohibition brings us face to face with those other opponents of scientific education, who are by no means in the moribund condition of the practical man, but alive, alert, and formidable.

It is not impossible that we shall hear this express exclusion of "literary instruction and education" from a College which, nevertheless, professes to give a high and efficient education, sharply criticized. Certainly the time was that the Levites of culture would have sounded their trumpets against its walls as against an educational Jericho.

How often have we not been told that the study of physical science is incompetent to confer culture; that it touches none of the higher problems of life; and, what is worse, that the continual devotion to scientific studies tends to generate a narrow and bigoted belief in the applicability of scientific methods to the search after truth of all kinds? How frequently one has reason to observe that no reply to a troublesome argument tells so well as calling its author a "mere scientific specialist." And, as I am afraid it is not permissible to speak of this form of opposition to scientific education in the past tense; may we not expect to be told that this, not only omission, but prohibition, of "mere literary instruction and education" is a patent example of scientific narrow-mindedness?

I am not acquainted with Sir Josiah Mason's reasons for the action which he has taken; but if, as I apprehend is the case, he refers to the ordinary classical course of our schools and universities by the name of "mere literary instruction and education," I venture to offer sundry reasons of my own in support of that action.

For I hold very strongly by two convictions: The first is, that neither the discipline nor the subject-matter of classical education is of such direct value to the student of physical science as to justify the expenditure of valuable time upon either; and the second is, that for the purpose of attaining real culture, an exclusively scientific education is at least as effectual as an exclusively literary education.

I need hardly point out to you that these opinions, especially the latter, are diametrically opposed to those of the great majority of educated Englishmen, influenced as they are by school and university traditions. In their belief, culture is obtainable only by a liberal education; and a liberal education is synonymous, not merely with education and instruction in literature, but in one particular form of literature, namely, that of Greek and Roman antiquity.

5

They hold that the man who has learned Latin and Greek, however little, is educated; while he who is versed in other branches of knowledge, however deeply, is a more or less respectable specialist, not admissible into the cultured caste. The stamp of the educated man, the University degree, is not for him.

I am too well acquainted with the generous catholicity of spirit, the true sympathy with scientific thought, which pervades the writings of our chief apostle of culture to identify him with these opinions; and yet one may cull from one and another of those epistles to the Philistines, which so much delight all who do not answer to that name, sentences which lend them some support.

Mr. Arnold tells us that the meaning of culture is "to know the best that has been thought and said in the world." It is the criticism of life contained in literature. That criticism regards "Europe as being, for intellectual and spiritual purposes, one great confederation, bound to a joint action and working to a common result; and whose members have, for their common outfit, a knowledge of Greek, Roman, and Eastern antiquity, and of one another. Special, local, and temporary advantages being put out of account, that modern nation will in the intellectual and spiritual sphere make most progress, which most thoroughly carries out this programme. And what is that but saying that we too, all of us, as individuals, the more thoroughly we carry it out, shall make the more progress?"

We have here to deal with two distinct propositions. The first, that a criticism of life is the essence of culture; the second, that literature contains the materials which suffice for the construction of such criticism.

I think that we must all assent to the first proposition. For culture certainly means something quite different from learning or technical skill. It implies the possession of an ideal, and the habit of critically estimating the value of things by comparison with a theoretic standard. Perfect culture should supply a complete theory of life, based upon a clear knowledge alike of its possibilities and of its limitations.

But we may agree to all this, and yet strongly dissent from the assumption that literature alone is competent to supply this knowledge. After having learnt all that Greek, Roman, and Eastern antiquity have thought and said, and all that modern literatures have to tell us, it is not self-evident that we have laid a sufficiently broad and deep foundation for that criticism of life, which constitutes culture.

Indeed, to any one acquainted with the scope of physical science, it is not at all evident. Considering progress only in the "intellectual and spiritual sphere," I find myself wholly unable to admit that either nations or individuals will really advance, if their common outfit draws nothing from the stores of physical science. I should say that an army, without weapons of precision and with no particular base of operations, might more hopefully enter upon a campaign on the Rhine, than a man, devoid of a knowledge of what physical science has done in the last century, upon a criticism of life.

When a biologist meets with an anomaly, he instinctively turns to the study of development to clear it up. The rationale of contradictory opinions may with equal confidence be sought in history.

It is, happily, no new thing that Englishmen should employ their wealth in building and endowing institutions for educational purposes. But, five or six hundred years ago, deeds of foundation expressed or implied conditions as nearly as possible contrary to those which have been thought expedient by Sir Josiah Mason. That is to say, physical science was practically ignored, while a certain literary training was enjoined as a means to the acquirement of knowledge which was essentially theological.

The reason of this singular contradiction between the actions of men alike animated by a strong and disinterested desire to promote the welfare of their fellows, is easily discovered.

At that time, in fact, if any one desired knowledge beyond such as could be obtained by his own observation, or by common conversation, his first necessity was to learn the Latin language, inasmuch as all the higher knowledge of the western world was contained in works written in that language. Hence, Latin grammar, with logic and rhetoric, studied through Latin, were the fundamentals of education. With respect to the substance of the knowledge imparted through this channel, the Jewish and Christian Scriptures, as interpreted and supplemented by the Romish Church, were held to contain a complete and infallibly true body of information.

Theological dicta were, to the thinkers of those days, that which the axioms and definitions of Euclid are to the geometers of these. The business of the philosophers of the middle ages was to deduce from the data furnished by the theologians, conclusions in accordance with ecclesiastical decrees. They were allowed the high privilege of showing, by logical process, how and why that which the Church said was true, must be true. And if their demonstrations fell short of or exceeded this limit, the Church was maternally ready to check their aberrations; if need were, by the help of the secular arm.

Between the two, our ancestors were furnished with a compact and complete criticism of life. They were told how the world began

7

and how it would end; they learned that all material existence was but a base and insignificant blot upon the fair face of the spiritual world, and that nature was, to all intents and purposes, the playground of the devil; they learned that the earth is the centre of the visible universe, and that man is the cynosure of things terrestrial, and more especially was it inculcated that the course of nature had no fixed order, but that it could be, and constantly was, altered by the agency of innumerable spiritual beings, good and bad, according as they were moved by the deeds and prayers of men. The sum and substance of the whole doctrine was to produce the conviction that the only thing really worth knowing in this world was how to secure that place in a better which, under certain conditions, the Church promised.

Our ancestors had a living belief in this theory of life, and acted upon it in their dealings with education, as in all other matters. Culture meant saintliness—after the fashion of the saints of those days; the education that led to it was, of necessity, theological; and the way to theology lay through Latin.

That the study of nature—further than was requisite for the satisfaction of everyday wants—should have any bearing on human life was far from the thoughts of men thus trained. Indeed, as nature had been cursed for man's sake, it was an obvious conclusion that those who meddled with nature were likely to come into pretty close contact with Satan. And, if any born scientific investigator followed his instincts, he might safely reckon upon earning the reputation, and probably upon suffering the fate, of a sorcerer.

Had the western world been left to itself in Chinese isolation, there is no saying how long this state of things might have endured. But, happily, it was not left to itself. Even earlier than the thirteenth century, the development of Moorish civilisation in Spain and the great movement of the Crusades had introduced the leaven which, from that day to this, has never ceased to work. At first, through the intermediation of Arabic translations, afterwards by the study of the originals, the western nations of Europe became acquainted with the writings of the ancient philosophers and poets, and, in time, with the whole of the vast literature of antiquity.

Whatever there was of high intellectual aspiration or dominant capacity in Italy, France, Germany, and England, spent itself for centuries in taking possession of the rich inheritance left by the dead civilisations of Greece and Rome. Marvellously aided by the invention of printing, classical learning spread and flourished. Those who possessed it prided themselves on having attained the highest culture then within the reach of mankind.

And justly. For, saving Dante on his solitary pinnacle, there was no figure in modern literature at the time of the Renascence to com-

8

pare with the men of antiquity; there was no art to compete with their sculpture; there was no physical science but that which Greece had created. Above all, there was no other example of perfect intellectual freedom—of the unhesitating acceptance of reason as the sole guide to truth and the supreme arbiter of conduct.

The new learning necessarily soon exerted a profound influence upon education. The language of the monks and schoolmen seemed little better than gibberish to scholars fresh from Virgil and Cicero, and the study of Latin was placed upon a new foundation. Moreover, Latin itself ceased to afford the sole key to knowledge. The student who sought the highest thought of antiquity, found only a second-hand reflection of it in Roman literature, and turned his face to the full light of the Greeks. And after a battle, not altogether dissimilar to that which is at present being fought over the teaching of physical science, the study of Greek was recognised as an essential element of all higher education.

Then the Humanists, as they were called, won the day; and the great reform which they effected was of incalculable service to mankind. But the Nemesis of all reformers is finality; and the reformers of education, like those of religion, fell into the profound, however common, error of mistaking the beginning for the end of the work of reformation.

The representatives of the Humanists, in the nineteenth century, take their stand upon classical education as the sole avenue to culture, as firmly as if we were still in the age of Renascence. Yet, surely, the present intellectual relations of the modern and the ancient worlds are profoundly different from those which obtained three centuries ago. Leaving aside the existence of a great and characteristically modern literature, of modern painting, and, especially, of modern music, there is one feature of the present state of the civilised world which separates it more widely from the Renascence, than the Renascence was separated from the middle ages.

This distinctive character of our own times lies in the vast and constantly increasing part which is played by natural knowledge. Not only is our daily life shaped by it; not only does the prosperity of millions of men depend upon it, but our whole theory of life has long been influenced, consciously or unconsciously, by the general conceptions of the universe, which have been forced upon us by physical science.

In fact, the most elementary acquaintance with the results of scientific investigation shows us that they offer a broad and striking contradiction to the opinion so implicitly credited and taught in the middle ages.

The notions of the beginning and the end of the world entertained by our forefathers are no longer credible. It is very certain that the

THOMAS HENRY HUXLEY

earth is not the chief body in the material universe, and that the
world is not subordinated to man's use. It is even more certain
that nature is the expression of a definite order with which nothing
interferes, and that the chief business of mankind is to learn that
order and govern themselves accordingly. Moreover this scientific
"criticism of life" presents itself to us with different credentials
from any other. It appeals not to authority, nor to what anybody
may have thought or said, but to nature. It admits that all our interpretations of natural fact are more or less imperfect and symbolic,
and bids the learner seek for truth not among words but among
things. It warns us that the assertion which outstrips evidence is
not only a blunder but a crime.

The purely classical education advocated by the representatives
of the Humanists in our day, gives no inkling of all this. A man may
be a better scholar than Erasmus, and know no more of the chief
causes of the present intellectual fermentation than Erasmus did.
Scholarly and pious persons, worthy of all respect, favour us with
allocutions upon the sadness of the antagonism of science to their
mediæval way of thinking, which betray an ignorance of the first
principles of scientific investigation, an incapacity for understanding what a man of science means by veracity, and an unconscious-
ness of the weight of established scientific truths, which is almost
comical.

There is no great force in the *tu quoque* argument, or else the
advocates of scientific education might fairly enough retort upon
the modern Humanists that they may be learned specialists, but that
they possess no such sound foundation for a criticism of life as deserves the name of culture. And, indeed, if we were disposed to be
cruel, we might urge that the Humanists have brought this reproach
upon themselves, not because they are too full of the spirit of the
ancient Greek, but because they lack it.

The period of the Renascence is commonly called that of the
"Revival of Letters," as if the influences then brought to bear upon
the mind of Western Europe had been wholly exhausted in the field
of literature. I think it is very commonly forgotten that the revival
of science, effected by the same agency, although less conspicuous,
was not less momentous.

In fact, the few and scattered students of nature of that day
picked up the clue to her secrets exactly as it fell from the hands of
the Greeks a thousand years before. The foundations of mathematics were so well laid by them, that our children learn their
geometry from a book written for the schools of Alexandria two
thousand years ago. Modern astronomy is the natural continuation
and development of the work of Hipparchus and of Ptolemy; modern physics of that of Democritus and of Archimedes; it was long

10

before modern biological science outgrew the knowledge bequeathed to us by Aristotle, by Theophrastus, and by Galen.

We cannot know all the best thoughts and sayings of the Greeks unless we know what they thought about natural phenomena. We cannot fully apprehend their criticism of life unless we understand the extent to which that criticism was affected by scientific conceptions. We falsely pretend to be the inheritors of their culture, unless we are penetrated, as the best minds among them were, with an unhesitating faith that the free employment of reason, in accordance with scientific method, is the sole method of reaching truth.

Thus I venture to think that the pretensions of our modern Humanists to the possession of the monopoly of culture and to the exclusive inheritance of the spirit of antiquity must be abated, if not abandoned. But I should be very sorry that anything I have said should be taken to imply a desire on my part to depreciate the value of classical education, as it might be and as it sometimes is. The native capacities of mankind vary no less than their opportunities; and while culture is one, the road by which one man may best reach it is widely different from that which is most advantageous to another. Again, while scientific education is yet inchoate and tentative, classical education is thoroughly well organised upon the practical experience of generations of teachers. So that, given ample time for learning and estimation for ordinary life, or for a literary career, I do not think that a young Englishman in search of culture can do better than follow the course usually marked out for him, supplementing its deficiencies by his own efforts.

But for those who mean to make science their serious occupation; or who intend to follow the profession of medicine; or who have to enter early upon the business of life; for all these, in my opinion, classical education is a mistake; and it is for this reason that I am glad to see "mere literary education and instruction" shut out from the curriculum of Sir Josiah Mason's College, seeing that its inclusion would probably lead to the introduction of the ordinary smattering of Latin and Greek.

Nevertheless, I am the last person to question the importance of genuine literary education, or to suppose that intellectual culture can be complete without it. An exclusively scientific training will bring about a mental twist as surely as an exclusively literary training. The value of the cargo does not compensate for a ship's being out of trim; and I should be very sorry to think that the Scientific College would turn out none but lopsided men.

There is no need, however, that such a catastrophe should happen. Instruction in English, French, and German is provided, and thus the three greatest literatures of the modern world are made accessible to the student.

11

French and German, and especially the latter language, are absolutely indispensable to those who desire full knowledge in any department of science. But even supposing that the knowledge of these languages acquired is not more than sufficient for purely scientific purposes, every Englishman has, in his native tongue, an almost perfect instrument of literary expression; and, in his own literature, models of every kind of literary excellence. If an Englishman cannot get literary culture out of his Bible, his Shakespeare, his Milton, neither, in my belief, will the profoundest study of Homer and Sophocles, Virgil and Horace, give it to him.

Thus, since the constitution of the College makes sufficient provision for literary as well as for scientific education, and since artistic instruction is also contemplated, it seems to me that a fairly complete culture is offered to all who are willing to take advantage of it.

But I am not sure that at this point the "practical" man, scotched but not slain, may ask what all this talk about culture has to do with an Institution, the object of which is defined to be "to promote the prosperity of the manufactures and the industry of the country." He may suggest that what is wanted for this end is not culture, nor even a purely scientific discipline, but simply a knowledge of applied science.

I often wish that this phrase, "applied science," had never been invented. For it suggests that there is a sort of scientific knowledge of direct practical use, which can be studied apart from another sort of scientific knowledge, which is of no practical utility, and which is termed "pure science." But there is no more complete fallacy than this. What people call applied science is nothing but the application of pure science to particular classes of problems. It consists of deductions from those general principles, established by reasoning and observation, which constitute pure science. No one can safely make these deductions until he has a firm grasp of the principles; and he can obtain that grasp only by personal experience of the operations of observation and of reasoning on which they are founded.

Almost all the processes employed in the arts and manufactures fall within the range either of physics or of chemistry. In order to improve them, one must thoroughly understand them; and no one has a chance of really understanding them, unless he has obtained that mastery of principles and that habit of dealing with facts, which is given by long-continued and well-directed purely scientific training in the physical and the chemical laboratory. So that there really is no question as to the necessity of purely scientific discipline, even if the work of the College were limited by the narrowest interpretation of its stated aims.

12

And, as to the desirableness of a wider culture than that yielded by science alone, it is to be recollected that the improvement of manufacturing processes is only one of the conditions which contribute to the prosperity of industry. Industry is a means and not an end; and mankind work only to get something which they want. What that something is depends partly on their innate, and partly on their acquired, desires.

If the wealth resulting from prosperous industry is to be spent upon the gratification of unworthy desires, if the increasing perfection of manufacturing processes is to be accompanied by an increasing debasement of those who carry them on, I do not see the good of industry and prosperity.

Now it is perfectly true that men's views of what is desirable depend upon their characters; and that the innate proclivities to which we give that name are not touched by any amount of instruction. But it does not follow that even mere intellectual education may not, to an indefinite extent, modify the practical manifestation of the characters of men in their actions, by supplying them with motives unknown to the ignorant. A pleasure-loving character will have pleasure of some sort; but, if you give him the choice, he may prefer pleasures which do not degrade him to those which do. And this choice is offered to every man, who possesses in literary or artistic culture a never-failing source of pleasures, which are neither withered by age, nor staled by custom, nor embittered in the recollection by the pangs of self-reproach.

If the Institution opened today fulfils the intention of its founder, the picked intelligences among all classes of the population of this district will pass through it. No child born in Birmingham, henceforward, if he have the capacity to profit by the opportunities offered to him, first in the primary and other schools, and afterwards in the Scientific College, need fail to obtain, not merely the instruction, but the culture most appropriate to the conditions of his life.

Within these walls, the future employer and the future artisan may sojourn together for a while, and carry, through all their lives, the stamp of the influences then brought to bear upon them. Hence, it is not beside the mark to remind you, that the prosperity of industry depends not merely upon the improvement of manufacturing processes, not merely upon the ennobling of the individual character, but upon a third condition, namely, a clear understanding of the conditions of social life, on the part of both the capitalist and the operative, and their agreement upon common principles of social action. They must learn that social phenomena are as much the expression of natural laws as any others; that no social arrangements can be permanent unless they harmonise with the requirements of social statics and dynamics; and that, in the nature of things, there is an arbiter whose decisions execute themselves.

But this knowledge is only to be obtained by the application of the methods of investigation adopted in physical researches to the investigation of the phenomena of society. Hence, I confess, I should like to see one addition made to the excellent scheme of education propounded for the College, in the shape of provision for the teaching of Sociology. For though we are all agreed that party politics are to have no place in the instruction of the College; yet in this country, practically governed as it is now by universal suffrage, every man who does his duty must exercise political functions. And, if the evils which are inseparable from the good of political liberty are to be checked, if the perpetual oscillation of nations between anarchy and despotism is to be replaced by the steady march of self-restraining freedom; it will be because men will gradually bring themselves to deal with political, as they now deal with scientific questions; to be as ashamed of undue haste and partisan prejudice in the one case as in the other; and to believe that the machinery of society is at least as delicate as that of a spinning-jenny, and as little likely to be improved by the meddling of those who have not taken the trouble to master the principle of its action.

In conclusion, I am sure that I make myself the mouthpiece of all present in offering to the venerable founder of the Institution, which now commences its beneficent career, our congratulations on the completion of his work; and in expressing the conviction, that the remotest posterity will point to it as a crucial instance of the wisdom which natural piety leads all men to ascribe to their ancestors.

14

matthew arnold

LITERATURE AND SCIENCE

The question is raised whether, to meet the needs of
our modern life, the predominance ought not now to pass from
letters to science; and naturally the question is nowhere raised with
more energy than here in the United States. The design of abasing
what is called "mere literary instruction and education," and of
exalting what is called "sound, extensive, and practical scientific
knowledge," is, in this intensely modern world of the United States,
even more perhaps than in Europe, a very popular design, and
makes great and rapid progress.

I am going to ask whether the present movement for ousting
letters from their old predominance in education, and for transferring the predominance in education to the natural sciences, whether
this brisk and flourishing movement ought to prevail, and whether
it is likely that in the end it really will prevail. . . .

Some of you may possibly remember a phrase of mine which
has been the object of a good deal of comment; an observation to
the effect that in our culture, the aim being *to know ourselves and
the world*, we have, as the means to this end, *to know the best
which has been thought and said in the world.*[1] A man of science,
who is also an excellent writer and the very prince of debaters,
Professor Huxley, in a discourse at the opening of Sir Josiah Mason's college at Birmingham,[2] laying hold of this phrase, expanded
it by quoting some more words of mine, which are these: "The
civilised world is to be regarded as now being, for intellectual and

From *Discourses in America* (Lecture 2: Literature and Science), 1883-
1884.
[1] Italicised phrases are from Arnold's essays "The Function of Criticism"
and "Culture and Anarchy." [Ed.]
[2] See above, Huxley's essay, "Science and Culture." [Ed.]

spiritual purposes, one great confederation, bound to a joint action and working to a common result; and whose members have for their proper outfit a knowledge of Greek, Roman, and Eastern antiquity, and of one another. Special local and temporary advantages being put out of account, that modern nation will in the intellectual and spiritual sphere make most progress which most thoroughly carries out this programme."

Now on my phrase, thus enlarged, Professor Huxley remarks that when I speak of the above-mentioned knowledge as enabling us to know ourselves and the world, I assert *literature* to contain the materials which suffice for thus making us know ourselves and the world. But it is not by any means clear, says he, that after having learnt all which ancient and modern literatures have to tell us, we have laid a sufficiently broad and deep foundation for that criticism of life, that knowledge of ourselves and the world, which constitutes culture. On the contrary, Professor Huxley declares that he finds himself "wholly unable to admit that either nations or individuals will really advance, if their outfit draws nothing from the stores of physical science. An army without weapons of precision, and with no particular base of operations, might more hopefully enter upon a campaign on the Rhine, than a man, devoid of a knowledge of what physical science has done in the last century, upon a criticism of life." . . .

When I speak of knowing Greek and Roman antiquity . . . as a help to knowing ourselves and the world, I mean more than a knowledge of so much vocabulary, so much grammar, so many portions of authors in the Greek and Latin languages; I mean knowing the Greeks and Romans, and their life and genius, and what they were and did in the world; what we get from them, and what is its value. . . .

. . . To know the best that has been thought and said by the modern nations, is to know, says Professor Huxley, "only what modern *literatures* have to tell us; it is the criticism of life contained in modern literature." And yet "the distinctive character of our times," he urges, "lies in the vast and constantly increasing part which is played by natural knowledge." And how, therefore, can a man, devoid of knowledge of what physical science has done in the last century, enter hopefully upon a criticism of modern life?

Let us, I say, be agreed about the meaning of the terms we are using. I talk of knowing the best which has been thought and uttered in the world; Professor Huxley says this means knowing *literature*. Literature is a large word; it may mean everything written with letters or printed in a book. Euclid's *Elements* and Newton's *Principia* are thus literature. All knowledge that reaches us through books is literature. But by literature Professor Huxley means *belles lettres.* He means to make me say, that knowing the best which has been thought and said by the modern nations is knowing their *belles lettres* and no more. And this is no sufficient equipment, he argues, for a criticism of modern life. But as I do not mean by knowing ancient Rome, knowing merely more or less of Latin *belles lettres,* and taking no account of Rome's military, and political, and legal, and administrative work in the world; and as, by knowing ancient Greece, I understand knowing her as the giver of Greek art, and the guide to a free and right use of reason and to scientific method, and the founder of our mathematics and physics and astronomy and biology,—I understand knowing her as all this, and not merely knowing certain Greek poems, and histories, and treatises, and speeches,—so as to the knowledge of modern nations also. By knowing modern nations, I mean not merely knowing their *belles lettres,* but knowing also what has been done by such men as Copernicus, Galileo, Newton, Darwin. . . .

There is, therefore, really no question between Professor Huxley and me as to whether knowing the great results of the modern scientific study of nature is not required as part of our culture, as well as knowing the products of literature and art. But to follow the processes by which those results are reached, ought, say the friends of physical science, to be made the staple of education for the bulk of mankind. And here there does arise a question between those whom Professor Huxley calls with playful sarcasm "the Levites of culture," [3] and those whom the poor humanist is sometimes apt to regard as its Nebuchadnezzars.[4]

The great results of the scientific investigation of nature we are agreed upon knowing, but how much of our study are we bound to give to the processes by which those results are reached? The results have their visible bearing on human life. But all the processes, too, all the items of fact, by which those results are reached and established, are interesting. All knowledge is interesting to a wise man, and the knowledge of nature is interesting to all men. It is very interesting to know, that, from the albuminous white of the egg, the chick in the egg gets the materials for its flesh, bones, blood, and feathers; while, from the fatty yolk of the egg, it gets the heat and energy which enable it at length to break its shell and begin the world. It is less interesting, perhaps, but still it is interesting, to know that when a taper burns, the wax is converted into carbonic acid and water. Moreover, it is quite true that the habit of dealing with facts, which is given by the study of nature, is, as the friends of physical science praise it for being, an excellent dis-

[3] *Levites:* See above, p. 1, Note 1. [Ed.]
[4] *Nebuchadnezzar:* A King of the ancient Babylonians who took the Israelites into captivity. [Ed.]

cipline. The appeal, in the study of nature, is constantly to observation and experiment; not only is it said that the thing is so, but we can be made to see that it is so. Not only does a man tell us that when a taper burns the wax is converted into carbonic acid and water, as a man may tell us, if he likes, that Charon[5] is punting his ferryboat on the river Styx, or that Victor Hugo[6] is a sublime poet, or Mr. Gladstone[7] the most admirable of statesmen; but we are made to see that the conversion into carbonic acid and water does actually happen. This reality of natural knowledge it is, which makes the friends of physical science contrast it, as a knowledge of things, with the humanist's knowledge, which is, say they, a knowledge of words. And hence Professor Huxley is moved to lay it down that, "for the purpose of attaining real culture, an exclusively scientific education is at least as effectual as an exclusively literary education." And a certain President of the Section for Mechanical Science in the British Association is, in Scripture phrase, "very bold," and declares that if a man, in his mental training, "has substituted literature and history for natural science, he has chosen the less useful alternative." But whether we go these lengths or not, we must all admit that in natural science the habit gained of dealing with facts is a most valuable discipline, and that every one should have some experience of it.

More than this, however, is demanded by the reformers. It is proposed to make the training in natural science the main part of education, for the great majority of mankind at any rate. And here, I confess, I part company with the friends of physical science, with whom up to this point I have been agreeing. . . .

All knowledge is, as I said just now, interesting; and even items of knowledge which from the nature of the case cannot well be related, but must stand isolated in our thoughts, have their interest. Even lists of exceptions have their interest. If we are studying Greek accents, it is interesting to know that *pais* and *pas,* and some other monosyllables of the same form of declension, do not take the circumflex upon the last syllable of the genitive plural, but vary, in this respect, from the common rule. If we are studying physiology, it is interesting to know that the pulmonary artery carries dark blood and the pulmonary vein carries bright blood, departing in this respect from the common rule for the division of labour between the

[5] *Charon:* According to the ancient Greek, Charon ferried the souls of the dead across the River Styx to the underworld. [Ed.]
[6] *Victor Hugo:* (1802-1885) Prolific poet and novelist of 19th century France. [Ed.]
[7] *Mr. Gladstone:* William Ewart Gladstone (1809-1898), eminent political leader and Prime Minister in Victorian England. [Ed.]

veins and the arteries. But every one knows how we seek naturally to combine the pieces of our knowledge together, to bring them under general rules, to relate them to principles; and how unsatisfactory and tiresome it would be to go on for ever learning lists of exceptions, or accumulating items of fact which must stand isolated.

Well, that same need of relating our knowledge, which operates here within the sphere of our knowledge itself, we shall find operating, also, outside that sphere. We experience, as we go on learning and knowing,—the vast majority of us experience,—the need of relating what we have learnt and known to the sense which we have in us for conduct, to the sense which we have in us for beauty. . . .

But, no doubt, some kinds of knowledge cannot be made to directly serve the instinct in question, cannot be directly related to the sense for beauty, to the sense for conduct. These are instrument-knowledges; they lead on to other knowledges, which can. A man who passes his life in instrument-knowledges is a specialist. They may be invaluable as instruments to something beyond, for those
• who have the gift thus to employ them; and they may be disciplines in themselves wherein it is useful for every one to have some schooling. But it is inconceivable that the generality of men should pass all their mental life with Greek accents or with formal logic. . . .

The natural sciences do not, however, stand on the same footing with these instrument-knowledges. Experience shows us that the generality of men will find more interest in learning that, when a taper burns, the wax is converted into carbonic acid and water, or in learning the explanation of the phenomenon of dew, or in learning how the circulation of the blood is carried on, than they find in learning that the genitive plural of *pais* and *pas* does not take the circumflex on the termination. And one piece of natural knowledge is added to another, and others are added to that, and at last we come to propositions so interesting as Mr. Darwin's famous proposition that "our ancestor was a hairy quadruped furnished with a tail and pointed ears, probably arboreal in his habits." . . .

Interesting, indeed, these results of science are, important they are, and we should all of us be acquainted with them. But what I now wish you to mark is, that we are still, when they are propounded to us and we receive them, we are still in the sphere of intellect and knowledge. And for the generality of men there will be found, I say, to arise, when they have duly taken in the proposition that their ancestor was "a hairy quadruped furnished with a tail and pointed ears, probably arboreal in his habits," there will be found to arise an invincible desire to relate this proposition to the sense in us for conduct, and to the sense in us for beauty. But this the men of science will not do for us, and will hardly even profess to do. They will give us other pieces of knowledge, other facts, about other animals and their ancestors, or about plants, or about stones, or about stars; and they may finally bring us to those great "general conceptions of the universe, which are forced upon us all," says Professor Huxley, "by the progress of physical science." But still it will be *knowledge* only which they give us; knowledge not put for us into relation with our sense for conduct, our sense for beauty, and touched with emotion by being so put; not thus put for us, and therefore, to the majority of mankind, after a certain while, unsatisfying, wearying.

Not to the born naturalist, I admit. But what do we mean by a born naturalist? We mean a man in whom the zeal for observing nature is so uncommonly strong and eminent, that it marks him off from the bulk of mankind. Such a man will pass his life happily in collecting natural knowledge and reasoning upon it, and will ask for nothing, or hardly anything, more. I have heard it said that the sagacious and admirable naturalist whom we lost not very long ago, Mr. Darwin, once owned to a friend that for his part he did not experience the necessity for two things which most men find so • necessary to them,—religion and poetry; science and the domestic affections, he thought, were enough.[8] To a born naturalist, I can well understand that this should seem so. So absorbing is his occupation with nature, so strong his love for his occupation, that he goes on acquiring natural knowledge and reasoning upon it, and has little time or inclination for thinking about getting it related to the desire in man for conduct, the desire in man for beauty. He relates it to them for himself as he goes along, so far as he feels the need; and he draws from the domestic affections all the additional solace necessary. But then Darwins are extremely rare. Another great and admirable master of natural knowledge. Faraday,[9] was a Sandemanian. That is to say, he related his knowledge to his instinct for conduct and to his instinct for beauty, by the aid of that respectable Scottish sectary, Robert Sandeman.[10] And so strong, in general, is the demand of religion and poetry to have their share in a man, to associate themselves with his knowing, and to relieve and rejoice it, that, probably, for one man amongst us with the

---

[8] Arnold was apparently unaware of Darwin's sentiments on poetry and the arts as expressed in the scientist's *Autobiography:* "If I had to live my life again, I would have made a rule to read some poetry or listen to some music at least once every week; for perhaps the parts of my brain now atrophied, would thus have kept active through use." [Ed.]

[9] *Faraday:* Michael Faraday (1791-1867), English physicist and chemist especially noted for his brilliant experiments with electricity. [Ed.]

[10] *Sandemanian:* A follower of Robert Sandeman (1718-1771) and John Glas (1695-1773), liberal Scottish theologians who advocated removing the more fanatical sectarian feeling from Calvinism, and held that the spirit of Christ alone could unify the diverse powers of man for good. [Ed.]

disposition to do as Darwin did in this respect, there are at least fifty with the disposition to do as Faraday.

Education lays hold upon us, in fact, by satisfying this demand. Professor Huxley holds up to scorn mediaeval education, with its neglect of the knowledge of nature, its poverty even of literary studies, its formal logic devoted to "showing how and why that which the Church said was true and must be true." But the great mediaeval Universities were not brought into being, we may be sure, by the zeal for giving a jejune and contemptible education. Kings have been their nursing fathers, and queens have been their nursing mothers, but not for this. The mediaeval Universities came into being, because the supposed knowledge, delivered by Scripture and the Church, so deeply engaged men's hearts, by so simply, easily, and powerfully relating itself to their desire for conduct, their desire for beauty. All other knowledge was dominated by this supposed knowledge and was subordinated to it, because of the surpassing strength of the hold which it gained upon the affections of men, by allying itself profoundly with their sense for conduct, their sense for beauty.

But now, says Professor Huxley, conceptions of the universe fatal to the notions held by our forefathers have been forced upon us by physical science. Grant to him that they are thus fatal, that the new conceptions must and will soon become current everywhere, and that every one will finally perceive them to be fatal to the beliefs of our forefathers. The need of humane letters, as they are truly called, because they serve the paramount desire in men that good should be for ever present to them,—the need of humane letters, to establish a relation between the new conceptions, and our instinct for beauty, our instinct for conduct, is only the more visible. The Middle Age could do without humane letters, as it could do without the study of nature, because its supposed knowledge was made to engage its emotions so powerfully. Grant that the supposed knowledge disappears, its power of being made to engage the emotions will of course disappear along with it,—but the emotions themselves, and their claim to be engaged and satisfied, will remain. Now if we find by experience that humane letters have an undeniable power of engaging the emotions, the importance of humane letters in a man's training becomes not less, but greater, in proportion to the success of modern science in extirpating what it calls "mediaeval thinking."

Have humane letters, then, have poetry and eloquence, the power here attributed to them of engaging the emotions, and do they exercise it? And if they have it and exercise it, *how* do they exercise it, so as to exert an influence upon man's sense for conduct, his sense for beauty? Finally, even if they both can and do exert an in-

21

fluence upon the senses in question, how are they to relate to them the results,—the modern results,—of natural science? All these questions may be asked. First, have poetry and eloquence the power of calling out the emotions? The appeal is to experience. Experience shows that for the vast majority of men, for mankind in general, they have the power. Next, do they exercise it? They do. But then, *how* do they exercise it so as to affect man's sense for conduct, his sense for beauty? And this is perhaps a case for applying the Preacher's words: "Though a man labour to seek it out, yet he shall not find it; yea, farther, though a wise man think to know it, yet shall he not be able to find it." [11] Why should it be one thing, in its effect upon the emotions, to say, "Patience is a virtue," and quite another thing, in its effect upon the emotions, to say with Homer,

"for an enduring heart have the destinies appointed to the children of men"? [12]

Why should it be one thing, in its effect upon the emotions, to say with the philosopher Spinoza, *Felicitas in eo consistit quod homo suum esse conservare potest*—"Man's happiness consists in his being able to preserve his own essence," and quite another thing, in its effect upon the emotions, to say with the Gospel, "What is a man advantaged, if he gain the whole world, and lose himself, forfeit himself"? How does this difference of effect arise? I cannot tell, and I am not much concerned to know; the important thing is that it does arise, and that we can profit by it. But how, finally, are poetry and eloquence to exercise the power of relating the modern results of natural science to man's instinct for conduct, his instinct for beauty? And here again I answer that I do not know *how* they will exercise it, but that they can and will exercise it I am sure. I do not mean that modern philosophical poets and modern philosophical moralists are to come and relate for us, in express terms, the results of modern scientific research to our instinct for conduct, our instinct for beauty. But I mean that we shall find, as a matter of experience, if we know the best that has been thought and uttered in the world, we shall find that the art and poetry and eloquence of men who lived, perhaps, long ago, who had the most limited natural knowledge, who had the most erroneous conceptions about many important matters, we shall find that this art, and poetry, and eloquence, have in fact not only the power of refreshing and delighting us, they have also the power,—such is the strength and worth, in essentials, of their authors' criticism of life,

[11] Ecclesiastes, 8:17.
[12] Iliad, xxiv, 49.

—they have a fortifying, and elevating, and quickening, and suggestive power, capable of wonderfully helping us to relate the results of modern science to our need for conduct, our need for beauty. Homer's conceptions of the physical universe were, I imagine, grotesque; but really, under the shock of hearing from modern science that "the world is not subordinated to man's use, and that man is not the cynosure of things terrestrial," I could, for my own part, desire no better comfort than Homer's line which I quoted just now,

"for an enduring heart have the destinies appointed to the children of men"!

And the more that men's minds are cleared, the more that the results of science are frankly accepted, the more that poetry and eloquence come to be received and studied as what in truth they really are,—the criticism of life by gifted men, alive and active with extraordinary power at an unusual number of points;—so much the more will the value of humane letters, and of art also, which is an utterance having a like kind of power with theirs, be felt and acknowledged, and their place in education be secured.

Let us therefore, all of us, avoid indeed as much as possible any invidious comparison between the merits of humane letters, as means of education, and the merits of the natural sciences. But when some President of a Section for Mechanical Science insists on making the comparison, and tells us that "he who in his training has substituted literature and history for natural science has chosen the less useful alternative," let us make answer to him that the student of humane letters only, will, at least, know also the great general conceptions brought in by modern physical science; for science, as Professor Huxley says, forces them upon us all. But the student of the natural sciences only, will, by our very hypothesis, know nothing of humane letters; not to mention that in setting himself to be perpetually accumulating natural knowledge, he sets himself to do what only specialists have in general the gift for doing genially. And so he will probably be unsatisfied, or at any rate incomplete, and even more incomplete than the student of humane letters only. . . .

If then there is to be separation and option between humane letters on the one hand, and the natural sciences on the other, the great majority of mankind, all who have not exceptional and overpowering aptitudes for the study of nature, would do well, I cannot but think, to choose to be educated in humane letters rather than in the natural sciences. Letters will call out their being at more points, will make them live more. . . .

eric larrabee

SCIENCE, POETRY, AND POLITICS

One of the paradoxes of the present period is that science, while relaxing metaphysical claims, has extended social ones. It is not unusual for the modern American scientist to find himself making demands on society that would formerly have been thought unnecessary to make—for financial support, for freedom from interference, for understanding of scientific aspirations and techniques on the part of the public. In protecting his own self-interest as a scientist he is compelled to enter arenas of value judgment from which science, as a philosophy, has progressively withdrawn itself. The principles on which claims might be based are no longer, if they ever were, generally accepted; and on every hand are signs of anti-scientific sentiment. Deprived of the protective devices that operate within the scientific fold, the scientist is confronted with the problem of how to conduct himself in the fields of nonscientific behavior, of which poetry and politics, one for individuals and the other for society as a whole, are two extremes.

If the need were merely for a better press, for "selling science to the people," then the AAAS [American Association for the Advancement of Science] could hire a competent public-relations counsel and leave the matter in qualified hands. Unfortunately it is nothing of the kind. The problem of Anti-science, though it may be a subdivision of the larger one of Anti-intellect, is not amenable to the manipulation of opinions. Palliative measures—like encouragements for more and better teaching and popularization of science —do not alter the conditions that have brought it into existence. They are, in fact, likely to be self-defeating and to alienate as

From *Science*, Vol. 117 (April 17, 1953), pp. 395-399. Reprinted by permission of the author and publisher.

often as they attract. The trouble is not too little publicity but too much, not its failure but its success. Scientists as a class, like nearly every other in contemporary America, are prone to exaggerate the degree to which they are persecuted, ignoring the existence of their own prestige in order to visualize themselves as underdogs. The vast admiration that science actually enjoys is not only more widely shared than the antipathies against it, it is partly responsible for them. At least one source of Anti-science lies in the deepening absorption of science by society, a further interpenetration of one by the other than had earlier existed. Anti-science is in many respects the friction that this process inevitably generates.

I do not mean to minimize the difficulties that scientists face, particularly since I write as an avowed generalist whose own problem is of a different, if not opposite, nature. But I write also in the conviction that they cannot be reduced without lay participation, that they involve propositions on which nonscientists have a responsibility to speak, and that science is much too important (to paraphrase Clemenceau) to be left to scientists alone. The limitations on a layman's prerogative are obvious and need neither be elaborated nor excused. This paper has no other justification than to offer scientists an outsider's view of their predicament. It is a sympathetic one, although it may not invariably appear so. The writer is fully aware how precarious his position is, but would rather take his chances than apologize for it, in the belief that science will be better served by friendly criticism than it is at present by its uncritical friends. Only from the outside, in any event, can the claims that science is now making beyond its proper sphere be validated.

II

The situation would be simpler to describe if those claims reached farther and were more vigorously engaged. "From nucleonics to sociology," writes the physiologist Ralph W. Gerard, "there exists in principle a continuum." Why stop at sociology? If there exists a definable boundary at which the orders of knowledge become qualitatively different, it must lie on the scale well beyond the region where the human personality begins overtly to intrude itself. If sociology is part of the scientific continuum, if only in principle, then so also must be the humanistic studies of behavior, which draw on poetry and politics, among other resources, for their factual evidence. Admittedly this is a wavering line of controversy, but it is the one from which science in the past quarter century has conducted a metaphysical retreat. The brave assertions of the behaviorists—like John B. Watson's "We need nothing to explain behavior but the ordinary laws of physics and chemistry"

—are no longer to be heard except in faint echoes among the Social Physicists. During the same period in which science has made its longest forward strides in both performance and public esteem, it has reduced its aims and shortened its philosophical reach.

To be sure, it would be unreasonable to expect science to be permanently associated with optimism, even about itself. An increase in knowledge, as we frequently are reminded, is also an increase in ignorance. Only the innovators of scientific method like Descartes and Bacon could assume that, if it were widely and truly applied, all conceivable questions about the cosmos would be answered in from six to sixty years. Yet it is curious that scientific self-confidence should fluctuate as it does, from one generation to the next, especially in its relationship to competing and conflicting doctrines. Nowhere is this more apparent than in the rhythm of changing tensions between science and religion, which at the moment have fallen slack and seem not to be of pressing importance. No one thinks it strange that the Pope should enunciate a doctrine of creation timed to an expanding universe or that a scientist of the stature of E. U. Condon should speak of the "truths of science" and the "truths of religion" as though they were complementary. Such circumspection must be both a puzzle and a relief to mature scientists now at work who can remember the Scopes trial, or who may indeed have grown up on Andrew White's *History of the Warfare of Science with Theology in Christendom.* Confronted with the current revival of religiosity among intellectuals, they must be tantalized by the ironical thought that science has won all the battles but lost the war.

Obviously such is not the case. A great deal of confidence in science—as, for that matter, of science in itself—is dormant, beneath the surface, taken for granted, and no less operative because it is unobtrusive. Despairing scientists in search of a more realistic impression of what has happened should perhaps observe more closely the morale of their opponents, who are compelled to admit, like the British theologian C. S. Lewis, that the war *is* over and that a materialist faith is everywhere triumphant. To the Anti-scientist, also thinking himself an underdog, this era seems saturated with a pragmatical disregard of supernatural sanctions. The easy-going empiricism of everyday life, in that sense, is both an index of science's success and a potential source of its strength, however little bearing it has on scientific philosophy at a sophisticated level. The point at issue here, however, is not the score of an intangible contest between ideologies. It is apparent that in science's house are many mansions, that there are many ways of "believing" in it or not, and that its forward progress about its main business does not depend directly on the regard in which it is held. Science has at best a negative or indirect effect on numerous currents in the climate of opinion, including some that have an effect on the intellectual reputability and what might be called the "political" status of science. Yet one could fairly deduce, I think, if only from the contemporary preoccupation of scientists with proselytizing and with self-protection, that in the near future no *status quo* for science, in its nonscientific situations, can be maintained.

III

For the purposes of the paragraphs which follow, it will be assumed that advance and retreat are the only alternative tactics and that of the two the former is preferred. Perhaps it is debatable whether science can ever serve as a universal organizing pinciple for those who are unable to apprehend its subtleties. Years of disciplined study, as Ernest Nagel has argued, are required for understanding the conceptions now employed at the outer edges of scientific advance. Perhaps the injunction of James B. Conant, that the uninformed public refrain from speculation of any kind about a subject (nuclear weapons, in this instance) on which essential facts must be concealed, reflects a typical pattern of divided knowledge to which we must become permanently reconciled. I should prefer not to think so, and not to accept the specialist's point of view, though it is valid in itself, without a generalist's modification. "Great scientific advances are not now," as Charles Singer writes, "nor have they ever been, of their own nature specially difficult of comprehension. . . . If those men of science be right who assume as inevitable their own unintelligibility to a public all too ready to accept this assumption, then is the outlook of our age gloomy indeed." Rather, let us assume that science has no theoretical limits, either of applicability or acceptance.

What, then, are the obstacles to advance? Many of them come quickly to mind—mistrust and resentment of a morally neutral position, of a specialist outside his specialty, of allegiance to principles above national jurisdictions, of disturbing opinions for which no individual can be held accountable, and so on. Leaving aside those persons who oppose science for simple doctrinaire or unconsidered reasons, there is clearly a complex of many attitudes involved for the thousands of educated and rational people who, to the seeming detriment of science, continue to hold nonscientific beliefs. Since their convictions have survived as much as half a century of concerted attack, it is unlikely that they will be converted overnight, or by a television program on recent developments in marine biology. Many of them are apparently satisfied with a working allegiance to technology, rather than to science, as the fount of material welfare. If forced to choose between cumu-

27

lative and noncumulative types of knowledge, many will reject the former in favor of the arts and letters that make life worth living and remain alive while science goes out of date. If science is to make any significant inroads on Anti-science in our lifetime, these are the people who must be convinced that science has music and color and poetry of its own.

I have not contrasted poetry with science in the naïve belief that all scientists are by definition insensitive to poetry. Yet disparagement of intuition in any form is a part of the scientific tradition, even if it is not universal or compulsory, or limited to scientists, for that matter. There is a certain thread of consistency in the response of scientists and poets to one another, from Bacon onward (how anyone, incidentally, who knew Bacon's low opinion of poetry could think he wrote the plays of Shakespeare is one of the real mysteries of nonscientific behavior). Newton was not alone among scientists in thinking poetry "a kind of ingenious nonsense," nor Blake among poets in calling science "the tree of death." Over a period of centuries, it is also a one-sided relationship, for the most part, with poets making the greater attempt to accommodate science than the other way around. They were more interested in Newton than he was in them, as in our own day T. S. Eliot has encompassed more science than science has encompassed him. While poets have struggled to preserve a place for value in a world of fact, few scientists have had to concern themselves with finding a place for fact in a world of value.

We might be better off today if more of them had. Many readers of this journal are presumably familiar with the deplorable state of isolation from its audience into which the poetic art is generally thought to have fallen. Many of them may be surprised to know, however, that several critics hold modern science responsible for this. The two most recent scholarly books on the subject—Douglas Bush's *Science and English Poetry* and Hyatt Howe Waggoner's *The Heel of Elohim: Science and Values in Modern American Poetry*—share the view that all modern poetry has been conditioned by science, even when seeming to react adversely, into avoiding clear and logical statement in favor of intentional complexity, ellipsis, and ambiguity. Mr. Waggoner puts it thus:

> Now if the observational and experimental techniques of science really constitute the only valid approaches to truth . . . then it follows that poetry, if it is to seem significant, should . . . appeal to the sensibility (defined as primarily if not wholly emotional) but not to reason. . . . It should, indeed it must, be this kind of poetry to be taken seriously: for we cannot take it seriously if it is only poor science (it is clearly very bad science). . . . It must be thus, then, because in a world in which a divorce has been arranged between

28

fact and value, poetry, which cannot compete with science in handling the kind of facts that science handles—and these are thought to be the only *facts* there are—poetry must keep strictly to the realm of value and leave the other realm to science.

"So much the better!" might be the reply of scientists who hold that science has no other responsibility than the untrammeled pursuit of its own ends. Yet if they choose to live and wish to be effective in a world in which poetry is also a fact, in which emotions undeniably exist and operate then their position is untenable. Since it is little better than verbal and essentially false, the distinction between fact and value crumbles at the touch. In a strictly observational fashion, it is impossible to find values that are free of fact or facts that are free of value: the notion that one may do so is merely a convenience, and it becomes increasingly less convenient the more we suffer its arbitrary and obnoxious consequences. If science builds its future on these shifting sands it will not only build poorly, it will invite the ultimate undermining of the structure by the forces thus removed from scientific sustenance and restraint.

Science, at its own peril, may continue to treat the intuitions of which poetry is the purest product as an unrelated avenue of experience. The materials on which the poetic intuition works are no less factual because they are not statistically handled, nor is the intuitive process less accurate because it is rapid and deals with probabilities, using a mental shorthand in which intermediary steps may not be consciously performed. Intuition is commonly called upon to manage an unlimited number of variables—the connotations, say, that a given word in a given poem will have for all possible readers—and to produce an approximate answer instantaneously. Intuitive conclusions may often be wrong, but not *because* they are intuitive or because any other method could have produced better ones. I trust these words will not be misinterpreted as a request that science scuttle mathematics and experiment forthwith, to rely henceforward on hunches and inspired guesswork—though much fruitful scientific work has had an assist from intuition in the past, and will presumably continue to enjoy its unpredictable and irreplaceable aid. Nothing need be abandoned that is now possible, nothing need be sacrificed that has proved its worth in any category, in lowering the artificial barrier that separates science from the proper studies of mankind. I do not presume that the sciences of the nonscientific which eventually result will be exact facsimiles of mid-twentieth-century models—or that they will need nothing more than "the ordinary laws of physics and chemistry"—but I do presume that they will be scientific in the best sense, in the traditional sense, which is science's only permanent legacy.

IV

Already there is a mounting body of evidence to suggest what the outcome will be if science hesitates to extend itself and withdraws into the security of only those "facts" that can be weighed and measured, or entered in the coding devices of electronic computers. In a mass-educated society people crave enlightenment, and, when they do not receive it from accredited sources, they will search elsewhere. Much of the faddist and crank behavior that perplexes and annoys the scientific community, often giving it the sense of being surrounded by a sea of irrationality, belongs in a grouping that might be titled "vacuum phenomena." Where an admiring but overdramatized picture of psychiatry is more widely accessible than reputable treatment, the result is dianetics. Where there is a pervasive sense of inadequate diet but only sporadic efforts to improve it, the result is Gayelord Hauser. Whenever large numbers of individuals are willing to make themselves ridiculous in the face of orthodox opinion, at a cost of which they are quickly made aware, there is likely to be an element among their motives that is not ridiculous at all. Much harm was caused by the liars and mental invalids who claimed to have seen flying saucers, but much harm was also caused by scientists who persisted in offering explanations that did not explain, insisting that no others were needed, and labeling all disagreement hysterical during the six years that elapsed before Donald Menzel's sympathetic, reflective, and apparently definitive book on flying saucers was published. If he is right, then the previous "explanations" were wrong; and they harmed science in their facile assumption that all nonscientists are equally susceptible to hallucinations, and that all science was called upon to do was rap a few knuckles.

Hence a pronouncement like that of Michael Polanyi—"a society which wants to foster science must accept the authority of scientific opinion"—seems to me to be subject to considerable qualification. There can be no question of the right, nay, the obligation of scientists to decide for themselves what textbooks and journals will be published under their own auspices, what appointments will be made to their faculties and institutions of research, or to what projects their own time and effort will be devoted. Yet there seems to me to be a very large question whether this is the same thing as the acceptance of "the authority of scientific opinion" by nonscientists, or whether there is any substitute for free and open discussion on any questions that affect the entire society. The amount of money to be allocated to a National Science Foundation is just such a question, and the unhappy incident that occurred the first time it came up is highly illustrative. Among certain disrespectful nonscientists of my acquaintance, there was unseemly but understandable mirth when scientists, as a pressure group, lined up at the public trough with other pressure groups and suddenly discovered that they exerted no pressure. It was a salutary lesson.

One cannot be effective in politics while remaining above it. One cannot wield political power without accepting political responsibility, which is primarily the responsibility to respect the politics of others. I am very much afraid that ever since the threat of atomic warfare brought American scientists into politics on a large scale—and into government employ on an even larger scale—there has been a marked tendency among them to patronize the political scene, to sneer at it, and at the same time to seek to dominate it as a privileged caste. Like the poet, the politician must develop a healthy respect for facts, which are no less real because they are imponderable. He must manage a number of variables at least as large as the number of his constituents, and if his intuitive statistical processes for so doing do not average out successful answers, he ceases to be a politician. Here, on the other hand, is a representative sample of a "scientific" verdict on politics, taken from a symposium on cytology published by a college press:

> We have to see to it that somehow future statesmen, members of the judiciary, the clergy, and other leaders of the people, the molders of public opinion, have a more "scientific" outlook than most now have. But in the meantime we scientists have also somehow got to take a larger part in the formulation of public policy than we have so far been doing. Here we run into a real problem: how determine policies without being a politician? And how can a good scientist be a good politician? For the essence of the politician's art is to make people think as he wants them to. . . .

Anyone who wonders why science has come upon hard times politically need only read that paragraph. It is loaded with emotional assumptions that put a nonscientist's teeth on edge, and that lead nonscientists who seek to defend science into black despair. I am reminded of a physicist with whom I once discussed the "problem" of Anti-science; he said that it seemed to him perfectly natural that people should resent the scientist's superiority. There is a word for this, gentlemen, and the word is arrogance. It has nothing to do with science proper, it is not required by the needs of dedicated and impartial investigation; and it is certainly not sustainable on an evidential basis. It is an archaic prop to the ego, a social and psychological bad habit left over from the bad manners of nineteenth-century academic life, and fortunately it is already on the way out. But it is still one of the first and most unnerving aspects of science that many laymen encounter, and it has done incalculable harm.

v

A scientist might conclude, presented with these arguments for modifying the rigid definitions that separate science from other forms of human activity, that an effort was being made by laymen to penetrate science and to take over its time-honored functions. The prospect that existing distinctions might be blurred suggests this fear to Dr. Polanyi: "It would not only become practically meaningless to describe anyone as a scientist, but even to refer to any statement as a scientific proposition. Science would become, in effect, extinct." In all respect, I cannot share the logic of this defensive orientation. The opposite danger, that science might lose the fertilizing and revivifying contributions which amateurs have always made to it, seems to me equally great if not greater. And for science to lose contact with society at large would be, of course, disastrous. Error we shall always have with us, within the sacred precincts as well as without, and a dreary record of historical failures underlines the fallacy of supposing that any one group may purify itself and live apart. Is it an abrogation of the scientist's independent judgment to rejoin the race of common folk on more workable terms of equality than now pertain?

The "mad scientist" who is so consistent a figure of modern folklore is not entirely the product of envy and ignorance. There is justice—poetic justice, if you like—in the popular view of the archetypical scientist as a warped and incomplete being, a man who has isolated one component of the universal experience and cultivated it to the exclusion of all others. Science itself, in a historical perspective, has achieved its triumphs as well as its tragedies by imposing an arbitrary but significant order on the undifferentiated flux of nature. There is a sense in which science consists legitimately of distortion, in which one can say that all great scientific discoveries appear initially to be contrary to common sense, and in which the Western civilization that science has profoundly shaped now dominates the world precisely because it is neurotic. But it seems highly unlikely that this pattern of dissociation can survive the coming fifty years without serious damage to both science and society, and of the powerful collective forces now coming into play none is more hopeful than the urge of scientists themselves toward synthesis, both of one special field of study with another and of one with all.

That is why, as a nonscientist who wishes to see science prosper, I am relatively undisturbed at the image of a world in which scientists would be indistinguishable from people, in which scien-

32

tists would be men and women first and scientists second, and in which—perhaps, in ways that scientists today may find difficult to visualize—everyone else will be scientists, too. The human condition is crowded with ambiguities, and all our acts have unintended consequences. The act itself of posing the scientific dilemma in these terms will suggest to the reader countless other terms in which it might also be posed, perhaps irritating him where it ought to soothe and offering consolation where it ought to kindle wrath. These are emotional objects of dispute, charged with old quarrels and haloed with the motivations we impute to one another. They are not, in that respect, "scientific," but I commend them to the attention of scientists, lest they be left indefinitely in other, and ultimately less sympathetic, hands.

archibald macleish

WHY DO WE TEACH POETRY?

There is something about the art of poetry which induces a defensive posture. Even in the old days when the primacy of poetry was no more challenged than the primacy of Heaven, which is now also challenged, the posture was habitual. If you published your reflections on the art in those days you called them a *Defense*.[1] Today, when the queen of sciences is Science,[2] you do not perhaps employ that term but you mean it. It is not that the gentlemen at the long table in the Faculty Club whose brains have been officially cleared to serve as depositories of scientific secrets of the eighth and thirteenth classes are patronizing in their manner. They are still gentlemen and therefore still modest no matter how great their distinction or how greatly certified. But one knows one's place. One knows that whereas the teachers of science meet to hear of new triumphs which the newspapers will proudly report, the teachers of poetry meet to ask old questions—which no one will report: such questions as, why teach poetry anyway in a time like this?

It is a relief in this general atmosphere to come upon someone who feels no defensiveness whatever: who is perfectly certain that poetry ought to be taught now as at any other time and who is perfectly certain also that he knows why. The paragon I have in mind is a young friend of mine, a devoted teacher, who was recently made headmaster of one of the leading American preparatory schools, and who has been taking stock, for some time past, of

Reprinted from *The Atlantic Monthly*, Vol. 197 (March, 1956), pp. 48-53. Copyright © 1956 by Archibald MacLeish.
[1] E.g. Sir Philip Sidney's *Apology for Poetry* (1595), P. B. Shelley's *Defense of Poetry* (1821).
[2] And not philosophy, as was formerly said.

his curriculum and his faculty. Poetry, as he sees it, ought to be taught "as a most essential form of human expression as well as a carrier throughout the ages of some of the most important values in our heritage." What troubles him is that few teachers, at least in the schools he knows, seem to share his conviction. He is not too sure that teachers themselves have "an abiding and missionary faith in poetry" which would lead them to see it as a great clarifier —a "human language" capable of competing with the languages and mathematics and science.

But though teachers lack the necessary faith, the fault, as my young friend sees it, is not wholly theirs. The fault is the fault of modern criticism, which has turned poetry into something he calls "poetry itself"—meaning, I suppose, poetry for poetry's sake. "Poetry itself" turns out to be poetry with its meanings distilled away, and poetry with its meanings distilled away is difficult if not impossible to teach in a secondary school—at least *his* secondary school. The result is that secondary school teachers have gone back, as to the lesser of two evils, to those historical and anecdotal practices sanctified by American graduate schools in generations past. They teach "poets and not poetry." With the result that "students become acquainted with poets from Homer to MacLeish" (quite a distance no matter how you measure it!) "but the experience doesn't necessarily leave them with increased confidence in what poetry has to offer." I can well believe it.

The reason why modern criticism has this disastrous effect, the reason why it produces "an almost morbid apathy toward 'content' or 'statement of idea,'" is its excessive "preoccupation with aesthetic values." Modern criticism insists that poems are primarily works of art; and when you insist that poems are primarily works of art you cannot, in my friend's view, teach them as carriers "throughout the ages of some of the most important values in our heritage." What is important about Homer and Shakespeare and the authors of the Bible is that they were "realists with great vision . . . whose work contains immensely valuable constructions of the meaning of life"; and if you talk too much about them as artists, those constructions of the meaning of life get lost.

Now this, you will observe, is not merely another walloping of the old horse who was once called the New Criticism. It goes a great deal farther. It is a frontal attack upon a general position maintained by many who never accepted the New Criticism or even heard of it. It is an attack upon those who believe—as most poets, I think, have believed—that a poem is primarily a work of art and must be read as a work of art if it is to be read at all. It is a high-minded and disinterested attack delivered for the noblest

35

of purposes, but an attack notwithstanding—and an effective one. What it contends is that an approach to poetry which insists that a poem is a work of art blocks off what the poem has to say, whereas what the poem has to say is the principal reason for teaching it. What the argument comes down to, in other words, is the proposition that it is a mistake, in teaching poetry, to insist that poetry is art, because, if you do so insist, you will not be able to bring your students to the meaning of the poem, the idea of the poem, what the poem has to tell them about man and world and life and death—and it is for these things the teaching of the poem is important.

Now, I can understand this argument and can respect the reasons for making it. Far too many of those who define poetry in exclusively artistic terms use their definition as a limiting and protective statement which relieves them of all obligation to drive the poem's meanings beyond the meanings of the poem: beyond the mere translation of the symbols and metaphors and the classical or other references—the whole apparatus of *explication du texte* [explanation of the text itself]. Far too many, indeed, of those who have to do with literature generally in our time, and particularly with modern literature, consider that meanings in any but a literary (which includes a Freudian) sense are not only outside, but beneath, their proper concern—that the intrusion of questions of morality and religion into the world of art is a kind of trespass and that works of literary art not only should but *can* be studied in a moral vacuum. Literature in the hands of such teachers is well on the way to becoming again that "terrible queen" which the men of the nineties raised above life and which Yeats, when he outgrew the men of the nineties, rejected.

But although I can understand this argument, and although I can respect its reasons, and although I believe it raises a true issue and an important issue, I cannot accept it; for it rests, or seems to me to rest, on two quite dubious assumptions. The first is the assumption, familiar in one form or another to all of us, that the "idea" of a work of art is somehow separable from the work of art itself. The most recent—and most egregious—expression of this persistent notion comes from a distinguished Dean of Humanities in a great institution of learning who is reported by the New York *Times* to have argued in a scholarly gathering that "the idea which the reader derives from Ernest Hemingway's *The Old Man and the Sea* comes after the reader has absorbed some 60,000 words. This takes at least an hour. . . . A similar understanding could come after a few minutes study of a painting by a skillful artist." Precisely, one imagines, as the Doré illustrations gave one the "idea" of the *Inferno* in a few easy looks!

II

It is the second assumption, however, which divides me most emphatically from my young friend. For the second assumption seems to be that *unless* idea and work of art are distinguished from each other in the teaching of a poem, the idea—and so the effectiveness of the teaching—will be lost. At this point my friend and I part company. I am ready, and more than ready, to agree that it is for the meanings of life that one reads (and teaches) poetry. But I am unable to see how there can be a distinction between a poem as a conveyer of such meanings and a poem as a work of art. In brief, the distinction between art and knowledge which is made throughout my friend's argument seems to me wholly without foundation. That it is a distinction almost universally recognized in our epoch I know well enough. Science makes it. Poetry makes it. And the world agrees with both. "Whatever can be *known*," says Bertrand Russell, "can be known by means of science." Poetry, say its professors, has no "messages" to deliver. And no one dissents from either. The exclusive proprietary right of science to know and to communicate knowledge is not only commonly recognized in our civilization: in a very real sense it is our civilization. For the characteristic of our civilization—that which distinguishes it from the civilizations which have preceded it—is the characteristic which knowledge-by-science has conferred upon it: its abstractness.

But though the agreement is general, the proposition is not one I can accept. I argue that the apologists for science are not justified in claiming, nor the apologists for poetry in admitting, the sole right of science to know. I insist that poetry is also capable of knowledge; that poetry, indeed, is capable of a kind of knowledge of which science is not capable; that it is capable of that knowledge *as poetry;* and that the teaching of poetry as poetry, the teaching of poem as work of art, is not only not incompatible with the teaching of poetry as knowledge but is, indeed, the only possible way of teaching poetry as knowledge.

To most of us, brought up as we have been in the world of abstractions which science has prepared for us, and in the kind of school which that world produces—schools in which almost all teaching is teaching of abstractions—the notion of poetry as knowledge, the notion of art as knowledge, is a fanciful notion. Knowledge by abstraction we understand. Science can abstract ideas about apple from apple. It can organize those ideas into knowledge about apple. It can then, by some means, introduce that knowledge into our heads—possibly because our heads are abstractions also. But poetry, we know, does not abstract. Poetry presents. Poetry pre-

37

ARCHIBALD MACLEISH

sents the thing as the thing. And that it should be possible to *know* the thing *as the thing it is*—to *know* apple *as* apple—this we do not understand; this, the true child of the time will assure you, cannot be done. To the true child of abstraction you can't know apple as apple. You can't know tree as tree. You can't know man as man. All you can *know* is a world dissolved by analyzing intellect into abstraction—not a world composed by imaginative intellect into itself. And the result, for the generations of abstraction, is that neither poetry not art can be a means to knowledge. To inspiration, yes: poetry can undoubtedly lead to that—whatever it is. To revelation, perhaps: there may certainly be moments of revelation in poetry. But to knowledge, no. The only connection between poetry and knowledge we can see is the burden of used abstractions—adages and old saws—which poetry, some poetry, seems to like to carry—adages most of which we knew before and some of which aren't even true.

But if all this is so, what then is the "experience of art"—the "experience of poetry"—which all of us who think about these things at all have known? What is the experience of *realization* which comes over us with those apples on a dish of Cézanne's or those three pine trees? What is the experience of realization which comes over us with Debussy's *Nuages*? What is the experience of realization which comes over us when Coleridge's robin sits and sings

> Betwixt the tufts of snow on the bare branch
> Of mossy apple-tree, while the nigh thatch
> Smokes in the sun thaw; . . .

or when his eave-drops fall

> Heard only in the trances of the blast,
> Or if the secret ministry of frost
> Shall hang them up in silent icicles,
> Quietly shining to the quiet Moon.

And if all this is so, why does one of the most effective of modern definitions of poetry (Arnold's in his letter to Maurice de Guérin) assign to that art the peculiar "power of so dealing with *things* as to awaken in us a wonderfully full, new, and intimate sense of them and of our relation with them"?

The answer is, of course, that the children of abstraction are wrong—and are impoverished by their error, as our entire time is impoverished by it. They are wrong on both heads. They are wrong when they think they *can* know the world through its abstractions: nothing can be known through an abstraction but the abstraction itself. They are wrong also when they think they *cannot* know the world as the world: the whole achievement of art is a demonstration to the contrary. And the reason they are wrong on both heads is the reason given, quite unintentionally, by Matthew Arnold. They are wrong because they do not realize that all true knowledge is a matter of relation: that we *really* know a thing only when we are filled with "a wonderfully full, new, and intimate sense of it" and, above all, of "our relation with" it. This sense—this *knowledge* in the truest meaning of the word knowledge—art can give but abstraction cannot.

There are as many proofs as there are successful works of art. Take, for obvious example, that unseen mysterious phenomenon, the wind. Take any attempt, by the familiar processes of abstraction, to "know" the wind. Put beside it those two familiar lines of George Meredith:—

> Mark where the pressing wind shoots javelin-like
> Its skeleton shadow on the broad-backed wave!

What will be the essential difference between the two? Will it not be that the first, the analytical, statement is or attempts to be a wholly objective statement made without reference to an observer (true everywhere and always), whereas an observer—one's self as observer!—is involved in the second? And will not the consequential difference be that a relation involving one's self is created by the second but not by the first? And will not the end difference be that the second, but not the first, will enable us to know the thing itself—to know what the thing is like?

It would be quite possible, I suppose, to semanticize this difference between knowledge by poetry and knowledge by abstraction out of existence by demonstrating that the word, know, is being used in two different senses in the two instances, but the triumph would be merely verbal, for the difference is real. It is indeed the realest of all differences, for what it touches is the means by which we come at reality. How are we to find the knowledge of reality in the world without, or in the shifting, flowing, fluid world within? Is all this a task for the techniques of abstraction—for science as it may be or as it is? Is it through abstraction alone that we are to find what is real in our experience of our lives—and so, conceivably, what is real in ourselves? Or do we need another and a different way of knowing—a way of knowing which will make that world out there, this world in here, available to us, not by translating them into something else—into abstractions of quantity and measure—but by bringing us ourselves to confront them as they are—man and tree face to face in the shock of recognition, man and love face to face?

ARCHIBALD MACLEISH

The question, I beg you to see, is not what we ought to do. There is no ought. A man can "live" on abstractions all his life if he has the stomach for them, and many of us have—not the scientists only, but great numbers of the rest of us in this contemporary world, men whose days are a web of statistics, and names, and business deals, held together by the parentheses of a pair of commuting trains with three Martinis at the close. The question is not what we ought to do. The question is what we have the choice of doing—what alternatives are open to us. And it is here and in these terms that the issue presents itself to the teacher of poetry.

III

Colleges and universities do not exist to impose duties but to reveal choices. In a civilization like ours in which one choice has all but overwhelmed the other, a civilization dominated by abstraction, in which men are less and less able to deal with their experience of the world or of themselves unless experience and self have first been translated into abstract terms—a civilization like a foreign language—in such a civilization the need for an understanding of the alternative is urgent. What must be put before the generation of the young is the possibility of a knowledge of experience *as* experience, of self *as* self; and that possibility only the work of art, only the poem, can reveal. That it is so rarely, or so timidly, presented in our schools is one of the greatest failures of our educational system. Young men and young women graduate from American schools and colleges by the hundreds of thousands every year to whom science is the only road to knowledge, and to whom poetry is little more than a subdivision of something called "literature"—a kind of writing printed in columns instead of straight across the page and primarily intended to be deciphered by girls, who don't read it either.

This sort of thing has consequences. Abstractions are wonderfully clever tools for taking things apart and for arranging things in patterns but they are very little use in putting things together and no use at all when it comes to determining what things are *for*. Furthermore, abstractions have a limiting, a dehumanizing, a dehydrating effect on the relation to things of the man who must live with them. The result is that we are more and more left, in our scientific society, without the means of knowledge of ourselves as we truly are or of our experience as it actually is. We have the tools, all the tools—we are suffocating in tools—but we cannot find the actual wood to work or even the actual hand to work it. We begin with one abstraction (something we think of as ourselves) and a mess of other abstractions (standing for the world) and we arrange and rearrange the counters, but who we are and what we are doing we simply do not know—above all what we are doing. With the inevitable consequence that we do not know either what our purpose is or our end. So that when the latest discoveries of the cyclotron are reported we hail them with the cry that we will now be able to control nature better than ever before—but we never go on to say for what purpose, to what end, we will control her. To destroy a city? To remake a world?

It was something of this kind, I imagine, that Adlai Stevenson had in mind when he startled a Smith Commencement last spring by warning his newly graduated audience of prospective wives that the "typical Western man—or typical Western husband—operates well in the realm of means, as the Roman did before him. But outside his specialty, in the realm of ends he is apt to operate poorly or not at all. . . . The neglect of the cultivation of more mature values," Mr. Stevenson went on, "can only mean that his life, and the life of the society he determines, will lack valid purpose, however busy and even profitable it may be."

As he has so often done before, Mr. Stevenson there found words for an uneasiness which has been endemic but inarticulate in the American mind for many years—the sense that we are getting nowhere far too fast and that, if something doesn't happen soon, we may arrive. But when he came to spell out the causes for "the neglect of the cultivation of more mature values" Mr. Stevenson failed, or so it seems to me, to identify the actual villain. The contemporary environment in America, he told his young listeners, is "an environment in which 'facts,' the data of the senses, are glorified and value judgments are assigned inferior status as 'mere matters of opinion.' It is an environment in which art is often regarded as an adornment of civilization rather than a vital element of it, while philosophy is not only neglected but deemed faintly disreputable because 'it never gets you anywhere.' " It is true that philosophy is neglected, and even truer that art is regarded in this country generally as it seems to be regarded by the automobile manufacturers of Detroit: as so much enamel paint and chromium to be applied for allegedly decorative purposes to the outside of a car which would run better without it. But the explanation is not, I think, that we set facts—even facts in quotation marks—above values, or that we glorify the data of the senses, unless one means by that latter phrase not what the senses tell us of the world we live in but what the statistics that can be compiled out of the data of the senses would tell us if we were ever in touch with our senses.

In few civilizations have the senses been less alive than they are with us. Look at the cities we build and occupy—but look at them! —the houses we live in, the way we hold ourselves and move; listen to the speaking voices of the greater part of our women.

And in no civilization, at least in recorded time, have human beings been farther from the *facts* we mean by that word, facets of
reality. Our indifference to ends is the result of our obsession with
abstractions rather than facts: with the ideas of things rather than
with things. For there can be no concern for ends without a hunger
for reality. And there can be no hunger for reality without a sense
of the real. And there can be no sense of the real in the world
which abstraction creates, for abstraction is incapable of the real:
it can neither lay hold of the real itself nor show us where to find
it. It cannot, that is to say, create the *relation* between reality and
ourselves which makes knowledge of reality possible, for neither
reality nor ourselves exist in abstraction. Everything in the world
of abstraction is object. And, as George Buttrick pointedly says,
we are not objects: we are subjects.

IV

But all this is a negative way of saying what a defender of poetry
should not be afraid of saying positively. Let me say it. We have
lost our concern with ends because we have lost our touch with
reality and we have lost our touch with reality because we are
estranged from the means to reality which is the poem—the work
of art. To most members of our generation this would seem an extravagant statement but it is not extravagant in fact and would
not have seemed so in another time. In ancient China the place of
poetry in men's lives was assumed as matter of course; indeed, the
polity was based on it. The three hundred and five odes or songs
which make up the Song-word Scripture survived to the fourth
century B.C., when Confucius is said to have collected them because they were part of the government records preserved in the
Imperial Archive. For thousands of years the examinations for the
Chinese civil service were examinations in poetry, and there is no
record that the results were more disappointing to the throne than
examinations of a different character might have been. Certainly
there is no record that a Chinese civil servant ever attempted to
deny an honor student in a military academy his commission in the
imperial army *or* navy because he was friendly with his own
mother! [3] Idiocies which the study of science and of other abstractions in contemporary institutions of naval education in the United
States seem to nourish were apparently cauterized from the mind
by the reading of poems.

It was not for nothing that Confucius told his disciples that the
three hundred and five songs of the Song-word Scripture could be
boiled down to the commandment: "Have no twisty thoughts."

[3] In August 1955 the United States government refused an ensign's
reserve commission to Midshipman Eugene Landy because he had been
"extremely close" to his mother, a former Communist.

You cannot have twisty thoughts if you are real and if you are thinking about real things. But if a mother is merely a biological event to you and if you yourself are merely a military event called an admiral, anything may happen: you may make your country ridiculous, humiliate a promising boy, and deprive the navy of a good officer, all in the twisted belief that you are being a wise man and a patriot.

One can see, not only in the three hundred and five songs, but in Chinese poetry of other periods, what Confucius meant. Consider two Chinese poems of the second century B.C. and the sixth of our era, both written by Emperors. The first is a poem of grief —of the sense of loss of someone loved: a poem therefore of that inward world of feeling, of emotion, which seems to us most nearly ourselves and which, because it is always in flux, always shifting and changing and flowing away, is, of all parts of our experience of our lives, most difficult to know. We cannot know it through science. We cannot know it by knowing things about it—even the shrewdest and most intelligent things, helpful though they may be to us in other ways. We cannot know it either by merely feeling it—by uttering its passing urgencies, crying out "I love" meaning "I think of myself as loving" or sobbing "I grieve" meaning "I think of myself as grieving." How then can we know it?

The Emperor Wu-ti wrote (this is Arthur Waley's beautiful translation):—

> The sound of her silk skirt has stopped.
> On the marble pavement dust grows.
> Her empty room is cold and still.
> Fallen leaves are piled against the doors.
>
> Longing for that lovely lady
> How can I bring my aching heart to rest?

Four images, one of sound, two of sight, one of feeling, each like a note plucked on a stringed instrument. Then a question like the chord the four would make together. And all at once we know. We know this grief which no word could have described, which any abstraction the mind is capable of would have destroyed. But we know more than this grief: we know our own—or will when it shall visit us—and so know something of ourselves.

The second is a poem of that emotion, that feeling, which is even more difficult to know than grief itself. The second is a poem of delight: youth and delight—the morning of the world—the emotion, of all emotions, most difficult to stop, to hold, to see. "Joy whose hand is ever at his lips bidding adieu" [John Keats, "Ode on Melancholy," lines 22-23]. How would you *know* delight in yourself and therefore yourself delighting? Will the psychiatrists tell you?

43

ARCHIBALD MACLEISH

Is there a definition somewhere in the folios of abstraction by which we attempt to live which will capture it for you? The Emperor Ch'ien Wen-ti (again Waley's translation) knew that there is only one mirror which will hold that vanishing smile: the mirror of art, the mirror of the poem:—

> A beautiful place is the town of Lo-yang:
> The big streets are full of spring light
> The lads go driving out with harps in their hands:
> The mulberry girls go out to the fields with their baskets
> Golden whips glint at the horses' flanks,
> Gauze sleeves brush the green boughs.
> Racing dawn and the carriages come home—
> And the girls with their high baskets full of fruit.

In this world within, you see, this world which is ourselves, there is no possibility of knowing by abstracting the meaning out—or what we hope will be the meaning. There we must know things *as* themselves and it must be *we* who know them. Only art, only poetry, can bring about that confrontation, because only art, only poetry, can show us what we are and ourselves confronting it. To be ignorant of poetry is to be ignorant therefore of the one means of reaching the world of our experience of the world. And to be ignorant of *that* world is to be ignorant of who and what we are. And to be ignorant of who and what we are is to be incapable of reality no matter what tools we have, or what intelligence, or what skills. It is this incapacity, this impotence, which is the tragedy of the time we live in. We are spiritually impotent because we have cut ourselves off from the poem. And the crowning irony is that it is only in the poem that we can know how impotent we have become.

Why do we teach poetry in this scientific age? To present the great alternative not to science but to that knowledge by abstraction which science has imposed. And what is this great alternative? Not the "messages" of poems, their interpreted "meanings," for these are abstractions also—abstractions far inferior to those of science. Not the explications of poetic texts, for the explication of a poetic text which goes no farther ends only in abstraction.

No, the great alternative is the poem as itself, the poem as a poem, the poem as a work of art—which is to say, the poem in the context in which alone the work of art exists: the context of the world, of the man and of the thing, of the infinite relationship which is our lives. To present the great alternative is to present the poem not as a message in a bottle, and not as an object in an uninhabited landscape, but as an action in the world, an action in which we ourselves are actors and our lives are known.

44

c. p. snow

THE TWO CULTURES

It is about three years since I made a sketch in print of a problem which had been on my mind for some time.[1] It was a problem I could not avoid just because of the circumstances of my life. The only credentials I had to ruminate on the subject at all came through those circumstances, through nothing more than a set of chances. Anyone with similar experience would have seen much the same things and I think made very much the same comments about them. It just happened to be an unusual experience. By training I was a scientist: by vocation I was a writer. That was all. It was a piece of luck, if you like, that arose through coming from a poor home.

But my personal history isn't the point now. All that I need say is that I came to Cambridge and did a bit of research here at a time of major scientific activity. I was privileged to have a ringside view of one of the most wonderful creative periods in all physics. And it happened through the flukes of war—including meeting W. L. Bragg in the buffet on Kettering station on a very cold morning in 1939, which had a determining influence on my practical life—that I was able, and indeed morally forced, to keep that ringside view ever since. So for thirty years I have had to be in touch with scientists not only out of curiosity, but as part of a working existence. During the same thirty years I was trying to shape the books I wanted to write, which in due course took me among writers.

There have been plenty of days when I have spent the working hours with scientists and then gone off at night with some literary

Reprinted by permission from Cambridge University Press from *The Two Cultures and the Scientific Revolution* by C. P. Snow © 1959.
[1] "The Two Cultures," *New Statesman,* 6 October 1956.

colleagues. I mean that literally. I have had, of course, intimate friends among both scientists and writers. It was through living among these groups and much more, I think, through moving regularly from one to the other and back again that I got occupied with the problem of what, long before I put it on paper, I christened to myself as the "two cultures." For constantly I felt I was moving among two groups—comparable in intelligence, identical in race, not grossly different in social origin, earning about the same incomes, who had almost ceased to communicate at all, who in intellectual, moral and psychological climate had so little in common that instead of going from Burlington House or South Kensington to Chelsea, one might have crossed an ocean.

In fact, one had travelled much further than across an ocean—because after a few thousand Atlantic miles, one found Greenwich Village talking precisely the same language as Chelsea, and both having about as much communication with M.I.T. as though the scientists spoke nothing but Tibetan. For this is not just our problem; owing to some of our educational and social idiosyncrasies, it is slightly exaggerated here, owing to another English social peculiarity it is slightly minimised; by and large this is a problem of the entire West.

By this I intend something serious. I am not thinking of the pleasant story of how one of the more convivial Oxford great dons —I have heard the story attributed to A. L. Smith—came over to Cambridge to dine. The date is perhaps the 1890's. I think it must have been at St. John's, or possibly Trinity. Anyway, Smith was sitting at the right hand of the President—or Vice-Master—and he was a man who liked to include all around him in the conversation, although he was not immediately encouraged by the expressions of his neighbours. He addressed some cheerful Oxonian chit-chat at the one opposite to him, and got a grunt. He then tried the man on his own right hand and got another grunt. Then, rather to his surprise, one looked at the other and said, "Do you know what he's talking about?" "I haven't the least idea." At this, even Smith was getting out of his depth. But the President, acting as a social emollient, put him at his ease, by saying, "Oh, those are mathematicians! We never talk to *them*."

No, I intend something serious. I believe the intellectual life of the whole of western society is increasingly being split into two polar groups. When I say the intellectual life, I mean to include also a large part of our practical life, because I should be the last person to suggest the two can at the deepest level be distinguished. I shall come back to the practical life a little later. Two polar groups: at one pole we have the literary intellectuals, who incidentally while no one was looking took to referring to themselves as "intellectuals" as though there were no others. I remember G. H. Hardy once remarking to me in mild puzzlement, some time in the 1930's: "Have you noticed how the word 'intellectual' is used nowadays? There seems to be a new definition which certainly doesn't include Rutherford or Eddington or Dirac or Adrian or me. It does seem rather odd, don't y' know." [2]

Literary intellectuals at one pole—at the other scientists, and as the most representative, the physical scientists. Between the two a gulf of mutual incomprehension—sometimes (particularly among the young—hostility and dislike, but most of all lack of understanding. They have a curious distorted image of each other. Their attitudes are so different that, even on the level of emotion, they can't find much common ground. Non-scientists tend to think of scientists as brash and boastful. They hear Mr T. S. Eliot, who just for these illustrations we can take an archetypal figure, saying about his attempts to revive verse-drama, that we can hope for very little, but that we would feel content if he and his co-workers could prepare the ground for a new Kyd or a new Greene. That is the tone, restricted and constrained, with which literary intellectuals are at home: it is the subdued voice of their culture. Then they hear a much louder voice, that of another archetypal figure, Rutherford, trumpeting: "This is the heroic age of science! This is the Elizabethan age!" Many of us heard that, and a good many other statements beside which that was mild; and we weren't left in any doubt whom Rutherford was casting for the role of Shakespeare. What is hard for the literary intellectuals to understand, imaginatively or intellectually, is that he was absolutely right.

And compare "this is the way the world ends, not with a bang but a whimper"—incidentally, one of the least likely scientific prophecies ever made—compare that with Rutherford's famous repartee, "Lucky fellow, Rutherford, always on the crest of the wave." "Well, I made the wave, didn't I?"

The non-scientists have a rooted impression that the scientists are shallowly optimistic, unaware of man's condition. On the other hand, the scientists believe that the literary intellectuals are totally lacking in foresight, peculiarly unconcerned with their brother men, in a deep sense anti-intellectual, anxious to restrict both art and thought to the existential moment. And so on. Anyone with a mild talent for invective could produce plenty of this kind of subterranean back-chat. On each side there is some of it which is

[2] This lecture was delivered to a Cambridge audience, and so I used some points of reference which I did not need to explain. G. H. Hardy, 1877-1947, was one of the most distinguished pure mathematicians of his time, and a picturesque figure in Cambridge both as a young don and on his return in 1931 to the Sadleirian Chair of Mathematics.

C. P. SNOW

not entirely baseless. It is all destructive. Much of it rests on misinterpretations which are dangerous. I should like to deal with two of the most profound of these now, one on each side.

First, about the scientists' optimism. This is an accusation which has been made so often that it has become a platitude. It has been made by some of the acutest non-scientific minds of the day. But it depends upon a confusion between the individual experience and the social experience, between the individual condition of man and his social condition. Most of the scientists I have known well have felt—just as deeply as the non-scientists I have known well—that the individual condition of each of us is tragic. Each of us is alone: sometimes we escape from solitariness, through love or affection or perhaps creative moments, but those triumphs of life are pools of light we make for ourselves while the edge of the road is black: each of us dies alone. Some scientists I have known have had faith in revealed religion. Perhaps with them the sense of the tragic condition is not so strong. I don't know. With most people of deep feeling, however high-spirited and happy they are, sometimes most with those who are happiest and most high-spirited, it seems to be right in the fibres, part of the weight of life. That is as true of the scientists I have known best as of anyone at all.

But nearly all of them—and this is where the colour of hope genuinely comes in—would see no reason why, just because the individual condition is tragic, so must the social condition be. Each of us is solitary: each of us dies alone: all right, that's a fate against which we can't struggle—but there is plenty in our condition which is not fate, and against which we are less than human unless we do struggle.

Most of our fellow human beings, for instance, are underfed and die before their time. In the crudest terms, *that* is the social condition. There is a moral trap which comes through the insight into man's loneliness: it tempts one to sit back, complacent in one's unique tragedy, and let the others go without a meal.

As a group, the scientists fall into that trap less than others. They are inclined to be impatient to see if something can be done: and inclined to think that it can be done, until it's proved otherwise. That is their real optimism, and it's an optimism that the rest of us badly need.

In reverse, the same spirit, tough and good and determined to fight it out at the side of their brother men, has made scientists regard the other culture's social attitudes as contemptible. That is too facile: some of them are, but they are a temporary phase and not to be taken as representative.

I remember being cross-examined by a scientist of distinction. "Why do most writers take on social opinions which would have

48

been thought distinctly uncivilised and démodé at the time of the Plantagenets? Wasn't that true of most of the famous twentieth-century writers? Yeats, Pound, Wyndham Lewis, nine out of ten of those who have dominated literary sensibility in our time—weren't they not only politically silly, but politically wicked? Didn't the influence of all they represent bring Auschwitz that much nearer?"

I thought at the time, and I still think, that the correct answer was not to defend the indefensible. It was no use saying that Yeats, according to friends whose judgment I trust, was a man of singular magnanimity of character, as well as a great poet. It was no use denying the facts, which are broadly true. The honest answer was that there is, in fact, a connection, which literary persons were culpably slow to see, between some kinds of early twentieth-century art and the most imbecile expressions of anti-social feeling.[3] That was one reason, among many, why some of us turned our backs on the art and tried to hack out a new or different way for ourselves.[4]

But though many of those writers dominated literary sensibility for a generation, that is no longer so, or at least to nothing like the same extent. Literature changes more slowly than science. It hasn't the same automatic corrective, and so its misguided periods are longer. But it is ill-considered of scientists to judge writers on the evidence of the period 1914-50.

Those are two of the misunderstandings between the two cultures. I should say, since I began to talk about them—the two cultures, that is—I have had some criticism. Most of my scientific acquaintances think that there is something in it, and so do most of the practising artists I know. But I have been argued with by non-scientists of strong down-to-earth interests. Their view is that it is an over-simplification, and that if one is going to talk in these terms there ought to be at least three cultures. They argue that, though they are not scientists themselves, they would share a good deal of the scientific feeling. They would have as little use—perhaps, since they knew more about it, even less use—for the recent literary culture as the scientists themselves. J. H. Plumb, Alan Bullock and some of my American sociological friends have said that they vigorously refuse to be corralled in a cultural box with people they wouldn't be seen dead with, or to be regarded as helping to produce a climate which would not permit of social hope.

[3] I said a little more about this connection in *The Times Literary Supplement*, "Challenge to the Intellect," 15 August 1958. I hope some day to carry the analysis further.
[4] It would be more accurate to say that, for literary reasons, we felt the prevailing literary modes were useless to us. We were, however, reinforced in that feeling when it occurred to us that those prevailing modes went hand in hand with social attitudes either wicked, or absurd, or both.

I respect those arguments. The number 2 is a very dangerous number: that is why the dialectic is a dangerous process. Attempts to divide anything into two ought to be regarded with much suspicion. I have thought a long time about going in for further refinements: but in the end I have decided against. I was searching for something a little more than a dashing metaphor, a good deal less than a cultural map: and for those purposes the two cultures is about right, and subtilising any more would bring more disadvantages than it's worth.

At one pole, the scientific culture really is a culture, not only in an intellectual but also in an anthropological sense. That is, its members need not, and of course often do not, always completely understand each other; biologists more often than not will have a pretty hazy idea of contemporary physics; but there are common attitudes, common standards and patterns of behaviour, common approaches and assumptions. This goes surprisingly wide and deep. It cuts across other mental patterns, such as those of religion or politics or class.

Statistically, I suppose slightly more scientists are in religious terms unbelievers, compared with the rest of the intellectual world —though there are plenty who are religious, and that seems to be increasingly so among the young. Statistically also, slightly more scientists are on the Left in open politics—though again, plenty always have called themselves conservatives, and that also seems to be more common among the young. Compared with the rest of the intellectual world, considerably more scientists in this country and probably in the U.S. come from poor families.[5] Yet, over a whole range of thought and behaviour, none of that matters very much. In their working, and in much of their emotional life, their attitudes are closer to other scientists than to non-scientists who in religion or politics or class have the same labels as themselves. If I were to risk a piece of shorthand, I should say that naturally they had the future in their bones.

They may or may not like it, but they have it. That was as true of the conservatives J. J. Thomson and Lindemann as of the radicals Einstein or Blackett: as true of the Christian A. H. Compton as of the materialist Bernal: of the aristocrats Broglie or Russell as of the proletarian Faraday: of those born rich, like Thomas Merton or Victor Rothschild, as of Rutherford, who was the son of an odd-job handyman. Without thinking about it, they respond alike. That is what a culture means.

[5] An analysis of the schools from which Fellows of the Royal Society come tells its own story. The distribution is markedly different from that of, for example, members of the Foreign Service or Queen's Counsel.

At the other pole, the spread of attitudes is wider. It is obvious that between the two, as one moves through intellectual society from the physicists to the literary intellectuals, there are all kinds of tones of feeling on the way. But I believe the pole of total incomprehension of science radiates its influence on all the rest. That total incomprehension gives, much more pervasively than we realise, living in it, an unscientific flavour to the whole "traditional" culture, and that unscientific flavour is often, much more than we admit, on the point of turning anti-scientific. The feelings of one pole become the anti-feelings of the other. If the scientists have the future in their bones, then the traditional culture responds by wishing the future did not exist.[6] It is the traditional culture, to an extent remarkably little diminished by the emergence of the scientific one, which manages the western world.

This polarisation is sheer loss to us all. To us as people, and to our society. It is at the same time practical and intellectual and creative loss, and I repeat that it is false to imagine that those three considerations are clearly separable. But for a moment I want to concentrate on the intellectual loss.

The degree of incomprehension on both sides is the kind of joke which has gone sour. There are about fifty thousand working scientists in the country and about eighty thousand professional engineers or applied scientists. During the war and in the years since, my colleagues and I have had to interview somewhere between thirty to forty thousand of these—that is, about 25 per cent. The number is large enough to give us a fair sample, though of the men we talked to most would still be under forty. We were able to find out a certain amount of what they read and thought about. I confess that even I, who am fond of them and respect them, was a bit shaken. We hadn't quite expected that the links with the traditional culture should be so tenuous, nothing more than a formal touch of the cap.

As one would expect, some of the very best scientists had and have plenty of energy and interest to spare, and we came across several who had read everything that literary people talk about. But that's very rare. Most of the rest, when one tried to probe for what books they had read, would modestly confess, "Well, I've *tried* a bit of Dickens," rather as though Dickens were an extraordinarily esoteric, tangled and dubiously rewarding writer, something like Rainer Maria Rilke. In fact that is exactly how they do regard him: we thought that discovery, that Dickens had been transformed into the type-specimen of literary incomprehensibility, was one of the oddest results of the whole exercise.

[6] Compare George Orwell's *1984*, which is the strongest possible wish that the future should not exist, with J. D. Bernal's *World Without War*.

C. P. SNOW

But of course, in reading him, in reading almost any writer whom we should value, they are just touching their caps to the traditional culture. They have their own culture, intensive, rigorous, and constantly in action. This culture contains a great deal of argument, usually much more rigorous, and almost always at a higher conceptual level, than literary persons' arguments—even though the scientists do cheerfully use words in senses which literary persons don't recognise, the senses are exact ones, and when they talk about "subjective," "objective," "philosophy" or "progressive," [7] they know what they mean, even though it isn't what one is accustomed to expect.

Remember, these are very intelligent men. Their culture is in many ways an exacting and admirable one. It doesn't contain much art, with the exception, an important exception, of music. Verbal exchange, insistent argument. Long-playing records. Colour-photography. The ear, to some extent the eye. Books, very little, though perhaps not many would go so far as one hero, who perhaps I should admit was further down the scientific ladder than the people I've been talking about—who, when asked what books he read, replied firmly and confidently: "Books? I prefer to use my books as tools." It was very hard not to let the mind wander—what sort of tool would a book make? Perhaps a hammer? A primitive digging instrument?

Of books, though, very little. And of the books which to most literary persons are bread and butter, novels, history, poetry, plays, almost nothing at all. It isn't that they're not interested in the psychological or moral or social life. In the social life, they certainly are, more than most of us. In the moral, they are by and large the soundest group of intellectuals we have; there is a moral component right in the grain of science itself, and almost all scientists form their own judgments of the moral life. In the psychological they have as much interest as most of us, though occasionally I fancy they come to it rather late. It isn't that they lack the interests. It is much more that the whole literature of the traditional culture doesn't seem to them relevant to those interests. They are, of course, dead wrong. As a result, their imaginative understanding is less than it could be. They are self-impoverished.

But what about the other side? They are impoverished too—per-

---

[7] *Subjective,* in contemporary technological jargon, means "divided according to subjects." *Objective* means "directed towards an object." *Philosophy* means "general intellectual approach or attitude" (for example, a scientist's "philosophy of guided weapons" might lead him to propose certain kinds of "objective research"). A "progressive" job means one with possibilities of promotion.

haps more seriously, because they are vainer about it. They still like to pretend that the traditional culture is the whole of "culture," as though the natural order didn't exist. As though the exploration of the natural order was of no interest either in its own value or its consequences. As though the scientific edifice of the physical world was not, in its intellectual depth, complexity and articulation, the most beautiful and wonderful collective work of the mind of man. Yet most non-scientists have no conception of that edifice at all. Even if they want to have it, they can't. It is rather as though, over an immense range of intellectual experience, a whole group was tone-deaf. Except that this tone-deafness doesn't come by nature, but by training, or rather the absence of training.

As with the tone-deaf, they don't know what they miss. They give a pitying chuckle at the news of scientists who have never read a major work of English literature. They dismiss them as ignorant specialists. Yet their own ignorance and their own specialisation is just as startling. A good many times I have been present at gatherings of people who, by the standards of the traditional culture, are though highly educated and who have with considerable gusto been expressing their incredulity at the illiteracy of scientists. Once or twice I have been provoked and have asked the company how many of them could describe the Second Law of Thermodynamics. The response was cold: it was also negative. Yet I was asking something which is about the scientific equivalent of: *Have you read a work of Shakespeare's?*

I now believe that if I had asked an even simpler question—such as, What do you mean by mass, or acceleration, which is the scientific equivalent of saying, *Can you read?*—not more than one in ten of the highly educated would have felt that I was speaking the same language. So the great edifice of modern physics goes up, and the majority of the cleverest people in the western world have about as much insight into it as their neolithic ancestors would have had.

Just one more of those questions, that my non-scientific friends regard as being in the worst of taste. Cambridge is a university where scientists and non-scientists meet every night at dinner.[8] About two years ago, one of the most astonishing experiments in the whole history of science was brought off. I don't mean the sputnik—that was admirable for quite different reasons, as a feat of organization and a triumphant use of existing knowledge. No, I mean the experiment at Columbia by Yang and Lee. It is an experiment of the greatest beauty and originality, but the result is so startling that one forgets how beautiful the experiment is. It makes

[8] Almost all college High Tables contain Fellows in both scientific and non-scientific subjects.

us think again about some of the fundamentals of the physical world. Intuition, common sense—they are neatly stood on their heads. The result is usually known as the contradiction of parity. If there were any serious communication between the two cultures, this experiment would have been talked about at every High Table in Cambridge. Was it? I wasn't here: but I should like to ask the question.

There seems then to be no place where the cultures meet. I am not going to waste time saying that this is a pity. It is much worse than that. Soon I shall come to some practical consequences. But at the heart of thought and creation we are letting some of our best chances go by default. The clashing point of two subjects, two disciplines, two cultures—of two galaxies, so far as that goes— ought to produce creative chances. In the history of mental activity that has been where some of the break-throughs came. The chances are there now. But they are there, as it were, in a vacuum, because those in the two cultures can't talk to each other. It is bizarre how very little of twentieth-century science has been assimilated into twentieth-century art. Now and then one used to find poets con- scientiously using scientific expressions, and getting them wrong— there was a time when "refraction" kept cropping up in verse in a mystifying fashion, and when "polarised light" was used as though writers were under the illusion that it was a specially admirable kind of light.

Of course, that isn't the way that science could be any good to art. It has got to be assimilated along with, and as part and parcel of, the whole of our mental experience, and used as naturally as the rest.

I said earlier that this cultural divide is not just an English phe- nomenon: it exists all over the western world. But it probably seems at its sharpest in England, for two reasons. One is our fanatical belief in educational specialisation, which is much more deeply ingrained in us than in any country in the world, west or east. The other is our tendency to let our social forms crystallise. This tend- ency appears to get stronger, not weaker, the more we iron out economic inequalities: and this is specially true in education. It means that once anything like a cultural divide gets established, all the social forces operate to make it not less rigid, but more so.

The two cultures were already dangerously separate sixty years ago; but a prime minister like Lord Salisbury could have his own laboratory at Hatfield, and Arthur Balfour had a somewhat more than amateur interest in natural science. John Anderson did some research in organic chemistry in Würzburg before passing first into the Civil Service, and incidentally took a spread of subjects which is now impossible.[9] None of that degree of interchange at the top of the Establishment is likely, or indeed thinkable, now.[10]

In fact, the separation between the scientists and non-scientists is much less bridgeable among the young than it was even thirty years ago. Thirty years ago the cultures had long ceased to speak to each other: but at least they managed a kind of frozen smile across the gulf. Now the politeness has gone, and they just make faces. It is not only that the young scientists now feel that they are part of a culture on the rise while the other is in retreat. It is also, to be brutal, that the young scientists know that with an indifferent degree they'll get a comfortable job, while their contemporaries and counterparts in English or History will be lucky to earn 60 per cent as much. No young scientist of any talent would feel that he isn't wanted or that his work is ridiculous, as did the hero of *Lucky Jim,* and in fact, some of the disgruntlement of Amis and his associates is the disgruntlement of the under-employed arts graduate.

There is only one way out of all this: it is, of course, by rethinking our education. In this country, for the two reasons I have given, that is more difficult than in any other. Nearly everyone will agree that our school education is too specialised. But nearly everyone feels that it is outside the will of man to alter it. Other countries are as dissatisfied with their education as we are, but are not so resigned.

The U.S. teach out of proportion more children up to eighteen than we do: they teach them far more widely, but nothing like so rigorously. They know that: they are hoping to take the problem in hand within ten years, though they may not have all that time to spare. The U.S.S.R. also teach out of proportion more children than we do: they also teach far more widely than we do (it is an absurd western myth that their school education is specialised) but much too rigorously.[11] They know that—and they are beating about to get it right. The Scandinavians, in particular the Swedes, who would make a more sensible job of it than any of us, are handicapped by their practical need to devote an inordinate amount of time to foreign languages. But they too are seized of the problem.

[9] He took the examination in 1905.
[10] It is, however, true to say that the compact nature of the managerial layers of English society—the fact that "everyone knows everyone else"—means that scientists and non-scientists do in fact know each other as people more easily than in most countries. It is also true that a good many leading politicians and administrators keep up lively intellectual and artistic interests to a much greater extent, so far as I can judge, than is the case in the U.S. These are both among our assets.
[11] I tried to compare American, Soviet and English education in "New Minds for the New World," *New Statesman,* 6 September 1956.

Are we? Have we crystallised so far that we are no longer flexible at all?

Talk to schoolmasters, and they say that our intense specialisation, like nothing else on earth, is dictated by the Oxford and Cambridge scholarship examinations. If that is so, one would have thought it not utterly impracticable to change the Oxford and Cambridge scholarship examinations. Yet one would underestimate the national capacity for the intricate defensive to believe that that was easy. All the lessons of our educational history suggest we are only capable of increasing specialisation, not decreasing it.

Somehow we have set ourselves the task of producing a tiny *élite*—far smaller proportionately than in any comparable country —educated in one academic skill. For a hundred and fifty years in Cambridge it was mathematics: then it was mathematics or classics: then natural science was allowed in. But still the choice had to be a single one.

It may well be that this process has gone too far to be reversible. I have given reasons why I think it is a disastrous process, for the purpose of a living culture. I am going on to give reasons why I think it is fatal, if we're to perform our practical tasks in the world. But I can think of only one example, in the whole of English educational history, where our pursuit of specialised mental exercises was resisted with success.

It was done here in Cambridge, fifty years ago, when the old order-of-merit in the Mathematical Tripos was abolished. For over a hundred years, the nature of the Tripos had been crystallising. The competition for the top places had got fiercer, and careers hung on them. In most colleges, certainly in my own, if one managed to come out as Senior or Second Wrangler, one was elected a Fellow out of hand. A whole apparatus of coaching had grown up. Men of the quality of Hardy, Littlewood, Russell, Eddington, Jeans, Keynes, went in for two or three years' training for an examination which was intensely competitive and intensely difficult. Most people in Cambridge were very proud of it, with a similar pride to that which almost anyone in England always has for our existing educational institutions, whatever they happen to be. If you study the fly-sheets of the time, you will find the passionate arguments for keeping the examination precisely as it was to all eternity: it was the only way to keep up standards, it was the only fair test of merit, indeed, the only seriously objective test in the world. The arguments, in fact, were almost exactly those which are used today with precisely the same passionate sincerity if anyone suggests that the scholarship examinations might conceivably not be immune from change.

In every respect but one, in fact, the old Mathematical Tripos seemed perfect. The one exception, however, appeared to some to be rather important. It was simply—so the young creative mathematicians, such as Hardy and Littlewood, kept saying—that the training had no intellectual merit at all. They went a little further, and said that the Tripos had killed serious mathematics in England stone dead for a hundred years. Well, even in academic controversy, that took some skirting round, and they got their way. But I have an impression that Cambridge was a good deal more flexible between 1850 and 1914 than it has been in our time. If we had had the old Mathematical Tripos firmly planted among us, should we have ever managed to abolish it? . . .

PART TWO

*Science and Literature
Since the Renaissance*

douglas bush

THE ELIZABETHANS:
THE MEDIEVAL HERITAGE

In this book I shall try to sketch the repercussions of science upon English poetry from the Elizabethan age to the present.[1] The subject is not so clear-cut and straightforward as it might seem to be. It embraces, obviously, the great body of poetry written in the last three and a half centuries, the development of various sciences during the same long period, and the direct response of poets to scientific thought and discovery. That is complex enough. But we are also obviously involved with the history of religion, metaphysics, and ethics and the increasing pressure of science upon traditional orthodoxies; with the growth of our mechanical and industrial civilization and its effects upon the life and spirit of man in general and poets in particular; and with the changes in the technique and texture as well as the content of poetry that have been brought about by the great changes in the poet's outer and inner world. And other related topics might be added.

These headings are large subjects in themselves, and many large books have been written on one or another of their multitudinous aspects. I can only acknowledge a congenital weakness for biting off more than I can chew; I have always had a fellow feeling for a graduate student I once heard of, who proposed doing a thesis on the influence of the eighteenth century on the nineteenth. As we

From *Science and English Poetry: An Historical Sketch, 1590-1950,* by Douglas Bush. Copyright 1950 by Indiana University Press. Reprinted by permission of Oxford University Press, Inc.
[1] The following selection is the introduction to the full-length book Bush here describes.

proceed, therefore, I shall doubtless be leaping like a circus rider
from horse to horse, or rather, perhaps, be imitating the hero who
mounted his horse and rode off in all directions. I do not pretend to
be offering any novel ideas, but I hope that, even if the topics discussed are familiar to students of literature and science, there may
be some interest in following, however inadequately, a story of
prime importance through some three hundred and fifty years. Of
course, if we had time, we might go back to Chaucer and beyond,
but it is only around 1600 that science begins to shake the faith
men live by, and it is poets' reactions to that conflict that will be
our main theme. Such a theme requires the use of poetry largely as
a series of documents, a procedure that is not approved by critics
who are less concerned with what a poet says than with how he
says it; I trust, however, that our preoccupation with poets' creeds
and philosophies will not seem to imply indifference to the *sine qua
non* of poetic power.

Finally, since the nature of the subject focuses attention upon
the obverse or destructive side of scientific progress, it might be
well to say, once for all, that I am aware that the history of science
is a great record of patient search, discovery, and illumination
(not to mention its material benefits), and that I am not at any
time playing the fatuous role of obscurantist. No one would suggest
that certain conceptions of God and man and human life, because
they were noble and long-lived, should have been permitted—if
that had been possible—to rest on illusion or delusion. In 1664 the
Cambridge Platonist, Henry More, one of the first philosophic
minds in England to grapple with the problem of science and religion, declared that "there is no real clashing at all betwixt any
genuine point of Christianity and what true philosophy and right
reason does determine or allow, but . . . there is a perpetual peace
and agreement betwixt truth and truth, be they of what nature or
kind so ever." That there can be no conflict between truth and truth
is surely axiomatic in every age. But in every age also there have
been, among scientists, religionists, and artists, inevitable errors,
uncertainties, and conflicting views of truth, and our journey lies
over that darkling plain. One could wish that there were a clear
light somewhere ahead of us.

The general problem can be briefly stated. A poet, granted
his special endowment, is a person devoted to achieving and expressing a view of human experience, and even that vague and
simple definition implies some degree of positive faith in the worth
and dignity of life and man. The poet's vision grows out of both his
imaginative intuition and his actual experience and knowledge, and
knowledge, in the modern centuries, has become increasingly

scientific. But science, which is devoted to the discovery of verifiable truth about nature and the means of controlling nature, is not at all concerned about the worth and dignity of life and man—though scientists, as men, may be. It is a commonplace that the effect of science has been to dislodge man from his supposedly central position in a divine order, to reduce him to a dubiously relevant—though unique—accident in an infinite universe and an infinite biological process, and, in recent times, to make him also a victim both of the mechanical forces that he has created and of the blind forces within himself that he has not created. In such a predicament, can man in general, and the artist as the quintessence of man, retain the belief in a supernatural order which all religions have affirmed and which naturalistic science denies? Can he at least continue to sustain himself with the belief that man and life have a dignity and meaning that transcend the chaotic succession of events? He may believe, with the scientist, that the truth shall make you free, but free from what? From error, no doubt, and also, perhaps, from any kind of faith or anchorage whatever. The scientist, setting such questions aside, may find complete spiritual satisfaction in his daily work in the laboratory; but the mass of men, and the poet, have no such alleviation or escape.

Science goes rapidly out of date, great literature is always alive; and some of the fundamental problems are as old as the Old Testament, or older. If the Hebrews attained the highest ancient conception of a providential God, they also put forth the grandest of all questionings of divine order and justice. When the Lord out of the whirlwind rebuked Job for his ignorant presumption and want of faith, he appealed to his own creation and government of the whole world of nature:

Where wast thou when I laid the foundations of the earth? declare, if thou hast understanding.

Who hath laid the measures thereof, if thou knowest? or who hath stretched the line upon it? . . .

Hast thou entered into the springs of the sea? or hast thou walked in the search of the depth?

Have the gates of death been opened unto thee? or hast thou seen the doors of the shadow of death? . . .

Canst thou bind the sweet influences of Pleiades, or loose the bands of Orion? . . .

Canst thou lift up thy voice to the clouds, that abundance of waters may cover thee?

Canst thou send lightnings, that they may go, and say unto thee, Here we are?

Who hath put wisdom in the inward parts? or who hath given understanding to the heart?

The twentieth-century scientist might answer modestly, "Yes, I can make rain, and I can send something more destructive than lightning," but the great questions remain questions.

Similar problems, conceived in a more philosophic way, were central in the Greek view of life. Is the race of men, Homer asks, no more than the generation of leaves, or do individual virtue and fortitude have a meaning in a dark world of strife and futility? Sophocles celebrates the inventive skill and prowess of man, who has conquered the beasts and the earth and the sea but cannot conquer death and time; yet he also sees the ephemeral race as guided and bound by the divine laws that never grow old. Some centuries later, Lucretius, with messianic fervor, preaches the science of Epicurean materialism which will free humanity from supernatural dread. And then comes Virgil, envying the man who could plumb the causes of things and tread under foot all fears and inexorable fate and the roar of greedy Acheron; and he arrives at the final vision that Tennyson summed up:

> Thou that seëst Universal Nature moved by Universal Mind;
> Thou majestic in thy sadness at the doubtful doom of human kind.

As the two Roman names at least remind us, even the special conflict that we are concerned with appeared very early in the history of thought. And long before Lucretius the Greeks had raised the questions of permanence and flux, reality and appearance, nature and convention. Plato, following upon many scientific thinkers and poets, achieved a reconciliation of opposites, a comprehensive orthodoxy that was ethical, metaphysical, and religious. But in Plato's own time, opposed to his central doctrine that God is the measure of all things, there was the doctrine, associated with the Sophist Protagoras, that man is the measure of all things; and we should not forget that other ancient father of modernism, Democritus, who saw the world as composed of atoms and a void. In that antithesis is the essence of all subsequent conflicts. If, according to the late Professor Whitehead, the European philosophical tradition consists of a series of footnotes to Plato, it might be said that the history of skepticism and naturalism is an elaboration of Protagoras and Democritus. But the conflict between those perennial modes of thought did not resume the center of the philosophic stage until the seventeenth century, when the revival of ancient skepticism and naturalism, assisted by some medieval heterodoxies, revived the old opposition in recognizably modern terms. We may remember also that the scientific renaissance of the sixteenth century owed much to the Platonic tradition; and as we go on we shall be observing how, when scientific rationalism becomes mechanistic and inhuman, the same Platonic tradition is a continual source of religious and poetic idealism.

Those things lie ahead. [Here] I want to speak, briefly, of [some] related topics: the "scientific" notions of the world and man inherited by Shakespeare and other Elizabethans; the religious and philosophic orthodoxy with which those notions were bound up; the Renaissance development of skepticism and naturalism which was beginning to challenge that orthodoxy. . . .

Although the year 1543 brought forth the great works of Copernicus and Vesalius, these and other scientific ideas made their way slowly even among the learned, and the Elizabethan view of the world and man remained fundamentally medieval and prescientific. This summary statement (like many other statements in this book) refers of course to the normal, not the exceptional, mind; in the Middle Ages there was far more scientific activity than was suspected two generations ago, and Shakespeare's England contained a number of mathematicians and scientists whose knowledge ranged far beyond the normal. But at that time, as in our time and in our minds, old and new ideas existed side by side, and the old greatly predominated. Of the strong persistence of medievalism, in Europe at large, we have concrete evidence in the printing and reprinting of such pseudo-scientific encyclopaedias as those of Isidore of Seville (seventh century) and Bartholomaeus Anglicus (thirteenth century). An enlarged and not very critical revision of this last was a handbook of Shakespeare's age. From *Batman upon Bartholome* of 1582 and Burton's *Anatomy of Melancholy*—which agree in many of the items to be mentioned—one may get a pretty good picture of the stock of information in the Elizabethan mind. Various works might of course be drawn upon, such as Sylvester's translation of Du Bartas' epic of creation, which was among other things a religious compendium of orthodox science and which remained popular through the first half of the seventeenth century.

In spite of books written by English Copernicans, the cosmology of Shakespeare and most of his fellows was the Ptolemaic or Aristotelian system, much patched up in the course of the centuries but still the same in essentials. Around a stationary earth a series of spheres carried the sun and moon and other planets; outside of these were a varying number of other spheres, and all were kept in motion by the outermost, the *primum mobile,* and were presided over, in Neoplatonic and Christian tradition, by angels. Astrology, whether in extreme or modified forms, was almost universally accepted, and by some of the chief thinkers of Europe. Even Kepler, the great lawgiver of astronomy, had mystical notions of the solar system. Along with astrology went belief in comets, meteors, and all sorts of unusual phenomena as divine portents. Physical nature and the human body were composed of the four elements, earth, water, air, and fire, which had the four qualities of heat and cold, dryness and moisture. The body contained four humors, analogous to the elements, namely, blood, phlegm, choler, and melancholy; according as one of these was present in excess, it would cause a sanguine, phlegmatic, choleric, or melancholy temper. The medium between body and soul was spirit. "Spirit," says Burton, "is a most subtle vapor, which is expressed from the blood, and the instrument of the soul, to perform all his actions." There are three kinds of spirit, natural, vital, and animal, begotten respectively in the liver, the heart, and the brain. The brain, to quote Burton again, "is a soft, marrowish, and white substance, engendered of the purest part of seed and spirits, included by many skins, and seated within the skull or brain-pan, and it is the most noble organ under heaven, the dwelling-house and seat of the soul, the habitation of wisdom, memory, judgment, reason, and in which man is most like unto God." (The range of that sentence goes well beyond modern textbooks of physiology or psychology.) "The common division of the soul is into three principal faculties, vegetal, sensitive, and rational, which make three distinct kinds of living creatures, vegetal plants, sensible beasts, rational men." In such mixtures of classical and medieval ideas, bits of empirical knowledge are elaborated and arranged in symmetrical patterns that are mainly a matter of logical or speculative theory.

The Renaissance man, like the medieval man, saw the natural world in several ways, which could be distinct or could run together. Those ways may be roughly labeled the everyday, the "scientific," and the religious. The scientific view has been briefly indicated. By the everyday view I mean that the world of nature was the world that presented itself to the senses and emotions, the familiar world of form and color and creative and destructive energies, not a set of problems to be investigated or of forces to be mastered; and that view was, until the seventeenth century, largely shared by philosophers. The religious view was more complex. For Aquinas and for Calvin alike, God revealed himself first through his word and secondarily through his works; and the unphilosophic St. Francis could, as one of a great family, praise the Lord God and all his creatures, our brother the sun and our sister the moon, our brothers the wind and fire, our sister the water, our mother the earth.

Of great importance for poetry was a special development of the religious view of nature and, in some sense, of the scientific view as well: that was the allegorical or emblematic conception. Because God maintains an active and intimate connection with his works, because all creatures and things and ideas flow from and back to one divine source, there is an unlimited network of correspondences binding together the physical and the spiritual, the earthly and the human and the celestial. Everything, concrete or abstract, is related, directly or by analogy, to everything else. The physical world, with its rivers and grass, is reflected in the microcosm, man, with his veins and hair. The basic unity of all things was presupposed in astrology and alchemy, and that speculative faith, however unscientific, has been partly realized by modern science. And the medieval or Renaissance man would have been delighted but hardly surprised by the view, put forth at one stage in modern physics, that the atom was a sort of miniature solar system. Because of this general belief in the divine unity of all creation, natural objects were seen not so much in themselves but as emblems or allegories of moral, religious, and metaphysical truth. From this mode of thought and feeling came the bestiaries, those collections of allegorical beast-fables and unnatural natural history which included the phoenix and the unicorn as well as animals known to the zoo. The same impulse engendered the hundreds of Renaissance emblem books, which revived this and other kinds of lore in a special literary and pictorial form, and which exerted a strong influence on many poets, such as Spenser, Shakespeare, Chapman, Donne, and George Herbert. Parallel manifestations in other areas were the often complex emblematic codes of graphic art and the allegorizing of pagan fiction, such as Ovid's tales, in terms of Christian truth.

Persons who use the word "medieval" as a synonym for "naive" and "credulous" of course regard all this sort of thing as wild nonsense, and, so far as it purports to be accurate information, no doubt it usually is. But, so far as it touches literature, to dismiss it as unscientific is no wiser than to dismiss a scientist's report of an experiment because it is not poetical. We might remember that this mode of apprehension and expression, on its highest level, produced the *Divine Comedy*. And, in general, we might remember that minds that worked in this allegorical way were not concerned with scientific ends. They were concerned with the religious nature and destiny of man in a divinely ordered world, and their imagination naturally and necessarily made use of more or less religious symbols. In short, the allegorical instinct is closely related to the poetic instinct, since a poet works through metaphor and symbol. If much of the traditional lore of nature that was considered true was not true, the fact of untruth had small bearing on the validity of the symbol. We might remember also that four hundred years after Copernicus we talk of the sunrise and the sunset, and we shall go on doing so; in the age of Einstein we do not make our daily appointments in accordance with the space-time continuum. In other words, our primary experience and responses, which are the main stuff of poetry, are outside the criteria of natural science.

*   *   *

basil willey

THE SEVENTEENTH CENTURY BACKGROUND

[A selection fom Chapter 1, "The Rejection of Scholasticism."] . . . It may be said, then, that for the [medieval theologians and] scholastics there was little or no distinction between
a "fact" and a theological or metaphysical "truth." For them the
important consideration was not how things behave, or what their
history might be, but how they were linked with Total Being, and
what, in a word, was their metaphysical status. This was satisfying
enough to a period in which men's interests were oriented towards
a transcendental "reality," but it was unfavourable to what, since
the Renaissance, has been called "science." This science has
achieved what it has achieved precisely by abstracting from the
whole of "reality" those aspects which are amenable to its methods.
There is no point in denying that only thus can "scientific" discovery be made. What we need to remember, however, is that we
have to do here with a *transference of interests* rather than with
the mere "exantlation" of new truth or the mere rejection of error.
All we can say is that at the Renaissance men began to wish for a
new life-orientation, and that this involved a hitherto unthought-of
degree of control over "things." Accordingly, the sort of knowledge
which dealt with the motions of bodies came to seem the most real,
the most genuine knowledge, and scientific "truth" the only genuine
"truth." "Truth" of some kind cannot be denied to the knowledge
on which modern civilisation rests, the knowledge which enables
us to construct aeroplanes and wireless-sets, to weigh the atom and
chart the mysterious universe. We have merely come to see that
this kind of knowledge does not exhaust reality, and that in the

From Basil Willey's *The Seventeenth Century Background,* Copyright
1942 by Columbia University Press, New York City, pp. 14-22, 226-229,
236-237, 238-240. Reprinted by permission of Columbia University Press.

unreduced remainder may lie "truths" "belonging to our peace."
Little now, in our "changing world," seems to matter except the
quality of our living. We have to try to live, somehow, amidst the
machines we have made and the débris into which they are falling; significance has somehow to be imparted to the "unwilling
dross." There can be no return, I believe, to the specific thought-
forms of scholasticism, but we are once more asking the fundamental questions. As soon as we try to live more wholly and more
deeply we become aware of all that experiment and observation
leave untouched. We must ask "What," "Whence" and "Why";
we differ from St Thomas mainly in having no direct replies to
give. All we can do is to reply in terms of "As If"; "live according
to the best hypotheses (whatever they may be)," thus runs our
reply to the questioner, "live thus, and see if you can live the hypotheses into 'truths' (truths for yourself, that is)."

With these considerations in mind, let us examine an actual
example of the rejection of scholasticism by a seventeenth century
scientist. The theory of motion was the keystone of seventeenth
century science: let us then compare the views of Galileo, the
pioneer of scientific investigation on this subject, with those of St
Thomas Aquinas.

St Thomas, following Aristotle, treats motion as a branch of
metaphysics; he is interested in why it happens, not how. He discusses it in terms of "act" and "potency," quoting Aristotle's definition of it (8 *Phys.* v. 8) as "the act of that which is in potentiality,
as such." [1] Motion exists, then, because things in a state of potentiality seek to actualise themselves, or because they seek the place
or direction which is *proper* to them.

> Everything moved, as such, tends as towards a divine likeness, to
> be perfect in itself; and since a thing is perfect in so far as it becomes
> actual, it follows that the intention of everything that is in poten-
> tiality is to tend to actuality by way of movement[2]

To every body in respect of its "form," is "due" a "proper place,"
towards which it tends to move in a straight line. Thus it is "due to
fire, in respect of its form, to be in a higher place," [3] or to a stone,
to be in a lower.

It is unnecessary to controvert theories of this kind as if they
were "untrue." Their "truth" is not of the empirical kind; it consists
in their being *consistent with a certain world-view*. For St Thomas
the world-view with which they were consistent was a datum sup-

---

[1] *Summa Contra Gentiles,* bk. i. ch. 13.
[2] *Ibid.,* bk. iii. ch. 22.
[3] *Ibid.,* ch. 23.

plied by divine authority. For us the notion of "revelation" may have acquired a different content, but it must be remembered that those of us who affirm the "reality," for example, of religious, or poetic experience, are appealing to a principle essentially similar. Possibly the survival-value of the "revelation" concept is due to its having symbolised our need to accept certain experiences as "true," not because they are empirically demonstrable, but simply because they are "given."

Galileo typifies the direction of modern interests, in this instance, not in refuting St Thomas, but in taking no notice of him. Motion might *be* all that the angelic doctor had declared it to be; Galileo nevertheless will drop weights from the top of a tower, and down inclined planes, to see how they behave. It is undeniable that the scholastic theory of motion informs us nothing of the manner in which bodies move in space and time, and this was precisely what Galileo wished to determine. He is concerned with quantities, not qualities; and his energy is thus devoted not to framing theories consistent with a rational scheme, but to *measuring* the speed of falling bodies in terms of time and space. After repeated measurements, he arrives at a mathematical formula expressing the "law" of their acceleration; he finds, for instance, that "their speed is proportional to the time of fall" and that "the space described increases as the square of the time." [4]

But the contrast between St Thomas and Galileo is even more instructive when we consider their views on an empirical question, the nature and movements of the heavenly bodies. In the scholastic doctrine of the heavenly bodies we have an illustration of the strange fact that a belief can be metaphysically "true" (in the sense of "coherent" or "consistent") and yet empirically false, that is, not in correspondence with what we call a "state of affairs." The received scholastic doctrine, for instance, taught that the heavenly bodies are unalterable and incorruptible. This belief seems to have rested on the assumption (*fact*, as it then appeared) that the motions of the heavenly bodies were circular. The "elements"—of fire, air, water and earth—of which all sublunary objects were compounded, moved in straight lines towards the places proper to them, fire and air "upwards," water and earth "downwards." The elements thus have "contraries," away from which they move; all straight-line movements, it was held, imply the existence of such a "contrary." But the heavenly bodies move in circles, thus their movement shows them to be without a "contrary." And that which was without a contrary must be exempt from generation and corruption, since, according to Aristotle, all generated objects proceed

[4] Dampier-Whetham, *Hist. of Science*, p. 144.

from their contraries and are corrupted again into contraries. It there-fore follows that the heavenly bodies are incorruptible.[5] Another way of expressing the same view was in terms of "matter" and "form." In all corruptible things the "form" fails to penetrate the "matter" completely—it does not quite inform its tenement of clay, therefore the object is in a state of potentiality, therefore it moves. But in the stars "the form fills the whole potentiality of matter, so that the matter retains no potentiality to another form." The stars "consist of their entire matter." [6] Their circular movement is the only kind of movement "proper" to such perfectly realised creatures as the heavenly bodies; circular movement being held, it must be remembered, to be inherently "noble," "perfect," or, as we might say, expressive of self-completeness.

It was against these and suchlike beliefs that the early upholders of Copernicanism had to contend. The Copernican theory was un-acceptable at first chiefly because it obliterated the traditional dis-tinction between corruptible and incorruptible, placing the earth, as it were, amongst the heavenly bodies. Accordingly we find Galileo tackling the "incorruptibility" theory at the beginning of his *System of the World*. The main purport of the First Dialogue is to refute Aristotle and the schools, and to demonstrate that the earth is one of the celestial bodies, "and as it were place it in Heaven, whence your Philosophers have exiled it." [7] He argues that though there may be no "contrary" to circular motion, "contrariety" of some kind can be found amongst the heavenly bodies; for example, "rarity" and "density." But the argument upon which he, like all the anti-scholastics of the seventeenth century, really relies, is the appeal to observation. It is through his Optic Glass that the Tuscan Artist[8] views the heavens, descrying new lands, rivers or mountains in the moon. By means of the telescope Galileo has *observed* genera-tion and corruption going on in the heavens.

> We have in our age new accidents and observations, and such, that I question not in the least, but if Aristotle were now alive, they would make him change his opinion.[9]

Comets have been observed which have been

> generated and dissolved in parts higher than the Lunar Orb, besides the two new Stars, Anno 1572 and Anno 1604, without contradiction

---

[5] See, e.g., *Summa Theologica*, pt. ii. qu. 85, art. 6.
[6] *S. Contra G.*, bk. iii. ch. 23.
[7] Galileo, *Mathematical Collections and Translations*, translated by Thomas Salusbury, 1661, p. 25.
[8] *Paradise Lost*, i. 288.
[9] Galileo, *op. cit.*, p. 37.

much higher than all the Planets; and in the face of the Sun itself, by help of the *Telescope,* certain dense and obscure substances, in substance very like to the foggs about the Earth, are seen to be produced and dissolved.[10]

Thus the metaphysical theory of the heavens is confronted by comets, new stars, and sun-spots seen through the telescope; and Salviatus, speaking for Galileo himself, makes much of an alleged saying of Aristotle that we ought to prefer sense-evidence to logic. Knowledge so gained is far more certain than any deduction from purely rational premises; it is more certain, therefore, that there are sun-spots, or mountains in the moon, than that the heavens are unalterable. This was then far from seeming the obvious "truth" that it has appeared to most people ever since. The Professor of Philosophy at Padua refused to look through Galileo's telescope, and his colleague at Pisa tried by means of logical arguments, to "charm the new planets out of the sky." [11] One must, however, make the effort to conceive a point of view from which the notion of lunar mountains, for example, would be abhorrent. They would be abhorrent to the Peripatetic as derogations from the moon's "perfection," which implied her perfect sphericity (the "sphere" being the most "perfect" of solids).[12] Galileo makes it his affair to deny that incorruptibility, inalterability and sphericity are necessary attributes of "perfection." It is more "noble" for the earth, for example, to be as it is than to be like a lump of crystal;[13] and if for the earth, why not for the stars? The far-reaching implications of this view must not be followed out here, but we should note this as a good early example of veneration for "things-as-they-are" rather than "things-as-they-can-be-conceived."

Again, scholasticism taught that the movements of the heavenly bodies implied the presence of a constant impelling force:

> Now one place is not more due to a heavenly body in respect of its form than another. Therefore nature alone is not the principle of the heavenly movement: and consequently the principle of its movement must be something that moves it by apprehension;[14]

—that is, an intellectual substance; in a word, the Unmoved Mover of Aristotle and St Thomas.

> And since whatever is moved by anything *per se,* and not accidentally, is directed thereby towards the end of its movement, and

---

[10] Galileo, *op. cit.,* pp. 37-8.
[11] Dampier-Whetham, *op. cit.,* p. 142.
[12] Galileo, *op. cit.,* p. 69.
[13] *Ibid.,* p. 45.
[14] S. *Contra G.,* bk. iii. ch. 23.

BASIL WILLEY

since the heavenly body is moved by an intellectual substance, and
the heavenly body, by its movement, causes all movement in this
lower world, it follows of necessity that the heavenly body is directed
to the end of its movement by an intellectual substance, and consequently all lower bodies to their respective ends.[15]

Against this comprehensive theory (indeed, it is more than a
theory, it is a religious affirmation) Galileo sets the new principle of
inertia. Constant exertion of force is *not* required to account for
the incessant motions of the heavens, since motion, like immobility,
once in being, will persist until affected by some force. Only the
primary impulse of the First Mover, then, need be postulated; not
his continual action. And it only remained for Newton to "explain"
why the motion of the heavenly bodies was circular (elliptical)
and not in straight lines. Galileo admitted that he knew nothing
about the ultimate nature of the forces he was measuring; nothing
about the cause of gravitation, or the origin of the Universe; he
deemed it better, rather than to speculate on such high matters, "to
pronounce that wise, ingenious and modest sentence, 'I know it
not.'" [16]

I have already hinted that I think we should cultivate the habit
of looking steadily at this intellectual revolution, vigorously check-
ing any propensity to an outrush of uncritical sympathy for either
side. We have to be on our guard, I think, as much against those
who represent the rejection of scholasticism as pure loss, as against
those who regard it as pure gain. It is only because for three hundred years almost everybody has united to extol it as pure gain,
that we may be forgiven for leaning a little (as Aristotle advises)
towards the opposite side, so as to restore the true mean. With this
reservation let us boldly declare that the rejection was not wholly
disastrous. We are compelled to deem it no mere calamity as long
as we believe that, though "truth" has many levels, it is at each and
every level preferable to "error." Do we really believe this? A good
way of testing our condition is to ask ourselves: do we or do we not
approve the action of the Paduan professor who refused to look
through Galileo's telescope? If we find that we condemn the professor, we have already decided on the main issue. To applaud him
is by no means impossible for a reasonable being. But we must
remember that if we do so, we are committed to a belief which
may prove inconvenient or even perilous if generally applied: the
belief, namely, that truth of a lower order may be neglected in
order that higher truths may be conserved.

*   *   *

[15] *Ibid.*, ch. 24.
[16] Dampier-Whetham, *op. cit.*, p. 146.

74

[A selection from Chapter 10, "The Heroic Poem in a Scientific Age."] . . . What I am especially concerned here to suggest, however, is that, at any rate after the failure of the Saints, it was not only the bent of his own nature but the intellectual climate of his age which impelled Milton towards a biblical theme for his heroic poem. It is true that Milton's outlook seems never to have been influenced by the post-Restoration and Royal Society atmosphere; he had nothing about him of the "experimental philosopher." Indeed, his work is much like an isolated volcano thrusting up through the philosophic plains, and drawing its fire from deeper and older levels of spiritual energy. But Milton was "protestant" to the core, and this meant that in the moral sphere he *was* an "experimenter," and had the same disdain for all that was not "truth" as the natural philosopher had in his. The protestant abhorrence of the tinsel ("carnality") of Laudian religion, well seen in Milton's anti-episcopal tracts, was the moral counterpart of the philosopher's scorn for scholastic verbiage. Intolerance of all except what seemed to him *most real* was, then, a characteristic of Milton which linked him with his age, and vitally affected his choice of poetic subject. In the conditions of the century, and to a man of Milton's temper, what kind of theme would appear worthy to be sung in new and lofty measure? Only one which he could feel to be in the highest sense "true" as well as "heroic." Milton's dismissal of "fabled Knights" and "battles feigned" and all the "tinsel trappings" of romance constitutes a rejection of "fiction" by the protestant consciousness, which is strictly comparable with the rejection of scholasticism by the scientific consciousness, and can be ascribed to the same underlying cause. The traditional sources of poetry were running dry; mythologies were exploded and obsolete; no poet with Milton's passion for reality could pour all the energies of his nature into such moulds any longer. But there still remained one source, and one only, from which the seventeenth century protestant poet could draw images and fables which were not only "poetic" but also "true": the Bible. Thanks to the work of several recent scholars, notably M. Saurat and Dr. Tillyard, we now appreciate the range and daring of Milton's speculation, and realise that it is unsafe to ascribe to him the purely naïve beliefs he was formerly thought to hold. Milton could twist Scripture to his purpose, or, as we have seen, override it on occasion.[1] Yet when all is said, Milton's attitude to the Bible was still that of protestantism. The Bible remained a numinous book for Locke, and Toland, and Swift, and Addison, and innumerable polite savants in the eight-

---

[1] Cf. "No ordinance, human or from heaven, can bind against the good of man." Quoted from *Tetrachordon* by Tillyard, *Milton* (Chatto & Windus, 1930), p. 164.

eenth century; how much more, then, must its authority have been felt as a fact by a man of Milton's stamp? That he deferred instinctively to it, even while "interpreting" it, is shown by his composing that laborious treatise, the *De Doctrina Christiana,* in which he is seen exercising the right, and discharging the duty, of every intelligent protestant to search the scriptures for himself and to construct his faith from its pages alone, without regard to the vain notions of other men, or the glosses of priestly tradition. To be left alone with Scripture might, indeed, mean to be left alone with one's own soul, for "Scripture" was wide enough to bear almost any construction. This may all along have been the inner logic of the protestant appeal to Scripture. But all this leaves unchanged the central fact that Milton, together with nearly every one else in his century, felt all proper contact with biblical material to be, in quite a special sense, contact with Truth. When contemporary history, which alone could have given "reality" to his Arthuriad, ceased to furnish matter for heroic and sacred song, Milton, too old, too disillusioned and too noble to spend his stored resources on anything but highest truth, could only turn to the Bible for his "fable." Science might dismiss old picture-thinking as phantasmal; Platonists might strive to wipe off the gross dews of the imagination from the clear glass of the understanding; puritans might banish as carnal the poetry of ritual and symbol: all these and other agencies might be at work, as they were, undermining and destroying older forms of religious and poetic experience; nevertheless here, in Scripture, God himself had condescended to be a poet, and his divine revelation could therefore still be sung by a Milton with undamaged assurance. The existence of the Hebrew scriptures, then, in the particular setting of seventeenth century protestantism, must be accounted, together with the idea of the heroic poem, as the cause which made possible a great serious poem at just the period when poetry was coming to be thought of as elegant and agreeable rather than "true." Poetry, like Popery, might be an affront to the common sense of a Locke or a Tillotson; but as Prophecy it was still admissible. Calliope could not defend the Thracian bard from the wild rout in Rhodope; and no mere Muse could protect a modern poet from the barbarous dissonance of Restoration England. But Milton invokes Urania, a higher than Calliope:

> So fail not thou, who thee implores:
> For thou art Heav'nly, she an empty dream.[2]

* * *

. . . *Paradise Lost* had in fact been, in spite of Dryden, the nearest realisation of the epic ideal that England would have. The

[2] *Paradise Lost,* preamble to bk. vii.

reasons for the solidity and lasting-power of Milton's epic lay outside the critical purview of Dryden or Boileau. It was based upon
the one "fable," the one piece of machinery, which could still be
"accredited" as real by almost everybody. True, it was bristling
with "inconveniences," but these were only those of the faith itself.
God the Father might argue like a school-divine; Satan might be
allowed an inexplicable degree of freedom; the whole business of
the Fall might seem an arraignment rather than a justification of
the ways of God to men; the geography and administration of
heaven and hell might be grossly pictorial and incompatible with
any rational theology; but all these difficulties were not created
by Milton: they were inherent in a religion which grafted an Aristotelian or Platonic theology upon a stock of Hebrew mythology.
Milton, like many in his own generation, was in the peculiar position of being able to hold advanced speculative views and yet at
the same time to "believe" in the traditional imagery of Christianity. The exact quality of that "belief" is difficult to define, but we
may perhaps help ourselves to conceive it by remembering the
instinctive deference of that age for ancient authority. If a Bacon
could guess at an antique wisdom embalmed in the classical myths,
how much rather could not a Milton infallibly *know* that divine
truth was contained in the sacred narratives? Like a good protestant, Milton held that every passage of Scripture has only one plain
sense, and that in all things necessary for salvation the Bible is
plain and perspicuous.[3] . . .

    . . . I do not think Milton read the first chapters of Genesis, as
Browne had suggested they might be read, *simply* as an allegory
illustrating the seduction of Reason by the Passions, though of
course the story could mean that also. Had the Fall of Man not
been for him a real historical fact as well as an allegory or dogma,
I do not believe he could have made it the central theme of his
greatest work. Similarly, "Christ" might be for Milton, as for John
Smith, a "type," a "principle," representing Right Reason, or the
executive power of God, yet one cannot doubt that for him that
principle was historically incarnated, in a unique sense, in Jesus
of Nazareth. Dr Tillyard has well noted [4] that in a famous passage
of *Areopagitica* Milton juxtaposes, without change of tone, the
legend of Psyche with the story of Genesis as if these were for
him on exactly the same plane of reality. One might add that in
the *Nativity Ode* there is nothing to mark the baroque figure of
the "meek-ey'd peace" as more fictional than the shepherds, the
Virgin blest, or the Babe. The "reality" of the false gods of heathen-
dom, was, we know, saved for Milton by their identification with

[3] Cf. *De Doctrina Christiana*, ch. xxx., Bohn, iv. p. 440-2.
[4] *op. cit.*, p. 223.

the defaulting angels. On the whole, however, I think we must conclude that whereas the pagan myths were to him but husks from which truth could be winnowed (as in the theory of Bacon and Reynolds), the biblical events, if allegorical at all, were the deliberate allegories of God himself; and when God allegorises he does not merely write or inspire parables, he also *causes to happen the events which can be allegorically interpreted.*[5] At the same time we may agree with Dr Tillyard that Milton's mind was not consciously preoccupied with the demarcation of truth from fiction. He did not belong to the scientific movement of the seventeenth century, which, as I have repeatedly indicated above, was pre-occupied with precisely this task. He lived in a moral rather than a physical world, and was ready to imbibe wisdom wherever he could find it. "Wisdom," for most Renaissance minds—and as we have seen, Milton's was of that, rather than of the "modern" or "philosophic" order—was to be sought above all in antiquity. Antiquity for the seventeenth century scholar meant two great traditions, the classical, in which he had been intellectually trained, and the Christian, in which he had been spiritually moulded. Great reverence was felt for both traditions—hence the apparent equipollence of Greek and Scriptural myths in parts of Milton's writings—but a special degree of belief was, I think, accorded to the Christian. To the end of the century, and beyond it, the events of the Christian revelation were saved as "real" by the belief that in them God had, for exceptional and non-recurrent reasons, made a deliberate infraction of the "laws of nature"; but that elsewhere and ever since for all time those laws would be found to operate in their ordinary course. It was only later, when science had familiarised a sharper division between "real" and "unreal" phe-nomena, that the miraculous elements of Christian doctrine could be attacked directly as "mere" fictions. . . .

[5] Cf. Saurat, *Milton, the Man and the Thinker*, p. 212.

marjorie hope nicolson

THE BREAKING OF THE CIRCLE

For three hundred years men have vainly tried to put together the pieces of a broken circle. Some have been poets, some philosophers, some artists. They have shared a common desire for a unity that once existed, and have sought a "return to medievalism," when life seemed integrated about a strong center, whether of the Church or of a monarch. Except for an occasional individual who has found peace in old religion, their efforts have proved fruitless. Poets and artists have deliberately revived old styles, but these attempts have been equally abortive. Modern critics have kidnapped to our times poets like Donne, in whom they find a "unified sensibility" of feeling and thinking. Philosophical poets—Pope, Wordsworth, Tennyson—have tried to express a world view, as did Lucretius for the ancients, Dante for the Middle Ages, Milton for the seventeenth-century Protestant. But all the king's horses and all the king's men cannot put Humpty-Dumpty together again. Mere fitting together of pieces may remake the picture in a jigsaw puzzle; it will not remake an egg. Nor can we reconstruct the old Circle of Perfection, broken by modern science and philosophy. Donne spoke truly when he said: "Nothing more endlesse, nothing sooner broke."

Since the seventeenth century the paths of literature and science have divided, and the ways of one have become strange to the other. Two main issues are involved, I think: one is a matter of language, the other of basic ways of thinking about the world and man. Since the Renaissance, "style" has become a self-conscious word. Francis Bacon, in the *Advancement of Learning*, protested the "literary" language of his own period as a vehicle for science. The Royal Society, in early Restoration years, deliberately adopted a program that hastened the division between two languages, urging members—many of whom were men of letters—to put aside the "language of Wits and Scholars" and adopt a clearer, simpler style modeled upon that of "Mechanicks and Artisans." Wordsworth, protesting the poetic diction of the eighteenth century, formulated another such program. All of us are aware of various reforms recommended by our own contemporaries. In Shakespeare's day, there was little distinction between styles, often none between prose and poetry, certainly only the rudiments of any self-conscious separation between the language of the poet and that of the scientist. Kepler, as we shall see, often spoke like Dante on the one hand, Marlowe on the other. The language of poetry and of science was one when the world was one.

A more profound change has come about in attitudes toward Nature. The earlier poets did not need to develop a self-conscious "philosophy of Nature," as did Wordsworth and Tennyson. They were inextricably involved in a world and a universe that lived as they lived, in which they found exact analogies for their organic and bodily functions and for the power of their souls. Man *was* in little all the sphere. As he grew and flourished, so did his world; as he decayed and died, so too his world. God's pattern was eternally repeated in macrocosm, geocosm, microcosm. Man's head was a copy of God and the universe, not only in its shape, but in its being the seat of Reason. Man, the epitome of God and the world, was rational; so were the world and the universe, into which God had imparted some of His own rationality. Each of the three worlds had its individuality, yet each was involved with the others, and all partook of God. Only since the seventeenth century has the poet felt the necessity of bringing together what the shears of a scientific philosophy cut apart.

The pencils of our historians are clear and sharp. The new mechanistic earth appeared as the result of teachings of Copernicus, Gilbert, Galileo, Descartes, Newton, all of whom, they imply, departed radically from the old superstition of a living earth. Historians are indulgent with the poets, if they mention them at all, for poets may be allowed to lag behind the times and repeat inherited metaphor. But historians are as severe as schoolmasters with any supposed "thinker" who is caught napping and still believes in the absurd idea of a living earth after Copernicus, Kepler, Galileo have bade the sun stand still and the earth move and take its place as a mechanical part of a mechanical universe.

These historians are quite correct, of course, about *what* happened. Some of them, I think, are on less firm ground when they tell us *when* and *how* it happened. We are led to believe that the scientist cast off overnight worn garments of thinking and rose in the morning to don a complete new outfit, leaving old superstition, old religion, old belief to the poets. The change was not so abrupt as that. In my introduction to these essays, I referred to Mr. Collingwood's statement about our own thinking: "Modern cosmology, like its predecessors, is based on an analogy. What is new about it is that the analogy is a new one." I say again that one of the most important differences between our modern attitude and the attitude of the Platonically-minded thinkers, from the ancients through the Renaissance, lies in our self-consciousness: we know that we are making analogies. Our ancestors believed that what we call "analogy" was *truth,* inscribed by God in the nature of things.

My purpose in this essay is twofold: I shall try to explain in more detail how and why the Circle of Perfection finally broke under the impact of seventeenth-century science, and at the same time suggest that old habits die hard, and that time-honored ways of thinking about the world and man did not change in a moment. The time-lag has sometimes been as clear in scientists as in poets. I am offering no apology for poets, who need none, though they often continue to live in a departed world or in a world made by their own imagination. Nor do I intend a critique of science. Perhaps I am really saying that many great scientists of the past were poets, and some of them mystics. They made their greatest discoveries by processes easily comprehensible to poets. They continued to speak a language that had been common to poet and scientist, when our forefathers still believed in a little world that was a copy of the great world and of God.

I

> Have not all soules thought
> For many ages, that our body is wrought
> Of Ayre and Fire, and other Elements?
> And now they thinke of new ingredients,
> And one Soule thinkes one, and another way
> Another thinkes, and 'tis an even lay.
>
> (*Second Anniversary,* II. 263-68)

So Donne in the *Second Anniversary.* Theories of the nature of man, like theories of the nature of the cosmos, were in confusion. Was man constituted of humors? Of elements? Were his imbalances to be corrected by the administration of "hot and dry," according to Galenic herbalists, or by chemicals, as Paracelsus declared? Paracelsus had opposed Galen; many opposed Paracelsus.

So far as the layman could see, one man's guess was as good as another's; it was "an even lay."

A revolution was to occur in physiology as in cosmology, and a little world of man was to die with the greater world and the universe. Human personality and character, as we have seen, had long been interpreted in terms in which the world and the universe were described. Physiology and psychology were one. Man's nature, like his body, was what the humors or the elements had made him. Later poets will not say with Shakespeare:

> His life was gentle, and the elements
> So mixed in him that Nature might stand up,
> And say to all the world, "This was a man!"

They will not pay tribute to a complete personality in such terms as Donne used of one of his "shees,"

> Shee whose Complexion was so even made,
> That which of her Ingredients should invade
> The other three, no Feare, no Art could guesse,
>
> (SA, ll. 123-25)

nor will they feel the close association between the humors of the body and mind and character that Donne took for granted when he wrote:

> Wee understood
> Her by her sight; her pure, and eloquent blood
> Spoke in her cheekes, and so distinctly wrought,
> That one might almost say, her body thought.
>
> (SA, ll. 243-46)

As man was cut off from Nature during the seventeenth century, so his mind was separated from his body. Most of all, the soul— in the medieval and Elizabethan sense—disappeared or was handed over by science to religion. It was symbolic of the new attitude that Descartes, still so close to his ancestors that he could not entirely dismiss the soul from his mechanical system as he could not entirely dismiss God, sought to localize the soul in the pineal gland. The Elizabethans were not afraid of the word *soul*. It was not something apart from the body or something that could be localized in it. It was man, the complete personality, the complex that made the individual an individual. But the time was coming when poets would no longer write, as did George Chapman in *Euthymiae Raptus,* of the happy state of the man in whom the soul had her proper empire:

> Then (like a man in health) the whole consort
> Of his tun'd body sings; which otherwise
> Is like one full of weiward maladies,
> Still out of tune.

Like his world and his universe, man had been a totality. Body, mind, and soul were one, "health" was a moral as well as a physical condition. Man was so involved in Nature that no separation was possible—nor would an Elizabethan have understood such separation. The Brights and the Burtons did not analyze melancholy purely as a state of mind; it was a state of the body, a state too of the soul. Timothy Bright approached his problem from his training as a physician, Robert Burton from his as a clergyman, but Burton was as competent a physician on this subject as was Dr. Bright; his was, in the truest sense of the phrase, "a cure of souls." The dissociation of sensibility, which critics have found in the modern world, was impossible among men to whom thinking and feeling were parts of the same process in body, mind, and spirit. But these are matters which we may understand better after we have seen the extent to which man, like the world and universe, gradually ceased to be part of an animate universe and became mechanism, a subject for objective analysis in terms of mechanical actions and reactions.

Donne could not have anticipated all this, of course, as he could not have grasped all the implications of the "new Philosophy." Yet some of his lines may serve as a guide to confusions in physiology which his age did realize, when men were living between an old world and a new. Let us go back to that passage of his, which seems to imply that while there were almost as many schools of medicine as doctors in those schools, the learned theorists had found no cure for the most common ills of man, as they had not been able to explain the basic problem of physiology:

> Knowst thou but how the stone doth enter in
> The bladders cave, and never breake the skinne?
> Knowst thou how blood, which to the heart doth flow,
> Doth from one ventricle to th' other goe?
> And for the putrid stuffe, which thou dost spit,
> Knowst thou how thy lungs have attracted it? . . .
> What hope have wee to know our selves, when wee
> Know not the least things, which for our use be?
>
> (SA, ll. 269-80)

*   *   *

Harvey's book, in which he announced the solution of the problem of circulation in 1628, is very different from most scientific

works of the earlier seventeenth century, consisting largely of careful reports of experiments with a minimum of theory, with almost
no philosophizing of the kind usually found in "natural histories"
of this period. There is no poetry here, and almost no overtones of
any sort, even in the introduction in which Harvey discussed the
usual belief "that the arteries carry the vital blood into the different
parts, abundantly charged with vital spirits, which cherish the
heat of these parts, sustain them when asleep, and recruit them
when exhausted." "No one denies," he wrote, almost with impa-
tience, "the blood as such, even the portion of it which flows in
the veins, is imbued with spirits." [1] But "spirituous blood is not
the less blood on that account"—and it was blood rather than
spirits that interested Harvey. As he cut up an eel, tied ligatures
about serpents, opened a live snake to watch the pulsation of the
heart, touched with his "finger wetted with saliva" the heart of a
pigeon, studied through a magnifying glass shrimps and crayfish,
to prove that they too had hearts, he was not moved to lyrical
rhapsody over these little worlds made cunningly, nor did he
ponder on the divine repetition of larger worlds in lesser. His
discovery "that there is a kind of rhythm" preserved between the
"two motions, one of the ventricles, the other of the auricles" might
have led that later physician, Sir Thomas Browne, to a charming
disquisition on the music of the spheres, the cosmic dance, or the
preestablished harmony of God. But Harvey—in more than chro-
nology—was the contemporary of Galileo, the predecessor of Descartes and Newton, with their world-machines. His mind turned
not to animism but to mechanism:

> Nor is this [harmony] for any other reason than it [the heart] is a
> piece of machinery, in which, though one wheel gives motion to
> another, yet all the wheels seem to move simultaneously; or in that
> mechanical contrivance which is adapted to firearms, where, the trig-
> ger being touched, down comes the flint, strikes against the steel,
> elicits a spark, which falling among the powder, ignites it, when the
> flame extends, enters the barrel, causes the explosion, propels the ball,
> and the mark is attained.[2]

Exact in his observations, empirical in his method, literal in his
style, Harvey seems as far removed from the poetical and mystical
tendencies of his age as any modern scientist could ask. Yet even
he could not completely dissociate himself from ways of thinking
ingrained in man for centuries. The analogy between macrocosm

[1] William Harvey, *Of the Motion of the Heart and Blood in Animals*,
trans. by Robert Willis, rev. by Alexander Bowie (London, 1889), Introduction.
[2] *Ibid.*, chapter V.

and microcosm still lingered in his mind; so too the Circle of Perfection. Indeed Harvey's capitalization in his startling announcement indicates the importance of the circle as the clue to the circulation of the blood. Originally he had taken for granted, like earlier physiologists, that the blood in the veins and the blood in the arteries were two separate streams; but the more he experimented, the more incapable he found himself of reaching a satisfactory explanation of the phenomena "unless the blood should somehow find its way from the arteries into the veins, and so return to the right side of the heart." "I began," he says, "to think whether there might not be a MOTION, AS IT WERE, IN A CIRCLE. Now, this I afterwards found to be true." Inevitably he went back to the macrocosm and microcosm: The motion of the blood is circular

> in the same way as Aristotle says that the air and the rain emulate the circular motion of the superior bodies; for the moist earth, warmed by the sun, evaporates; the vapours drawn upwards are condensed, and descending in the form of rain, moisten the earth again. By this arrangement are generations of living things produced; and in like manner are tempests and meteors engendered by the circular motion, and by the approach and recession of the sun.[3]

As in the great world, so in the small: through the motion of the blood, all parts of the body "are nourished, cherished, quickened by the warmer, more perfect, vapours, spirituous, and, as I may say, alimentive blood," which, having made its circular journey "returns to its sovereign, the heart, as if to its source, or to the inmost home of the body, there to recover its state of excellence and of perfection."

Harvey had discovered the process of circulation in terms of the mechanism of the heart; but he had not solved the greater mystery of the heart. He needed no "ethereal spirits" in order to chart the course of the circulation, yet he sought the aid of such spirits in order to explain the passage of heat from the sun, who warmed and nourished the world, to the heart, source of blood that warmed and nourished the animal. Only in the sections in which he discusses such mysteries does Harvey resort to what scientists would consider rhetoric. As the sun to the universe, so the heart to the little world:

> The heart . . . is the beginning of life; the sun of the microcosm, even as the sun in his turn might well be designated the heart of the world. . . . It is the household divinity which, discharging its func-

[3] *Ibid.*, chapter VIII.

tion, nourishes, cherishes, quickens the whole body, and is indeed the foundation of life. . . . Since death is a corruption which takes place through deficiency of heat, and since all living things are warm, all dying things cold, there must be a particular seat and fountain, a kind of home and hearth, where the cherisher of nature, the original of the native fire, is stored and preserved; from which heat and life are dispensed to all parts as from a fountain head. . . . Now, that the heart is this place, that the heart is the principle of life, . . . I trust no one will deny.[4]

There is little other rhetoric in the bare, clear unadorned style of Harvey's volume; and—except on these few occasions—little universal analogy. In so far as man could break with the past, Harvey put aside older ways of thinking, as older ways of writing. The body of man was not to him "the Marvel of Marvels," the "Mundum Magnum, a world to which all the rest of the world is subordinate." The body of man, like the bodies of eels, serpents, crayfish, was a "subject" for dissection, exposed upon a laboratory table before a scientist who objectively studied its processes and found in the little world a series of machines, operating upon mechanical principles.

Harvey was speaking a new language to ears still attuned to the old. The early reception of his theory was far from spectacular. As he himself said, "Some chid and calumniated me, and laid it to me as a crime that I had dared to depart from the precepts and opinions of all anatomists." Others, more willing to listen, did not at first believe that he had proved his case. His ideas met with skepticism on the Continent, and for a time evoked little general enthusiasm in the more receptive England. After his death in the mid-century, all that was changed, and Restoration England (as capable of thinking in terms of mechanical hearts as of mechanical universes), claimed him as "her boast and pride." . . .

II

In his own day William Gilbert of Colchester enjoyed more fame than did William Harvey in his. They were to go down to posterity together, praised by their countrymen as the two greatest British pre-Newtonian scientists. Proud of its part in exploration and discovery, England was equally proud that the great developments in the magnetic needle and in the study of magnetism were English.

* * *

Had Gilbert lived a generation later, he would undoubtedly have interpreted the power of his loadstone and of his magnetic

[4] *Ibid.*

earth in terms of mechanism. But Gilbert was an Elizabethan. His earth was still the animate earth he had inherited from Thales through a long train of philosophers and scientists. He was Elizabethan, too, in that it seemed to him entirely natural that the earth should have its "soul." That soul he also read over from earth again into his *terrella*. "The Magnetic Force," he began one of his most important chapters, "is Animate, or Imitates a Soul; in many Respects it Surpasses the Human Soul while that is United to an Organic Body." Gilbert had cast aside the adornments of rhetoric, but he could not write of the soul of his little earth without emotion:

> Wonderful is the loadstone shown in many experiments to be, and, as it were, animate. And this one eminent property is the same which the ancients held to be a soul in the heavens, in the globes, and in the stars, in sun and moon. . . . And I wonder much why the globe of earth with its effluences should have been by Aristotle and his followers condemned and driven into exile and cast out of all the fair order of the glorious universe, as being brute and soulless. . . . As for us, we deem the whole world animate, and all globes, all stars, and this glorious earth, too, we hold to be from the beginning by their own desinate souls governed and from them also to have the impulse of self-preservation. . . . Pitiable is the state of the stars, abject the lot of earth, if this high dignity of soul is denied them, while it is granted to the worm, the ant, the roach, to plants and morels. . . . Wherefore not without reason, Thales . . . declares the loadstone to be animate, a part of the animate mother earth and her beloved offspring.[5]

Gilbert was writing science, and his place in the history of science is secure. Yet he still thought as poets thought, and in spite of himself he often wrote as poets wrote of a living world and a living universe, and of the mysterious power God had implanted in their souls, which he found repeated even in the tiny *terrella* "sympathizing with the whole," that "natural little body endowed with a multitude of properties whereby many abstruse and unheeded truths of philosophy, hid in deplorable darkness, may be more readily brought to the knowledge of mankind."

Gilbert did not live to prove the importance in the cosmic scheme of that force and power he found in the loadstone and in the earth, emanating from a center to a circumference which was everywhere. He was too close to the beginnings of the "new Philosophy" to understand the full import of his own teaching. Kepler, Galileo, Descartes were still to come before Newton formulated the law of the universe. Gilbert, of course, knew only Copernicus, whose

[5] *Ibid.*, v.xii. pp. 308-12.

theories he did not accept *in toto*, though he devoted the last long section of the *De Magnete* to insistence upon the truth of one aspect of Copernicanism—the diurnal rotation of the earth.

III

Gilbert's conclusion leads us back again to the problem of the "new Philosophy" that called all in doubt to Donne eleven years after Gilbert had published his work. Let us pause over some of Donne's details before going on to discover the basic presuppositions of another important scientist who was largely responsible for the breaking of the cosmic circles in which Donne had found evidence for beauty, symmetry, and proportion:

> And new Philosophy calls all in doubt,
> The Element of fire is quite put out;
> The Sun is lost, and th' earth, and no mans wit
> Can well direct him where to looke for it.
>
> (*First Anniversary*, II. 205-8)

That "the Sun is lost, and th' earth" is clear enough: Copernicus had changed the places of both, and man looked at the heavens with unfamiliar eyes. If the planets still moved in circles, they moved about another center, including in their cosmic dance the earth which had become merely a planet. But what of the line immediately preceding? In the *Second Anniversary* Donne returned to this problem when he said, in his description of the progress of the soul to heaven,

> she stayes not in the ayre,
> To looke what Meteors there themselves prepare;
> She carries no desire to know, nor sense,
> Whether th' ayres middle region be intense;
> For th' Element of fire, she doth not know,
> Whether she past by such a place or no.
>
> (SA, ll. 189-94)

But in 1611 Donne had found additional reason for despondency when he realized that "the element of fire is quite put out." Tycho and others had declared that there was no such circle of fire between the earth and the moon as Aristotle had presupposed and men generally had believed, but it was less Tycho than his younger assistant Kepler who brought that truth home to such men as Donne, by a simple optical demonstration that "if there were a sphere of fire under the moon, considerable refraction of the rays emitted from the stars should be evident." [6] The orb of fire was

---

[6] See Charles Monroe Coffin, *John Donne and the New Philosophy* (New York, 1938), p. 169.

destroyed, as were those other solid orbs in which man had long believed. Still another circle had broken. But what of the great circles of the planets? Did they not remain, even though the solid orbs were gone, even though the center of the planets was now the sun?

> We thinke the heavens enjoy their Sphericall,
> Their round proportion embracing all.
> But yet their various and perplexed course,
> Observ'd in divers ages, doth enforce
> Men to finde out so many Eccentrique parts,
> Such divers downe-right lines, such overthwarts,
> As disproportion that pure forme. . . .
>   nor can the Sunne
> Perfit a Circle, nor maintaine his way
> One inch direct; but where he rose to-day
> He comes no more, but with a couzening line,
> Steales by that point, and so is Serpentine. . . .
> So of the Starres which boast that they doe runne
> In Circle still, none ends where he begun.
>
>   (*FA*, ll. 251-76)

This is not all "new Philosophy"; indeed many of Donne's lines deal with astronomical ideas known to the ancients; while others refer to Ptolemaic conceptions. The new astronomy had served only to sharpen problems and discrepancies already implicit in the old. Old and new together, however, they "disproportioned that pure forme" which laymen had believed existed in the heavens. Charles Monroe Coffin has analyzed all these lines in detail, and I shall pause over only one idea, which he does not stress, but which I believe lay behind Donne's feeling that the "Sphericall" and "round proportion" once enjoyed by the heavens could no longer be proved. In 1609 Kepler had published *De Motibus Stellae Martis*, his commentary on the planet Mars, in which he set down the first two of what we now call "Kepler's laws," demonstrating the fact that the planets move about the sun not in circles but in ellipses, formulating the law governing their motion. The existence of the most perfect circles of all had been disproved, ironically enough by a scientist who had felt the beauty and the mystery of the circle more profoundly than had Donne and professed poets.

Modern historians of science usually approach Kepler with some misgiving, unless they belong to the group that reads its early science only in extracts carefully selected by anthologists for their scientific value. Newton disturbs the others somewhat: he should not have been more concerned over his apocalyptical interpretations than he was about the law of gravity; he should not have been influenced by such a mystic as Jacob Boehme—yet he was. But Kepler bewilders them even more. They cannot deny the importance of his laws, but they deplore his superstition and his mysticism. The *furor poeticus* may be all very well in a poet, but a scientist should not have interlarded his serious work with poetry, nor intoxicated himself with words, as did Kepler. Kepler believed that the earth was alive and that its nature corresponded to the nature of a living universe; he believed in the sacred mystery of numbers, particularly the numbers THREE, FIVE, SEVEN; he believed in God. His way of thinking did not seem strange to Sir Thomas Browne, who wrote his most famous work to prove that a scientist may be deeply religious and felt with Kepler that an undevout astronomer must be mad. If Kepler was obsessed, it was not with superstition but with religion, religion of a sort that has long disappeared from modern science.

If we were not familiar with both the ideas and the language, we might well share the bewilderment of modern scientists when we read such a passage as this:

As the body produces hair on the skin, so the earth produces plants and trees, and as in the former lice are generated, so in the latter caterpillars, crickets, and many other insects and sea-monsters. As the body exudes moisture in tears and sweat through the pores, so does the earth exude amber and bitumen. As urine from the bladder, rivers flow from the mountains. As the body discharges winds that reek of sulphur and are inflammable, so the earth has its sulphur in subterranean fires, in thunder and lightning. As in the veins of living beings are formed blood and sweat, exuded through the passages of the body, so in the veins of the earth are metals and petrifactions, and from them issue steamy torrents. As other living beings take into their bodies food and drink, the earth, through its channels, draws into itself stuff of which much is concocted. It swallows the waters of the sea so that the ocean, in spite of the constant flowing of rivers, never overflows.[7]

This is not Paracelsus Bombast; it is a section of Kepler's "The Earth as a Living Being" in the *Harmonice Mundi*, a section, indeed, leading to one of his statements on the "dynamic power" of matter, which he called "energy." We read in the histories that "Kepler replaced the notion of soul, the animism of the earlier thinkers, by the notion of physical energy." Such was his effect, yet his passages on energy are usually embedded, as here, in others developing his belief that the world possesses both a living body

[7] My quotations from Kepler (with the exceptions noted) are based upon a translation made by my former colleague, Professor Anita Ascher of Smith College.

with senses and a soul with memory, which, as he says here, like a pregnant woman, has the potency of producing from itself something apart from itself. The soul of the earth is a flame "in which the image of the Divine Countenance is imprinted." The earth-soul reflects the cosmic soul: "For the Creator has in himself not only the geometrical archetypes of all things that He has made, but also the divine plan for all the phenomena still to be created. Hence the earth-soul reflects in itself the image of the zodiac and of the firmament, evidence of the interrelation and the homogeneity of terrestrial and celestial things." In the energy of the earth is the essence of the soul: "It is the steady burning of a flame." God himself is the "essence of energy," and, as the "essence of the flame is in its burning, so the essence of the image of God lies in its activity, its energy."

His conception of God is central to everything Kepler ever wrote. It was religion rather than science that first attracted the young Kepler to Copernicanism. As E. A. Burtt has pointed out, both Copernicus and Kepler were sun-worshipers. I borrow from Professor Burtt a passage he has translated from the *De Revolutionibus* of Copernicus:

> Then in the middle of the all stands the sun. For who, in our most beautiful temple, could set this light in another or better place, than that from which it can at once illuminate the whole? Not to speak of the fact that not unfittingly do some call it the light of the world, others the soul, still others the governor. Tremegistus calls it the visible God; Sophocles' Electra, the All-seer. And in fact does the sun, seated on his royal throne, guide his family of planets as they circle round him.[8]

In one of his youthful works, Kepler went farther than Copernicus:

> Of all the bodies in the universe the most excellent is the sun, whose whole essence is nothing else than the purest light, than which there is no greater star; which singly and alone is the producer, conserver, and warmer of all things; it is a fountain of light, rich in fruitful heat, most fair, limpid and pure to the sight . . . called king of the planets for his motion, heart of the world for his power, its eye for his beauty, and which alone we should judge worthy of the Most High God, should he be pleased with a material domicile, and choose a place in which to dwell with the blessed angels.[9]

From such sun-worship Kepler never recovered. Throughout his works the Sun is equated with the Father. Lover of the mystic

---

[8] Edwin A. Burtt, *Metaphysical Foundations of Physics* (New York, 1932), p. 45.
[9] *Ibid.*, p. 48.

THREE, he persistently read the Trinity into the phenomena of the heavens, as when he wrote in the *Harmonice Mundi:* "The number THREE is represented in the sphere by the surface, the centre, the content; in the stationary world by the fixed stars, the sun and the ether; in the divine Trinity by the Father, the Son and the Holy Ghost. As the Sun dwells in the midst of the planets, at rest, yet the source of motion, he is the image of God the Father, the Creator. The relation of God to his creation is that of the Sun to motion; and as the Father is the Creator in the Trinity, so the Sun is the source of motion among the stars."

Commenting upon the Nineteenth Psalm, which deals with Creation, Kepler said: "Clearly the Psalmist was not pretending to speak as an astronomer, for otherwise he would not have failed to mention the five planets, since there is no more admirable, more beautiful, more suitable evidence to thinking men of the wisdom of the Creator than their motions." He described his "rapture" when he realized that Plato's five regular solids afforded a clue to the distance between the orbits of the planets. Yet much as he loved those five regular solids, which play so large a part in his system, he loved the circle more. "Nothing has been created by God without design," he wrote in the *Harmonice Mundi.* "Among geometrical bodies, six have been distinguished with special significance: the sphere, and the five regular solids. The spherical is part of the outermost heaven, for the world is twofold, both moving and at rest. The latter is an image of the Divine Being, considered in itself, the former an image of God the Creator. The curved line is to be compared with God, the straight with his creatures." "Why did God, in adorning the universe," he asked in the *Mysterium Cosmographicum,*

consider and heed the difference between the straight and the curved, and [prefer] the nobleness of the curved? Because the most perfect Architect must of necessity create a work of the greatest beauty. Since the Creator conceived in his mind the idea of the universe, and since that idea contained what is existent and perfect, in order that the work created might likewise be perfect . . . he could not have taken the idea for the pattern of the universe from anything but his own Being. . . . This image of himself, this idea, God imprinted upon the universe, that this might be the best and most beautiful world. . . . So the wisest of Creators created dimensions and devised quantities, the nature of which coincides with the difference between the straight and the curved. . . . And the curved represents to us God.

Like the world and the universe, the soul of the world and the universe is a circle; and the soul of man, too, is at least potentially circular. Kepler takes us back to that circle whose circumference is nowhere, whose center is everywhere. Since the soul possesses energy, it moves from its seat, the center, to the circle. When it reaches out to "feel" external objects, these "acts of sensation are grouped about it circularly." "Every soul carries the circle in itself, not only abstracted from matter, but also in a way from dimension, so that centre and circle fall together, and the soul is an extended circle, as well as a centre without circumference."

Lover of the circle as of the sun, Kepler long took for granted that the planets must inevitably move in that perfect form. Indeed he was retarded in his study of planetary motion by this presupposition. When gradually the mathematician was forced to the conclusion that the planets moved in ellipses, the mystic was bewildered. One who reads his passages sympathetically against the background of their time will appreciate his dilemma and better understand the work in which he announced his first two laws. I hope I do not misrepresent his feeling when I paraphrase him thus: circular motion still remains the perfect motion, and the circle is always a symbol of God. If the planets do not move in circles, the limitation is not in the Creator but in the creature; the planets sought the circle, but in so far as they are not only spirit but matter, possessing limitations of grossness not shared by the Creator who is pure spirit, they move not in perfect circles but in ellipses, "imitating" so far as their natures permit "the beauty and the nobleness of the curved." Reluctantly and against his own desire Kepler broke the perfect Circle in the heavens.

Kepler's place as mathematician is secure. If his approach to mathematics was by way of a God who always geometrizes, his conclusions have stood the test of time. As metaphysician he seems on very shaky ground, so far as modern philosophers are concerned. He was a mystic, not a philosopher: mystically he found a way to truth even though the truth which modern science accepts in his work is only a small part of the whole. Kepler's "new Philosophy" was not that of a logician or metaphysician. Like the poets his was an aesthetic response, a gratification in a beautiful and glorious universe erected by the Great Geometer in which Kepler found the "mystical Mathematicks of the City of Heaven."

> Nature and Nature's laws lay hid in night.
> God said, "Let Newton be!" and all was Light.

Pope wrote the perfect epitaph for the Newton who was the father of modern science, the Newton who in his *Principia* formulated the fundamental law of the universe and described that universe as it continued to be described until yesterday. The Newton who gave the final death-blow to the old theory of an animate earth, who proved that both the world and the earth are mechanism, was the direct descendant of Galileo and Descartes. But there was another Newton, more concerned with his interpretations of Daniel [10] than with the mechanical laws of the universe, a Newton who was the son of Kepler, the mystic. It was the other Newton who added the last mysterious passages to the *Principia,* and who in both *Principia* and *Opticks* presupposed a "cosmic spirit" pervading all things, exciting sensation and volition in men and animals who were less mechanical than animate. I have often wondered whether that Newton felt that his formulation of the law of gravitation was not so much the beginning of something new as the climax of something very old. Here was the ultimate proof that the microcosm does reflect the macrocosm, that there is a repetition, interrelationship, interlocking between parts and whole, long surmised by classical, medieval, Renaissance scientists, poets, mystics: the law that governs the planets and restrains the stars in their macrocosmic courses is the same law that controls the falling of a weight from the Tower of Pisa or the feather from the wing of a bird in the little world, of which man still remains the center.

IV

. . . New Philosophy, as we have seen, was far from being the only cause of pessimism in 1611. The discoveries of Galileo, with implications that were read into them, served merely to bring to a climax attitudes which had been persistent for many years, as the death of Elizabeth had sharpened awareness that the old order was changing—for the worse, conservatives believed—in the little world of England.

Donne turned not to new but to old philosophy when he asked: "But keeps the earth her round proportion still?" and answered his own question in the negative. The perfect sphere of the earth was distorted and ugly through the sin of man. So far as astronomy was concerned, here too the new served to dramatize to laymen confusions and inconsistencies which astronomers had already found in the old. Galileo's telescopic observations proved what Copernicus, and Greek philosophers long before him had surmised, that the sun was lost and the earth, and no man's wit could well direct him where to look for it. The discovery not only of two *novae* but of unseen stars in profusion was merely a climax to ideas of decay and disintegration that had been persistent in classical, Jewish, and Christian thinking. The suggestion that some of these changes indicated decay in sun or moon was only another prophecy

[10] The great importance of apocalyptical interpretation in this period is abundantly proved by Ernest Lee Tuveson, *Millennium and Utopia* (Berkeley and Los Angeles, 1949).

of the end of the world, long anticipated by religious teachers. One circle had broken in the commonwealth of England; another in the irregularity of earth's surface; the greatest of all in the movements of the heavenly bodies. All was in pieces, all coherence gone for Donne, in whose life these changes in the external world and universe coincided with a period of unusual personal difficulty. After all, as Theodore Spencer pointed out, Donne and Hamlet were men of about the same age, experiencing the same world-sorrow at crucial moments in their own careers.

But John Donne did not live to see the final crashing down of the *flammantia moenia mundi,* the utter disruption of the Circle of Perfection. He went only so far as to say:

> And freely men confess that this world's spent,
> When in the Planets, and the Firmament
> They seeke so many new.
>
> (*FA*, ll. 209-11)

In my *Voyages to the Moon* I have traced that theme in detail, trying to show how old literary and philosophical ideas of other worlds than this came back with new meaning after Galileo's proof that the moon was a world like our world, with mountains and valleys, perhaps with water. Though Galileo later denied that last possibility, other important thinkers accepted it, and human imagination was stirred by the possibility that somehow, some time, man might travel to the moon, to find other living beings like or unlike himself. In the *Second Anniversary* Donne's voyaging soul on its way to heaven paid no more attention to the new world in the moon than to the circle of fire:

> She baits not at the Moone, nor cares to trie
> Whether in that new world, men live, and die,
>
> (Lines 195-96)

But Milton's Satan and Milton's Angel considered the possibility of a world in the moon,

> if land be there,
> Fields and inhabitants? Her spots thou seest
> As clouds, and clouds may rain, and rain produce
> Fruits in her softened soil for some to eat,
> Allotted there.
>
> (*Paradise Lost,* viii.144-48)

Others went further than Milton, and the idea of a world in the moon became a theme for romance and satire, but a theme, too, with immensely serious implications for man who had once been the sole son of God. If not in the moon, then perhaps in the planets, life might exist, and if not in our cosmic universe, then beyond in the myriads of cosmic universes created by a "new Philosophy," which was an old philosophy.

Copernicus and his immediate followers sowed a wind; the next generation reaped a whirlwind. The complete shattering of the circle was the result of an old idea that came back with new meaning and apparent proof: *the idea of the infinity of the universe and an infinity of worlds.* That conception had little to do with the Copernican hypothesis as we understand the phrase, though it was implied in the Copernican system. To what extent it was precipitated in England by Giordano Bruno, time may tell, for the problem of the influence of Bruno in seventeenth-century England is a teasing one, yet unsolved. But whether the ideas of infinity, so widely discussed, rejected, accepted, came from Bruno or Copernicus, from Nicholas of Cusa or his Greek antecedents, or whether they emerged by spontaneous generation makes little difference to us here. The time-spirit of which Bruno was only one exponent was abroad in the land, and poetic minds were responsive to the combination of philosophy, science, and poetry that Bruno welded into a whole.

As elsewhere in these essays, I shall employ a poet, rather than a scientist, as our guide to old ways of thinking, Henry More. . . . More was a Cambridge Platonist, with all the connotations and contradictions that the word *Platonism* involved in the seventeenth century. Like his fellow-student at Christ's College, John Milton, he read into Plato much that would have surprised that philosopher. His Platonism was a fusion of many sources: the mysticism of Pythagoras, the magic of the Hermetic books, interpretations of Ficino, Pico della Mirandola, Porphyry, most of all "Plotin," as he called Plotinus. His was the Platonism, too, of Kepler, by whose mysticism More was influenced. His God was the Deity of Plenitude, creating with lavish and unwithdrawing hand. But we need not enter into these matters of philosophy and theology in detail. One of the great appeals of Platonism to More was that it afforded a philosophical basis for acceptance of the new astronomy. Vestiges of the old astrology remain in More's thinking, as in Milton's; he never lost his feeling for the "true consent" of planet and element. Yet Platonism could be made compatible with the Copernican and Galilean astronomy, as with the expansion of the universe taught by the Brunoesque philosophy. Indeed to Platonists like More— as to Copernicus himself—the new astronomy was not new, but a welcome return to cosmology earlier than that of Ptolemy, taught by Pythagoras, Democritus, Leucippus, and many others.

❋　　❋　　❋

. . . The telescopic heavens enthralled rather than disturbed him. He did not feel with Donne that new astronomy had "disproportioned the pure form" of the heavens.

> Tell me therefore
> When you behold with your admiring eyes
> Heavens Canopie all to be spangled o're
> With sprinkled stars, what can you well devise
> Which causen may such careless order in the skies.[11]

* * *

. . . The goodness of God has not been limited to one creation of one universe. Time was infinite, creation a continuing process:

> long ago there Earths have been
> Peopled with men and beasts before this Earth,
> And after this shall others be again
> And other beasts and other humane birth . . .
> Another Adam once received breath,
> And still another in endlesse repedation . . .
>
> (Stanza 76)

Beyond and beyond our universe, stretching in space and time, are, were, and might be other worlds, filled with the creatures of God. Let man begin to understand the unbounded universe of which he is part and he will cease to talk about the "disorder" and the "disproportion" of the heavens, think rather in terms of new order and new proportion, new distances for which mathematicians and astronomers were only beginning a new language, and grasp in some small degree the extraordinary and astounding new harmony of the skies.

Religious philosopher that he was, Henry More created his infinite universe from the Infinite God in whom he believed, a God of plenitude, whose nature was to create to super-abundance:

> Wherefore this precious sweet Ethereall dew
> For ought we know, God each where did distill,
> And thorough all that hollow Vastnesse threw,
> And the wide gaping drought therewith did fill,
> His endlesse overflowing goodnesse spill
> In every place; which streight he did contrive
> Int' infinite severall worlds, as his best skill
> Did him direct and creatures could receive:
> For matter infinite needs infinite worlds must give . . .

[11] Henry More. *Infinity of Worlds*, in *Complete Poems*, ed. by Alexander Grosart (1878), stanza 53.

> And that even infinite such worlds there be,
> That unexhausted Good that God is hight,
> A full sufficient reason is to me,
> Who simple Goodness make the highest Deity.
>
> (Stanzas 50-51)

Such a Deity could not have created one world, one universe, once and once only; His world, His universe, His cosmos must reach to infinity, without limitation of time or space, must be as diverse, as full, as varied as its limitations would permit. Not for Henry More, generous and exuberant by nature, the Aristotelian Unmoved Mover, the Self-Sufficient who had no need for self-expression in creation. More's Deity was far more lavish than the Nature praised by Comus, expressing Himself not in the spawn of the sea and silkworms but in worlds unnumbered. . . .

As Milton had no vocabulary for the vast illimitable ocean without bound, Henry More had none for the infinite universe. In his metaphysics, he transferred to Space some twenty adjectives and epithets that had formerly been applied only to Deity. The new universe made him "drunk with Divinitie," "brent with eager rage"; his "heart for joy doth spring"; his soul was exalted by "an inward triumph"; his "spirits move with pleasant trembeling." He exulted in the experience, yet he trembled with emotion compounded of delight and awe. A generation later men began to find words for such experience, responding with mingled pleasure and "trembeling" to the vast in the universe, later still to the vast in the world. Henry More had always loved beauty, but beauty had been associated in his mind with the finite, the limited, the proportioned. Beauty satisfied the emotions; it did not confound them. Infinity overwhelmed. In his conversion to infinity Henry More had had an experience he was never to forget. If he could not write as a poet, he felt as a poet, and felt something no poet before him had attempted to express. He was the first English poet who attempted to put into language man's feeling for what was not yet called Sublime—a Sublime which came from the "new Philosophy" that no longer called all in doubt, but rather released human imagination to a spaciousness of thought man had not known before. The Idea of Infinity had demolished the Circle of Perfection.

ralph crum

POETRY SOLEMNLY SURVEYS THE
NEWTONIAN WORLD MACHINE

In 1687 Newton's *Principia Mathematica* was published,
and thus was opened for the whole field of human thought the
mathematical ideal of science. Its underlying philosophy is that the
universe is a vast machine and that the goal of science is to discover the mathematical relations which hold in every part of that
great mechanism. This is to be accomplished mainly through reasoning deductively from mathematical principles already discovered, but also by making facts derived empirically fit under some
mathematical law, perhaps still undiscovered.[1] Thus was strengthened the position of Descartes, taken over forty years before, that
man himself had been formed by mechanical means, though always under the governing power of God, and that he acts and re-
acts according to a complicated system of springs. Less than a
quarter of a century after Descartes, Spinoza was attempting, in
his *Ethics,* to deal with man's passions and motives, as if they were
part of a geometric system. The idea that man was furnished with
a sure guide in his conscience (i.e., a source of revelation of the
divine will) was rudely shattered in 1690 with the publication of
Locke's *Essay Concerning Human Understanding*, which denied
the doctrine of innate ideas, and which made sensation the only
source of knowledge. This knowledge was gained mechanically,
inasmuch as man's mind was considered a blank tablet upon which
experience wrote. Thus the new science and the philosophy which
underlay it offered a challenge to the conception of man as a free
moral agent.

From *Scientific Thought in Poetry* by Ralph Crum, copyright © 1931
by Columbia University Press.
[1] Preface to *Principia Mathematica.*

It would appear that such a doctrine of mechanism must tend to crowd out everything mysterious, supernatural, or divine. Logically it would do so, except for the fact that there must have been a Master Mechanic to build the Mechanism and to start it going. Newton argued that the world machine was not quite perfect and that it was constantly requiring regulation. The most classical expression of the argument from design came over a hundred years afterwards, in William Paley's *Natural Theology* (1802), in which he argued that the forms which organized bodies bear prove the necessity of an intellectual designer. This Deistic movement which aimed to preserve the ancient religion by making it rational, believed, in the main, that by taking out of religion the mysterious element, or nearly all of it, the reason, through scientific knowledge of how Nature works, would establish logically the existence of God. It attempted, in brief, a synthesis between orthodox religion and the new science. In England Deism continued to mark the most liberal religious thought until the last quarter of the eighteenth century, when we find the views of Hume and those of Gibbon, Tom Paine, and William Godwin coming to the fore. In France, however, as we shall note in the next chapter, a more atheistic point of view gained ground with greater rapidity.

Our purpose here is to note how English poetry in certain of the more outstanding instances reacted to these changes in philosophical and religious thought, in so far as this was itself acted upon by the new science. Poetry, as we have noted, has been sensitive at least in some of its aspects, to the philosophical and religious thought of the time. That eighteenth-century poetry was sensitive, in part at least, to these changing factors is evidenced by comparing Bernard de Mandeville's "Grumbling of the Hive" (1705), with Pope's *Essay on Man* (1732-34). Mandeville upheld the idea of Hobbes, which we noted was current among some poets in the latter part of the seventeenth century, that selfishness and not the moral sense, is the sole principle by which man should be governed. Nay more, Nature herself is relentless, subjecting all her creatures to the vagaries of a ruthless chance. But in Pope's poem we have a versified exposition of the deistic position, as Pope understood it from Bolingbroke. Here nature is conceived in a very different light from that which prompted those seventeenth-century poets and Mandeville himself. Although Nature is a "mighty maze," it is "not without a plan." [2] Like Milton, he is going to attempt to "vindicate the ways of God to Man." Since man can see only a part and not the whole, he cannot know God's plan. Man's time is a moment and his space is only a point. The universe in all its parts works harmoniously and keeps a fixed order, which

[2] *Essay on Man.*

only the "madness, pride, impiety," of "a vile worm" could expect
to have changed for his special benefit. Therefore, "whatever is,
is right." Man should not presume to scan God, but "the proper
Mankind is Man." Then follows a section in which the
leavored to fit the physical sciences into his scheme of
nd in which he concludes that this knowledge is of little
the individual himself. Of the two principles of man,
and Reason, both are equally necessary, but it is the
Reason to distinguish between the good and the bad. "The
Nature was the reign of God." Reason teaches that man
mself best who serves the welfare of society. The Univer-
acts by general laws, and happiness subsists not in one
. "Order is Heav'n's first law." Faith, Law, Morals, all end
of God and Love of Man. Self-love wakes the virtuous
ction, extending to friend, parent, neighbor, country, and
whole human race.

content to rest upon the assurance which his reason gives
there is a "Great First Cause" about which he can know
beside which he feels very insignificant and blind, but
cause of the law and order that he finds in the world, he
be right and good.[3]

t of "faith," as we must term it in contradiction to
e," seems to contain nothing contradictory so far as the
are. But can we blame the poet, when so many philoso-
theologians of his time were falling into the same fallacy
from design? Or, ought we to term this a "rationaliza-
he sense that James Harvey Robinson defines the term,
ontaneous and loyal support of our preconceptions"?[4]
, Hume had not yet pointed out the fallacy in this argu-
ther it is to the credit of the poets that they have stead-
ed to accept the mechanical explanation as the final one,
on that will naturally be answered according to one's
eed or one's philosophy. It is a fact, however, that Pope
declined to endorse this principle in its entirety. So
that there is a divine plan of some kind towards which
is working, and also because the thoroughly scientific
its implications at least refuses to take account of this,
ndemns what he considers the presumptions of science.
ounts "where Science guides," and measures earth,
and states the tides, et cetera, is like him who attempts
ternal Wisdom how to rule."[5]

rsal Prayer," Globe Edition of Pope, p. 227.
Kinds of Thinking," in *The Mind in the Making.*
m, II.

101

> Superior beings, when of late they saw
> A mortal Man unfold all Nature's law,
> Admir'd such wisdom in an earthly shape,
> And shew'd a Newton as we shew an Ape.[6]

He warns the Scientist that he must be modest. If we would see what Science really is,

> First strip off all her equipage of Pride;
> Deduct what is but Vanity, or Dress,
> Or Learning's Luxury, or Idleness;
> Or tricks to shew the stretch of human brain,
> Mere curious pleasure; or ingenious pain;
> Expunge the whole, or lop th' excrescent parts
> Of all our Vices have created Arts;
> Then see how little the remaining sum,
> Which serv'd the past, and must the time to come![7]

The tendency of modern science to rely too much upon the testimony of the senses is apt to promote false pride in us, because,

> To observations which ourselves we make
> We grow more partial for th' Observer's sake;
> To written Wisdom, as another's less:
> Maxims are drawn from Notions, those from Guess.[8]

Furthermore,

> How little, mark! that portion of the ball,
> Where faint at best, the beams of Science fall.[9]

Indeed, many of the scientists whom he has observed, or conjured up in his imagination, deserve, he thinks, to be classified among the dunces, and Science itself is pictured as groaning beneath the footstool of the Goddess of Dullness. These dull ones,

> Full in the midst of Euclid dip at once,
> And petrify a Genius to a Dunce:
> Or set on Metaphysic ground to prance,
> Show all his paces, not a step advance.[10]

[6] *Ibid.*, II.
[7] Epistle II.
[8] *Moral Essays*, Epistle I. "To Sir Richard Temple," Globe Edition.
[9] *Dunciad*, III.
[10] *Ibid.*, III.

A gloomy clerk, "whose pious hope aspires to see the day when Moral Evidences shall quite decay," dogmatizes upon the meaning of contemporary science thus:

> Let others creep by timid steps, and slow,
> On plain Experience lay foundations low,
> By common sense to common knowledge bred,
> And last, to Nature's cause thro' Nature led,
> All-seeing in thy mists, we want no guide,
> Mother of Arrogance, and Source of Pride!
> We nobly take the high Priori Road
> And reason downward, till we doubt of God;
> Make Nature still encroach upon his plan;
> And shove him off as far as e'er we can:
> Thrust some Mechanic cause into his place;
> Or bind in Matter, or diffuse in Space.[11]

Is not the poet here deploring that characteristic which he feels is lying implicit, at least in eighteenth-century science, "Of naught so doubtful as of Soul and Will," and which is tending to see God as Lucretius saw him, a God,

> Wrapt up in Self, a God without a Thought,
> Regardless of our merit or default.[12]

Many other poets and writers in the eighteenth century felt that the scientists were presumptuous and filled with overweening pride. Swift's ridicule of the philosophers and the scientists in Gulliver's voyage to Laputa is a case in point. Dr. Arbuthnot, likewise, while finding much to praise in mathematics, nevertheless ridicules the abuses of learning and pedantry in his contribution to the Scriblerus Club (1713-14).

Mark Akenside, however, composed a "Hymn to Science" in which he bade Science descend and "illumine each bewildered thought" and "bless" his "laboring mind," disperse phantoms, scholasts' learning, sophists' cant, visionary bigot's rant, monk's philosophy.

> Let thy powerful charms impart
> The patient head, the candid heart,
> Devoted to thy sway.

But he also prays that he may proceed cautiously

[11] *Ibid.*, IV.
[12] *Ibid.*, IV.

> And from the dead, corporeal mass,
> Through each progressive order, pass
> To Instinct, Reason, God.

Science is warned, moreover, against soaring "too high, in that divine abyss," and admonished to be content to lend "thy beams" to faith and

> Make me the judge of my desires,
> The master of my heart.

Akenside showed a discrimination in his handling of the problem, that appeared all too rare. He pointed out that there were three classes of truth: "matter of fact, experimental, or scientifical truth; which last is either metaphysical or geometrical, either purely intellectual or perfectly abstracted." [13]

Among the poets who championed science, James Thomson (1700-48) is worthy of an important place, not because he wrote one of the many poems on Newton, but because of the knowledge of science he displayed in that poem, and the attitude which he manifested. The poet, writing just after Newton's death in 1727, who speaks of himself as aspiring like the "ethereal flames . . . in Nature's general symphony to join," [14] does not, as Cowley did, depict Newton Apollo-like chasing Daphne into the secret heart of man, but as one who,

> . . . from motion's simple laws
> Could trace the secret hand of Providence
> Wide-working through the universal frame.[15]

He "sat not down and dreamed Romantic schemes," but

> . . . with heroic patience years on years
> Deep-searching, saw at last the system dawn,
> And shine, of all his race, on him alone.

The poet then enumerates more specifically what Newton contributed to science: the principle of gravitation, a declaration concerning the influence of the moon upon the tides, the fact that the stars are all suns, subject to the laws of gravitation as our own solar system, that the comet pursues a long elliptic curve, that

[13] "Pleasures of Imagination," 1765, Book II.
[14] "To the Memory of Sir Isaac Newton," I.
[15] *Ibid.,* I.

sound proceeds by waves, that a ray of sunlight can be broken up into its component parts by passing it through a prism, and innumerable other things. Thomson asks:

> Did ever poet imagine aught so fair,
> Dreaming in whispering groves by the hoarse brook?

Another virtue displayed by the scientist is the order-bringing characteristic of his work, restoring "whirling vortices and circling spheres to their first great simplicity." Surely such a great man, the poet says in effect, must be more than a "finer breath of spirits dancing through the tubes awhile, and then forever lost in vacant air." Indeed, in the case of this renowned scientist, the poet boasts, "his devotion swelled responsive to his knowledge":

> For could he
> Whose piercing mental eye diffusive saw
> The finished university of things
> In all its order, magnitude and parts
> Forbear incessant to adore that Power
> Who fills, sustains, and actuates the whole?

The poet can eulogize the scientist because the scientist recognizes something more than mere mechanism. The issue between a world-machine and a loving, personal God is not at all clearly drawn; but we feel, if it were, the poet would be upon the side of religion.

About seventeen years after Thomson penned his lines, and about a decade after Pope's *Essay on Man*, another poet was turning the same problems over in his mind. Edward Young (1683-1765) wrote *The Complaint, or Night Thoughts*, in 1742-44, the occasion of some of these gloomy thoughts being the deaths of his wife and his step-daughter. Although he often mused conventionally, as shown in the following lines,

> Not deeply to discern, not much to know
> Mankind was born to wonder, and adore,

yet during the course of his thinking he found himself beset with many doubts. In the first place, the great sense of space which the new science has revealed rather terrifies him:

> What involution! what extent! what swarms
> Of worlds, that laugh at earth? immensely great!
> Immensely distant from each other's spheres
> What, then, the wondrous space thro' which they roll?
> At once it quite engulf's all human thought;
> 'Tis comprehension's absolute defeat.

and furthermore,

> The boundless space, thro' which these rovers take
> Their restless roam, suggests the sister thought
> Of boundless time.

On the other hand, however, the conception of the world as a machine seems a comfort:

> Nor think thou seest a wild disorder here;
> Through this illustrious chaos to the sight,
> Arrangement neat, and chastest order reign.
> The path prescrib'd inviolably kept,
> Upbraids the lawless sallies of mankind.

There seems to be, then, a great plan in nature:

> We rave, we wrestle, with great nature's plan:
> We thwart the Deity; and 'tis decreed,
> Who thwarts his will, shall contradict their own.
> Hence our unnatural quarrels with ourselves;
> Our thoughts at enmity, our bosom broils . . .

In that case the cure for all this melancholy and doubt is to "read Nature" which "bids dead matter aid us in our creed."
So many scientists, he complains, fail to read the moral truth which lies in nature:

> And dive in science for distinguisht names,
> Dishonest fomentation of your pride;
> Sinking in virtue, as you rise in fame.
> Your learning, like the lunar beams, affords
> Light, but not heat; it leaves you undevout,
> Frozen at heart, while speculation shines.

And anyway, there is something in the scientific temper of his time that appears more curious than devout,

> More fond to fix the place of heaven, or hell,
> Than studious this to shun, or that secure.

But, from his religion comes the thought that:

> Humble love,
> And not proud reason, keeps the door of heaven;
> Love finds admission, where proud science fails.
> Man's science is the culture of his heart;

> And not to lose his plummet in the depths
> Of nature, or the more profound of God.

Indeed,

> Take God from nature, nothing is left;
> Man's mind is in a pit, and nothing sees.

The poet finds comfort that in the wondrous motions of the heavenly bodies a design is to be seen. He cannot bear the thought that the world is simply a vast machine. The planets, cast off from the sun, feel something of the great central love.

> By sweet attraction, no less strongly drawn;
> Aw'd, and yet raptur'd; raptur'd, yet serene:

The forces which the scientist labels as mechanical are thus personified by Young in terms of an egocentric world. In his thinking he has not even yet sensed the deep significance of the Newtonian physics. He has, perhaps, a premonition of what it may mean, but against the logical implication of the idea he rebels. And with reason, I think it must be admitted, because according to the classical tradition, the poet should seek to express beauty. It is true, as Thomson pointed out, that the scientist may also express beauty; but as Lucretius found, it is difficult to make a mechanical idea of life appear beautiful to people who have been nourished upon the other conception. The scientist has to close his eyes and heart to most of his natural inclinations and desires; he is a scientist, primarily through great mental discipline. The poet, on the other hand, at least according to the traditions he has inherited, must address man's feelings as well as his intellect. The relative proportions of feeling and intellect which have gone into poetry, have of course, varied from time to time, and to a certain extent, with man and man within any given period. In the main, however, one period demands more of one element than the other. In this sense, at least, the eighteenth century, especially the first half, tended to exact more of the intellectual element in poetry than the element of feeling. The poets in the main, however, in England— and this appears to be a very vital fact in our discussion—could not bring themselves to sing whole-heartedly about a mechanical world. It remains for us, then, to consider to what extent the traditional elements in poetry can account for this fact.

It will be recalled that for Aristotle poetry was an ideal imitation of truth and that its aim was aesthetic pleasure. While this theory, to be sure, did not attract a great deal of attention in either the ancient or the medieval periods, it became very prominent in

Italy during the sixteenth century, spread to France in the seventeenth, and was reflected in English criticism during the first half of the eighteenth. This pseudo-classicism came to have implications which the original theory never intended. These principles were regarded in the light of laws formulated by the ancients, but which had all the force of the scientific laws of a Newton. Indeed, they were regarded in much the same light.

> Those Rules of old discovered, not devis'd,
> Are Nature still, but Nature methodiz'd.[16]

Therefore,

> Learn hence for ancient rules a just esteem
> To copy Nature is to copy them.[17]

The poet owed little or nothing to that very intangible thing known as "inspiration." Poetry was an art, the rules of which had been supplied by the Ancients. One could become a poet almost mechanically, then, by following the precepts and examples of these legislators.

If there was something rather machine-like in that idea of poetry, there was at the same time, something which marked a difference in attitude between the poet and the scientist. Thus, while the true poet must look backward for his guide and counsel, the scientist (when he was most worthy of that name) was looking forward to new formulations and discoveries in the future. This difference in outlook tended naturally to keep the work of the scientist and the poet apart, even though both might be equally rational. Poetry in looking back, was fostering respect for a traditional past; science, on the other hand, was shaking off the shackles of that same past. No wonder, then, that poetry should feel itself more in harmony with theological and traditional philosophy than with science. Hence, the poet Thomson pictures poetry as

> Tutored by Philosophy and informing the page
> With music, image, sentiment, and thought,
> Never to die; the treasure of mankind,
> Their highest honour, and their truest joy![18]

One of the best expositions of the pseudo-classicism in England was that given by Samuel Johnson, after the full force of the movement had already spent itself. He, it will be recalled, maintained

[16] Pope's "Essay on Criticism." I.
[17] *Ibid.*
[18] "Summer," 1, 1753 f.

that the function of art was to express the typical rather than the particular and that only the best examples should be exhibited.[19] It is necessary to imitate only those parts of nature "which are proper for imitation." [20] The theory which primarily keeps science and poetry apart, however, is the fact that

> Poetry cannot dwell upon the minute distinctions, by which one species differs from another, without departing from that simplicity of grandeur which fills the imagination; nor dissect the latent qualities of things without losing its general power of gratifying every mind, by recalling its conceptions.[21]

Johnson, however, was not a slave to rules. "Whatever part of an art," he writes in one connection, "can be executed or criticized by rules, that part is no longer the work of genius, which implies excellence out of the reach of rules." [22] Indeed, his allowance for genius, for enthusiasm,[23] for novelty,[24] may not be orthodox pseudo-classicism, but it does not tend to bring science and poetry any nearer. On the contrary, it is looking in the direction of a further revolt.

Are we justified in concluding, then, that the English poet's respect for tradition in the first half of the eighteenth century is a sufficient explanation of the fact that he does not whole-heartedly praise the conception of a mechanical world? Or are we to assume with William Blake, considerably later, that imagination and reason are really inimical, though perhaps not necessarily irreconcilable?

Believing that his poems, or at least large portions of them, were truly the products of supernaturalism, William Blake (1757-1827) very naturally could not rest content with ideas built entirely upon human experience.[25] It is true, as some critics have pointed out, that many of his poems have received careful and painstaking revision at his hands, yet believing in inspiration as he did, he condemned what he considered the mocking spirit of Voltaire and Rousseau against religion:

> The Atoms of Democritus
> And Newton's Particles of Light

---

[19] *The Rambler,* No. 4.
[20] *Ibid.*
[21] *The Rambler,* No. 36, "The Reasons that Pastorals Delight."
[22] *The Adventurer,* No. 76.
[23] *Ibid.,* No. 79.
[24] *Ibid.,* No. 82.
[25] He testifies that many passages of his poems were dictated to him directly by spirits. See Diary, Reminiscences, and Correspondence of Henry Crabbe Robinson. Boston. 1880, Vol. 2, pp. 34, 38-39.

Are sands upon the Red Sea Shore,
Where Israel's tents do shine so bright.[26]

Yet, it is hardly fair to Blake to attribute his antagonism to science entirely to religion, for with him it went very much deeper than any creed. He was concerned very much more with the limitations of the reasoning power itself:

The Reasoning Power in Man . . . is a false Body,
an Incrustation over my Immortal Spirit, a selfhood
which must be put off and annihilated alway.[27]

He is, moreover, attacking a particular power of the mind—that of drawing generalizations from sense data and regarding these as sufficient explanations of final causes. And right there, it seems to me, lies Blake's special significance for this study. He definitely connected that attitude of mind with the Baconian and Newtonian philosophy in a time when such a clear understanding of the matter, particularly upon the part of a poet, was all too rare.

For Bacon and Newton, sheath'd in dismal steel, their terrors hang
Like iron scurges over Albion, Reasoning like vast Serpents
Enfold around my limbs, bruising my minute articulations.[28]

Furthermore, he states definitely that he is opposed to a "Philosophy of Five Senses . . . complete," which was given "into the hands of Newton and Locke." [29] Note, in addition, how he characterizes the machine-age:

I turn my eyes to the Schools and Universities of Europe,
And there behold the Loom of Locke, whose Woof rages dire,
Wash'd by the Water-wheels of Newton: black the cloth
In heavy wreaths folds over every Nation: cruel works
Of many Wheels I view, wheel without wheel, with cogs tyrannic,
Moving by compulsion each other; not as those in Eden, which,
Wheel within wheel, in freedom revolve, in harmony and peace.[30]

Whatever we may feel about Blake's visionary propensities, it is indeed clear that he understood the character of the Newtonian science and its implications better than the other poets we have been considering in this chapter, and better, I believe, than any English poet contemporary with him. The issue that the accept-

[26] "Mock on, mock on, Voltaire, Rousseau."
[27] "Milton," f. 42.
[28] A Vision of Albion,—from "Jerusalem," f. 15.
[29] "The Song of Los."
[30] "Jerusalem," f. 15.

ance of the mechanical conception of the universe also implied logically the rejection of all forms of supernaturalism was clearly perceived by him:

> But the spectre, like hoar-frost and a mildew, rose over Albion,
> Saying, "I am God, O Sons of Men! I am your Rational Power
> Am I not Bacon and Newton and Locke, who teach humility to Man,
> Who teach Doubt and Experiment? and my two wings, Voltaire,
>   Rousseau?
> Where is that Friend of Sinners, that Rebel against my Laws,
> Who teaches Belief to the Nations, and an unknown Eternal Life?
> Come hither into the desert and turn these stones to bread!
> Vain, foolish Man wilt thou believe without Experiment,
> And build a World of Phantasy upon my great Abyss,
> A World of Shapes in craving lust and devouring appetite?" [31]

The consequences of such a philosophy are very apparent to him, for if our knowledge is to be limited to only what our five senses reveal to us and these generalizations are to be taken as the final words then "the Philosophic and Experimental would soon be at the Ratio of all things; and stand still, unable to do other than repeat the same dull round over again." [32] But from this, we are saved, he declares, by the "Poetic or Prophetic Character." Indeed, the real world is the world of Imagination, of which "this Vegetable Universe is but the faint shadow." [33]

This explains, in part, at least, his opposition to classicism, for the "Grecian is Mathematic Form: Gothic is Living Form. Mathematic Form is eternal in the Reasoning Memory: Living Form is Eternal Existence." [34] "We do not want either Greek or Roman models if we are but just and true to our Imaginations." [35] He does not mean to imply, however, that the ancient writers were not inspired. In the new age "those grand works of the more ancient and consciously and professedly inspired men will hold their proper rank and the Daughters of Memory shall become the Daughters of Inspiration." [36] In brief, poetry is not to be regarded as the handmaid of science or philosophy. Instead, "let the Philosopher always be the servant and scholar of Inspiration." [37]

Even though Blake's attitude appears at first to be one that definitely places poetry and science in opposition, he does not, it will be noted, state that the poet should eschew science. Rather, his

[31] "Jerusalem," f. 54.
[32] Oxford Edition of Blake's *Poetical Works,* p. 426.
[33] "Jerusalem," f. 77.
[34] "On Virgil."
[35] "Milton," from the Preface.
[36] *Ibid.*
[37] From *Descriptive Catalogue,* see "Poems," p. 439.

own concern for, and his discussions of, space, time, and infinity, and the limitations of the scientific attitude of mind would belie any such conclusion had he made it.[38] His main quarrel with the scientific point of view is, as we have already seen, that it is all too content to rest upon the assumption that the dictums derived from sense experience and from experimentation constitute the one and only truth. He steadfastly refuses, for example, to accept the idea of mechanism as being the whole explanation of human existence. Instead, this higher truth, he believes, is revealed through poetry, which pierces beyond the veil of semblance and discovers the true essence beyond.

But how is poetry to reveal this truth which transcends human experience? That was Blake's problem, to which he addressed himself assiduously. Poetry, of course, must express beauty. The poet, therefore, must strive to render this transcendent truth in sensuous form, to translate his conception into an image which shall serve as a key or a symbol, just as the luminous eye of the tiger symbolizes the whole tiger in a dark jungle,

> Tiger! Tiger burning bright
> In the forests of the night.[39]

He tried, in brief,

> To see a World in a grain of sand,
> And a Heaven in a wild flower.[40]

It scarcely needs to be pointed out that this is a dangerous pathway to tread, because it so easily leads into the morass of visions imperfectly realized and of obscurities which are apparently meaningless, and this was the fate which overtook many of the so-called prophetic books of Blake in the latter part of his life.

In these prophetic books he sought myths to express, not the latest philosophical truths, but the truth which is itself the source of philosophy—the immediate revelation of which poets and prophets partake. Since these works cover a comparatively long period of time, his mythological characters, symbolizing the higher truth, undergo many modifications in the course of his labors; but in the main it is fairly clear, thanks to some recent researches,[41] what Blake was attempting to accomplish. When, for example, he

---

[38] "Poems," pp. 372, 373, 378, 387.
[39] "The Tiger."
[40] "Auguries of Innocence."
[41] *The Prophetic Writings of William Blake*, by D. J. Sloss and J. P. R. Wallis, in two volumes, published by the Clarendon Press, Oxford, in 1926, is a work that is especially illuminating on this point.

wished to symbolize the "Eternal Essence," he sometimes referred to it as "Jesus" and sometimes as the "Four Zoas," of which he says:

> What are the Natures of those Living Creatures the Heavenly Father
>   only
> Knoweth! No individual Knoweth, nor Can Know in all Eternity.[42]

From this Eternal Essence, he represents the creator of men (symbolized as Urizen) separating himself and existing in time. So Time (symbolized by Los) came to have a separate existence from the Eternal Essence; and Space (personified as Enitharmon), by seceding from Time, is still further removed from Eternal Truth. Thus, the assertion of selfhood tends to take one further away from the initial Truth, and this fact he represents symbolically by the Fall of Man.

Whatever we may feel about Blake's success in accomplishing what he set out to do, we must acknowledge that his attempt was at least significant, because obviously he was trying to make poetry perform a very difficult task: to present not merely abstract truths in sensuous imagery, but also mystical, intuitive perceptions, and

> . . . to open the immortal Eyes
> Of Man inwards into the Worlds of Thought, into Eternity
> Ever expanding in the Bosom of God, the Human Imagination.[43]

If our conclusion is that Blake did not succeed entirely in his purpose, that decision does not, of course, imply that the task is impossible. With that question we are not here immediately concerned. But with his objections to representing the mechanical conception in poetry and in insisting that true poetry must deal with sensuous images and not abstractions, he is running counter to much of the poetic theory of the eighteenth century. Nor is his insistence that poetry and science are essentially different due to his respect for poetic tradition, or entirely to religious scruples, but rather to his steadfast belief that the poetic power transcends the powers of the human mind.

Are we to accept his declaration that the poet presents a truer picture of reality than the scientist? And are we to conclude that his objection to the mechanical ideal which eighteenth-century science had set for itself, along with the protestations of the other poets we have been considering, is valid? . . .

[*In another chapter Crum goes on to explore these questions further by examining how the mechanistic scheme of the universe was rigorously applied in the French literature of the 18th century.*]

[42] "Four Zoas," I.
[43] Blake, *Jerusalem*, 5.

ernest de selincourt

THE INTERPLAY OF LITERATURE AND SCIENCE

. . . The mind of man was the main region of Words-worth's song, and in the mind of man, as he knew it within himself, he found elements that the mechanistic conception of nature was wholly incompetent to explain. From youth up he had been haunted by mysterious presences in the sky and in the hills, and his experience convinced him of the reality of a vast world which can only be comprehended by a quality which he terms imagination, a quality not irrational, but one which transcends mere reason, or rather may be termed "reason in her most exalted mood," a subtle combination of reason and emotion; for the higher forms of emo-tion, which are a kind of imaginative instinct, will often prove a guide to truth where pure reason fails. Seeking, then, for an inter-pretation of the universe that comprehends those elements in our nature which science, intent on her more limited purpose, is jus-tified in neglecting, he dethrones reason from absolute monarchy among the faculties of man, and puts science in her justly subordi-nate place.

Wordsworth's attitude to science is entirely misconceived by those who regard him as its ignorant or contemptuous enemy. Among the inspirations of his life at Cambridge none was more last-ing than the memory of the statue of Newton, with his prism and silent face—

From "The Interplay of Literature and Science During the Last Three Centuries" by Ernest de Selincourt in the *Hibbert Journal* (1938), volume 37, reprinted in *Wordsworth and Other Studies* by Ernest de Selincourt, © 1947 by George Allen and Unwin Ltd. Reprinted here by permission of George Allen and Unwin, Ltd.

> The marble index of a mind for ever
> Voyaging through strange seas of thought, alone,

and no one has paid more eloquent tribute than he to mathematics and "its independent world, created out of pure intelligence." He had indeed a poetic premonition of the part which mathematical physics would play in the advance of human knowledge, whilst to his mind, "beset with images and haunted by itself," he knew the fascination and the relief afforded by mathematical abstraction:

> With awe and wonder did I meditate
> Upon the alliance of those simple, pure
> Proportions and relations with the frame
> And Laws of Nature, how they would become
> Herein a leader to the human mind . . .
> Yet from this source more frequently I drew
> A pleasure calm and deeper, a still sense
> Of permanent and universal sway
> And paramount endowment in the mind,
> An image not unworthy of the one
> Surpassing Life, which out of space and time,
> Nor touched by welterings of passion, is
> And hath the name of God. Transcendent peace
> And silence did await upon these thoughts.

The poet and the man of science were to him "twin labourers, and heirs of the same hopes," and in his *Prelude* he has recorded a dream which, as De Quincey puts it, "reaches the very *ne plus ultra* of sublimity, expressly framed to illustrate the eternity . . . of those two hemispheres, as it were, that compose the total world of human power, mathematics on the one hand, and poetry on the other."

But since man is a spiritual being, poetry, with all it stands for, takes precedence of science. For just as in his youth Wordsworth had been conscious of influences of which science takes no account, so in the crisis of his life, when his hopes for humanity had failed him and his spiritual life ran dry, he found that the abstract truths of mathematics, to which he turned in despair as the one rock of certainty, availed him nothing; and only gradually did he regain his mental equilibrium when those elements in his nature which he had ruthlessly sought to expel, reasserted their sovereignty.

Yet this experience did not lead him to repudiate science, but rather to define the just limits of her domain. With this intent he exposes the shallowness of the mind that is wholly satisfied with mechanical analysis; hence his oft-quoted aphorism "we murder to dissect;" hence, too, those lines that have pained the susceptibilities of many a scientist, in which the physician is held up to scorn as a "fingering slave,

> One who would peep and botanise
> Upon his mother's grave."

But this is no more an attack on botanical science than the portrait which precedes it, of the "man of purple cheer, right plump to see", is an attack on the Church of England. The offending lines, read in their context, are merely a satirical exposure of scientific curiosity where, as most of us would agree, it is out of place. Elsewhere Wordsworth expresses strong disagreement with those who held that the habit of analysing and anatomizing was necessarily destructive of other and higher faculties. On the contrary,

"Admiration and love," he says, "to which all knowledge truly vital must tend, are felt by men of real genius in proportion as their discoveries in natural philosophy are enlarged; and the beauty of form in plant or animal is not made less but more apparent as a whole by more accurate insight into its constituent properties and powers."

This is indeed one of the greatest gifts of science:

> Happy is he who lives to understand
> Not human nature only, but explores
> All natures,—to the end that he may find
> The law that governs each; and where begins
> The union, the partition where, that makes
> Kind and degree, among all visible Beings . . .
> Up from the creeping plant to sovereign man.

Every isolated step in the advance of knowledge has its own intrinsic value: its supreme value depends on its correlation with the sum of human knowledge, so that it corrects and enriches our understanding of life as a whole. So conceived, the triumphs of science may become as fruitful a theme for the poet as any other field of human adventure; nay, without the poet's aid they will not be fully realized. The scientist, as such, excludes all sense of ultimate values—they are not his concern; whereas, says Wordsworth, it is the peculiar function of the poet "to carry sensation into the midst of the objects of science itself," or to transfer pure thought into that world of imagination, of combined thought and feeling, in which the life of the spirit is lived. For "poetry is the breath and finer spirit of all knowledge, the impassioned expression which is on the countenance of all science."

And as Wordsworth recognized the place of scientific knowledge in the sum of man's intellectual experience, so he welcomed its application to the relief of man's estate:

> I exult to see
> An intellectual mastery exercised
> O'er the blind elements; . . . almost a soul
> Imparted to brute matter. I rejoice,
> Measuring the force of these gigantic powers
> That by the thinking mind have been compelled
> To serve the will of feeble-bodied Man.

But he protested against the identification of progress with their indiscriminate employment, which, ignoring paramount human values, sacrificed the claims of both beauty and humanity to "gain, the master idol of the realm."

In all this Wordsworth showed true prophetic insight. For just as many a social reform of to-day is a tardy attempt to correct or arrest the harm to our civilization which he foresaw, so science has herself outgrown that mechanistic view of the world against which he so passionately revolted. His belief in an "active principle" subsisting in all natures, in whose creative power lies the true freedom of the universe, his mystical intuition of

> A motion and a spirit that impels
> All thinking things, all objects of all thoughts,
> And rolls through all things,

suggests a point of view not wholly incompatible with the latest speculations of the physicist. With confidence, therefore, Wordsworth welcomes the progress of knowledge. He has no desire to recall the illusions of the past, nor to shirk those

> Truths whose thick veil Science has drawn aside;

he knows that "the universe is infinitely wide," and however far science may extend her frontiers, beyond them there will always remain a gulf, which "imaginative faith alone can overleap."

Of such a faith his age had need. The rapid advance of technology which marked the early nineteenth century, with its contributions to wealth and daily comfort, inevitably strengthened the hold of a facile materialism; the advance in scientific theory had already begun to shake, as never before, the foundations of religious belief. That spirit of unrest which two centuries earlier had haunted the mind of the poet Donne, was now to infect the whole educated world.

The sonnet of Wordsworth from which I have just quoted was

117

written in 1833; it was his response to the epoch-making pronouncements of Lyell on the antiquity of the earth. Evolutionary conceptions of organic life were already in the air; they gained some popular vogue in 1844 from Robert Chambers's *Vestiges of Creation,* and in 1859 received their exhaustive and authoritative exposition in Darwin's *Origin of Species,* of which Huxley said with justice: "It is doubtful whether any single book, except Newton's *Principia,* ever worked so great and so rapid a revolution in science, or made so deep an impression on the general mind." The creation of the world, which theological tradition had confidently dated 4004 B.C., was now put back into a past infinitely remote, Adam and Eve and their "delicious garden" were relegated to the pleasant, if instructive, land of myth. And if the historicity of the Bible were thus impugned in one capital instance, how much else of its contents invited a similar interpretation? Obviously it could no longer be regarded as the unimpeachable repository of literal fact; its true value must largely depend, like that of other great literatures, on the measure of its power to stimulate and satisfy the religious imagination. Moreover the inexorable laws of the struggle for existence and the survival of the fittest forced into prominence a nature "red in tooth and claw"—no new discovery indeed, but hitherto little emphasized, and hard to reconcile with the notion of a beneficent Creator.

> Without whose tender care
> No sparrow falleth to the ground;

and lastly, man's inclusion in the evolutionary scheme raised problems that admit no easy solution, as to man's spiritual life, his origin and destiny, as to how far he can be a free agent, or claim a personal relation with the Deity.

Faced by these insistent questions only the most obscurantist of ecclesiastics could emulate the ostrich: the thinkers and poets were impelled to reconsider the foundations of their belief. It was no easy task, and great literature was born of the conflict. A later generation, to whom the ideas of Lyell and Darwin are common-places, has prated ignorantly of Victorian complacency; but a little perception should help us to enter into the minds of men who felt the ground on which they had securely rested cut from under their feet, and to sympathize with their spiritual nostalgia at the loss of that more definite creed which their reason forced them to renounce:

> The Sea of Faith,
> Was once too at the full, and round earth's shore
> Lay like the folds of a bright girdle furl'd;
> But now I only hear

Its melancholy, long, withdrawing roar,
Retreating to the breath
Of the night wind, down the vast edges drear
And naked shingles of the world.

Thus Matthew Arnold and his friend Clough, "between two worlds, one dead, one powerless to be born," sought, in a creedless Christianity, a peace they could not find.

But the prevalent mood of the time found its well-nigh perfect expression in the poetry of Tennyson, and the spell that he exerted, not merely over the general public, but equally over the acutest thinkers and men of science, sprang from their recognition that in his search for a faith beyond the forms of faith he voiced their own doubts and aspirations.

"It lay," wrote the philosopher Henry Sidgwick, "in the unparalleled combination of intensity of feeling with comprehensiveness of view and balance of judgement, shown in presenting the *deepest* needs and perplexities of humanity. We were absorbed in struggling for freedom of thought from the trammels of a historical religion; and what we sympathised with most, apart from the personal feeling, was the defence of honest doubt, the reconciliation of faith and knowledge, and generally the *forward* movement of the whole."

Tennyson had always been deeply interested in natural science; Huxley, indeed, pronounced his insight into scientific method equal to that of the greatest experts. But the more obvious inferences drawn from scientific investigation:

The stars, she whispers, blindly run,

❋   ❋   ❋

So careful of the type she seems
So careless of the single life,

ran counter to the instincts of his spiritual consciousness. The answer, he felt, could only lie in more knowledge; and pending that knowledge, man's sole refuge was in faith—a faith which is no stolid adherence to what science has disproved, but rather a faith in that which is beyond both proof and disproof.

The modern sceptic pours scorn on Tennyson for sheltering behind a faith he could not justify; but a faith fully justified would not be faith at all, but knowledge. And yet, provided that faith is no mere lazy acceptance of tradition, but the lively outcome of his whole inner experience, a man has no more power, or right, to abjure it than he has to reject the inferences of his intellect. The two may seem inconsistent to an outsider, he may himself be haunted

119

with the fear that they are inconsistent, and it was that fear that gave to Tennyson's poetry its peculiar plangency of feeling. Moreover, as he wavers in his faith, so too, at times, he will doubt the validity of the verdict his reason urges him to accept. Is our knowledge of the physical universe, confessedly incomplete as it is, to have the last word on the spiritual life and destiny of man?

> Who loves not knowledge? Who shall rail
>   Against her beauty? May she mix
>   With men and prosper! Who shall fix
> Her pillars? Let her work prevail.
>
> But on her forehead sits a fire,
>   She sets her forward countenance
>   And leaps into the future chance,
> Submitting all things to desire.

Science, hardly less than theology, is tainted with arrogant assumptions; her laws of nature are, after all, no more than hypotheses which for the moment seem best to fit the facts before her, and faced by other facts she will propound other laws incompatible with her former tenets. In her ceaseless quest for truth, she is forced continually to modify, even to renounce, her cherished theories:

> Our little systems have their day;
>   They have their day and cease to be:
>   They are but broken lights of thee,
> And thou, O Lord, art more than they.

Yet if science was thus disturbingly revolutionary in the sphere of religion, in other regions of thought its influence was both optimistic and conservative. Evolution, to Tennyson as to many others, implied progress, but a progress which had its roots deep down in the past; it thus encouraged an historical perspective in the approach to all social and human problems; it emphasized, as never before, the influence of heredity and of environment; whilst in the approach to literature it enforced the value of tradition as opposed to ephemeral caprice.

But the advance of knowledge makes not for unanimity but for diversity of human opinion, and how differently different minds may react to the same scientific data can be seen by contrasting their influence upon some of the greatest among Tennyson's younger contemporaries. George Meredith wholeheartedly welcomed the evolutionary doctrine, and drew from it a buoyant optimism, untempered by any hankerings after the supernatural. Earth was to him the great Mother of all living things; the principle by which she educates her children—natural selection through a conflict of types, is but "her cherishing of the best endowed." Through this conflict man has developed from mere animalism, or "blood," as Meredith terms it, to that compound of blood, heart, and brain whose perfect adjustment is the fulfilment of his life's purpose. But he can only attain this harmony by keeping close to reality; to ignore his kinship with Earth is folly: to yearn beyond Earth for personal relation with the Lord of Earth is delusion. By accepting her discipline, and in mystical union with her, man gains all that he needs, the knowledge

> Of good and evil at strife,
> And the struggle upward of all,
> And [his] choice of the glory of life.

Thomas Hardy confronts the same universe with the obstinate questionings of tragic despair. The infinitude of space and time only emphasizes for him the helpless insignificance of man, the progress of the type only stresses the remorseless indifference to the individual. His hope for the future, and it is a dim hope, lies in "evolutionary meliorism," which he defines as "a minimum of loving-kindness, operating through scientific knowledge, and actuated by that modicum of free-will conjecturally possessed by organic life."

A different outlook from either Meredith's or Hardy's characterizes Robert Bridges. Like Wordsworth, he realized how much that bears essentially on the riddle of life lay wholly outside the purview of science, and with a full appreciation of what science had accomplished in the years that divided them, he restated for his own age, and with a similar solution, the problem that Wordsworth had faced a century before.

Like Wordsworth, he admits no quarrel between science and poetry; he delights to record how science, "comforting man's animal poverty, and leisuring his toil, hath humanized manners and social temper"; and no one has paid more lovely tribute than he to science's latest achievements. But science does not attempt to satisfy the spirit of man. When we ask how it is that our material bodies are capable of consciousness, of thought, and spiritual aspiration, she refuses to answer, not because she denies these mysteries, but because she can make nothing of them. But what if the clue lie in those very conditions of thought which pure reason rejects as delusive, i.e. in our instincts? Instinct in the animals is purposeful, though the animal does not understand the purpose; why should not man's higher instincts be as true as those of the animals on their lower plane? And prime among these instincts is the instinct for beauty—

ERNEST DE SELINCOURT

> The quality of appearances that thro' the senses
> wakneth spiritual emotion in the mind of man:
> And art, as it createth new forms of beauty
> awakneth new ideas that advance the spirit
> in the life of Reason to the wisdom of God.

Beauty is not illusory because it lies outside the scope of science. To accept its suggestions as reality is indeed an act of faith, but the scientist too works by faith—faith in the validity of the mind's logical processes, in the ultimate explicability of the physical world, in the order of nature; the further faith of the poet, that there is a purpose in that order, and that the order is good, is but "a reasonable trust in our deeper nature and better desires, to doubt which were destructive of reason herself":

> For beauty being the best of all we know
> sums up the unsearchable and secret aims
> of nature, and on joys whose earthly names
> were never told, can form and sense bestow;
> and man hath sped his instinct to outgo
> the steps of science, and against her shames
> imagination stakes out heavenly claims,
> building a tower above the head of woe.

The warmth of the welcome accorded to Bridge's *Testament of Beauty*, far in excess of that which has greeted any other serious imaginative work of our time, bore clear testimony to the value, in a troubled world, of his lofty and comprehensive spiritual experience; more recent literature has given us nothing comparable to it either in range or vision; and it is an arresting paradox that at a time when contemporary science has discarded its former materialistic outlook and when theories of evolution, instead of throwing all their emphasis on man's affinity with lower types of life, trace a line of escape from the prison of matter to the full freedom of the spirit, imaginative literature should, as a whole, be deaf to its suggestions.

But the causes are not far to seek. In the first place the trend of scientific thought is largely obscured by its own materialistic triumphs. Science has become the victim of her own success. Dazzled by the wonder of the gifts which she deals out with so lavish a hand, man insults the dignity of her quest of truth by paying regard only to its practical by-products. In the second place the speculations of physical science have become so abstruse that they pass beyond the comprehension of the lay intelligence. The achievements of Copernicus, of Newton, of Darwin, were, at least in broad outline, explicable to the plain man; and while they destroyed his former illusions, gave him something in their place which, after his first disconcerting shock of surprise, proved more acceptable to his reason than the illusions they destroyed. But only a mind scientifically trained can grasp the quantum theory or relativity; and hence some time must elapse before the new ideas can be sufficiently assimilated by the layman to admit of adequate translation into the untechnical language of the literary artist, and thereby become a part of that intellectual and emotional experience which it is the function of literature to disseminate. It is true that eminent men of science, conscious of the difficulty, have attempted the task themselves, and some of their attempts have achieved the proud distinction of best sellers. But I am a little sceptical as to the number of readers who have fully understood either their arguments or their conclusions, nor is it derogatory to their scientific genius to suggest that they have not the supreme literary gift of "carrying truth alive into the heart by passion."

And further, the present distracted state of the world is not conducive to the absorption of new ideas. A generation that has grown up beneath the dark shadows of a disastrous war and a still more disastrous peace, breathes an atmosphere of disillusionment; it tends instinctively to call in question the meaning of life, to doubt, indeed, whether life can have a meaning. Justly critical of those whose folly and ignorance brought things to such a pass, they have seen the world as a Waste Land, peopled by hollow men; and realizing what man has made of man, they distrust the validity of the higher human impulses, and are attracted not to the more optimistic suggestions of physical speculation but to that branch of science which seems to justify their distrust. It was inevitable that biology should extend its researches from man's body to his mind, and explore the influence of physical upon mental states. But no department of science is fraught with more dangerous pitfalls for the amateur; and a dabbling in psycho-physics, by authors whose gifts are literary rather than scientific, has often warped their estimate of life and character. It is significant that their finest literary achievement has been in satire: alike in biography and in fiction the physical has been exaggerated at the expense of the spiritual; while criticism of the great literatures of the past has been tainted with a crude neurology, and its authors, ignorant of the sanity of true genius, have thrown more light upon their own personal frailty than upon the potential greatness of the human soul.

It is the calamity of our modern civilization, and may well prove its tragedy, that too large a portion of the world's available genius is absorbed by science, to the impoverishment not only of literature, but, even more, of that realm of practical affairs in which ideas are applied to life. More than a century ago, Shelley, himself a passionate devotee of science, diagnosed the malady of a world whose predicament was far less perilous than our own.

"We want," he said, "the creative faculty to imagine what we know, we want the generous impulse to act what we imagine, we want the poetry of life. Our calculations have outrun conception—we have eaten more than we can digest. The cultivation of the sciences, which have enlarged the empire of man over the external world, has, for want of the poetic faculty, proportionally circumscribed those of the internal world, and man, having enslaved the elements, remains himself a slave."

The gifts of science are double-edged, as we know to-day to our cost: it is not the fault of science that they are abused.

"It may be a forlorn hope," wrote Thomas Hardy shortly before his death, "that of an alliance, by means of the interfusing of poetry, between religion, which must be retained unless the world is to perish, and complete rationality, which must come unless also the world is to perish."

But if contemporary literature has not yet risen to its great opportunity, it may be, as Hardy further suggests, because "advance is never in a straight line, and may have moved back *pour mieux sauter*—drawn back for a spring." And the signs are not without hope. In the meantime we have our heritage from the past. Great literature has this advantage over science, that it has a permanence co-extensive with human life and passion and aspiration. The science of yesterday is no longer science: it has already become history. Literature is always literature. Ptolemy's astronomy is out of date: the ecstasy with which he beheld the starlit heavens awakens its response in us to-day. Newton's *Principia* is in part superseded: but Shakespeare, despite modern psychology, does not "abide our question." Even where the ideas on which it is based are proved illusory, literature retains its power. The cosmography of the *Divine Comedy*, of *Paradise Lost*, of the Bible, has long been exploded, and in exploding it science has done them a service, for it has thrown into bolder relief their true poetic and spiritual content. In the past, their readers have often mistaken the husk for the kernel, and, battening on their dogma, failed to catch their inspiration: for us their power is manifest—"to raise the thoughts above sublunary cares and pleasures."

In truth, man is a complex creature. Science was born from the insatiable curiosity of his intellect,

> To measure every wandering planet's course,
> Still climbing after knowledge infinite:

and science has flourished exceedingly. But man is also a poetical animal, and it has been wisely said that "a savant who is not also a poet in soul and a religionist at heart is a feeble and unhappy creature." On the balanced development of both parts of his nature depends his worth as an individual; in their just fusion as motive forces in society lies the measure of human progress.

b. ifor evans

WORDSWORTH AND SCIENCE

An illuminating volume which explores, as one of its themes, the relation of literature and the sciences is A. N. Whitehead's *Science and the Modern World,* to which reference has already been made. Yet this volume, so masterly in its attempt to explain simply the complex advances of modern science, is disappointing when it approaches literature. Whitehead does not seem to have examined the texts, or to have consulted those who have examined them; it is as if he did not consider the arts worthy of the methods which he applied in such a masterly way in exploring the sciences. "In English literature," he wrote with reference to the romantics, "the deepest thinkers of this school were Coleridge, Wordsworth and Shelley. Keats is an example of literature untouched by Science. We may neglect Coleridge's attempt at an explicit philosophical formulation. It was influential in his own generation, but in these lectures it is my object only to mention those elements of the thought of the past which stand for all time. Even with this limitation, only a selection is possible. For our purposes Coleridge is only important by his influence on Wordsworth. Thus Wordsworth and Shelley remain.

"Wordsworth was passionately absorbed in nature. It has been said of Spinoza that he was drunk with God. It is equally true that Wordsworth was drunk with nature. But he was a thoughtful, well-read man, with philosophical interests and sane even to the point of prosiness. In addition, he was a genius. He weakens his evidence by his dislike of science. We all remember his scorn of the poor man whom he somewhat hastily accuses of peeping and botanising on his mother's grave. Passage after passage could be quoted from

Reprinted with permission from Humanities Press, New York, from B. Ifor Evans' *Literature and Science,* copyright 1950.

him, expressing this repulsion. In this respect, his characteristic thought can be summed up in his phrase 'we murder to dissect.' "

In these two paragraphs, the only statement which could not be challenged is that Shelley was a thinker and interested in science. All the rest could be challenged, and, having been challenged, would be found wanting. I have already discussed Keats, and I have shown that the suggestion that he is "untouched" by science is not supported by the evidence. The patronising reference to Coleridge is typical of the period at which Whitehead is writing, though it would not now be accepted as valid. One cannot avoid the suspicion that Whitehead was depending on the critics, and not on the text of Coleridge, for his alert mind would have seen further than this if he had examined the texts for himself. Coleridge was the friend of scientists, and knew the language of science, and more than any other creative writer of his time sought some reconciliation between science and literature.

There remains Wordsworth. Wordsworth is important in the whole argument. I must admit that Professor Douglas Bush, himself a distinguished historian of the romantic period, writing in his admirable *Science and English Poetry*, uses language very similar to Whitehead's. "Wordsworth's thought or feeling," Professor Bush writes, "is altogether non-scientific, and is not concerned with evidences of design or indeed with much except his own response to the idea of unity of Being." For Professor Bush's work I have the profoundest respect, but here, on Wordsworth, I feel that his approach is devoid somewhat of that sense of justice which is normally such a feature of his criticism. Indeed, despite the fact that the best biography of Wordsworth was composed by Professor Harper of Princeton, I would venture the suggestion that no American, unless he has long lived in England, can do justice to Wordsworth, for Wordsworth's thought and the experience on which that thought is based, is intensely English in its origin.

It is surprising, though, to find Professor Bush describing *A Poet's Epitaph* as an anti-intellectual and anti-scientific outburst. The whole point of the poem, as I understand it, is that the poet was interested in individuals, and in experiences, and being Wordsworth, particularly in experiences derived from nature. He was not being in any precise sense of the term anti-scientific, but he was attacking all those who regarded humanity as a collective phenomenon from whom data may be derived:

> Art thou a Statist in the van
> Of public conflicts trained and bred?
> —First learn to love one living man;
> *Then* may'st thou think upon the dead.

127

B. IFOR EVANS

> A Lawyer art thou?—draw not nigh!
> Go, carry to some fitter place
> The keenness of the practised eye,
> The hardness of that sallow face!

Incidentally Wordsworth used the word "Statist" in its older sense of "politician" or one skilled in affairs of State. The only stanza which has any direct relation to science is:

> Physician art thou?—one, all eyes,
> Philosopher!—a fingering slave,
> One that would peep and botanize
> Upon his mother's grave?

This is the very stanza to which Whitehead was referring in his extraordinary passage that Wordsworth, "weakens his evidence by his dislike of science. We all remember his scorn of the poor man whom he somewhat hastily accuses of peeping and botanising on his mother's grave." But this, as I understand it, is not the meaning of the passage. Wordsworth in this and the other stanzas was asserting, as I have suggested above, that the individual life and the validity of human experience and the sentiments that arise from them are important, whatever may be the call to abstract investigation by statesman, or lawyer, or doctor. He was claiming that the poet who regards each man as a separate person has a more valuable point of view than experts who categorize humanity on one mechanical basis or another. Science as such has but little place in the argument.

Wordsworth, it is true, was conscious of experiences, derived directly from nature which seemed to him to have a mystical quality and so penetrate more deeply into the burden of the mystery of the world than was in any other way possible. In some of the early poems he spoke boldly, recklessly if you will, in support and confirmation of these experiences. But the artist will follow the single experience or intuition and see where it leads him, particularly if his creative power permits him to give it a separate existence in a poetic design. So it was in *The Tables Turned,* the poem from which Whitehead quoted the phrase "We murder to dissect." The mood is clear if the poem is read as a whole, along with the companion poem "Expostulation and Reply."

> One impulse from a vernal wood
> May teach you more of man,
> Of moral evil and of good,
> Than all the sages can.

128

> Sweet is the lore which Nature brings;
> Our meddling intellect
> Mis-shapes the beauteous forms of things:—
> We murder to dissect.

This is a mood, a poem of "sentiment and reflection": it does not represent Wordsworth's normal, and certainly not his total attitude to learning.

Whitehead speaks of "Wordsworth's greatest poem" by far as "the first book of *The Prelude*." Yet it is the whole of *The Prelude* that is Wordsworth's greatest poem, and it is there, among numerous other places, that he expressed his admiration for science, and particularly for Newton. Wordsworth was an undergraduate at St. John's College, Cambridge. His bedroom window looked out on to the Chapel of Trinity. Newton's association with Trinity made a profound impression upon Wordsworth. The early version of *The Prelude* has a comment on Newton's statue in Trinity College:

> And from my Bedroom, I in moonlight nights
> Could see, right opposite, a few yards off,
> The Antechapel, where the Statue stood
> Of Newton with his Prism and silent Face.

Later, on revision, Wordsworth expanded this passage until it read:

> . . . . where the statue stood
> Of Newton with his prism and silent face,
> The marble index of a mind for ever
> Voyaging through strange seas of Thought, alone.[1]

In the Sixth Book of *The Prelude* Wordsworth returned to reflect upon his own studies in mathematics, which he contemplated with a proper modesty, while emphasising the possibilities of the science in its more mature forms. His mind had still Newton at the background, and that he had closely considered the passage can be seen from the degree to which he revised it. I quote its opening sections here from the final version of 1850:[2]

> Yet may we not entirely overlook
> The pleasure gathered from the rudiments
> Of geometric science. Though advanced
> In these inquiries, with regret I speak,
> No farther than the threshold, there I found

---

[1] Book III, ll. 60-63.
[2] Book VI, ll. 115-141.

Both elevation and composed delight:
With Indian awe and wonder, ignorance pleased
With its own struggles, did I meditate
On the relation those abstractions bear
To Nature's laws, and by what process led,
Those immaterial agents bowed their heads
Duly to serve the mind of earth-born man;
From star to star, from kindred sphere to sphere,
From system on to system without end.

More frequently from the same source I drew
A pleasure quiet and profound, a sense
Of permanent and universal sway,
And paramount belief; there, recognised
A type, for finite natures, of the one
Supreme Existence, the surpassing life
Which—to the boundaries of space and time,
Of melancholy space and doleful time,
Superior, and incapable of change,
Nor touched by welterings of passion—is,
And hath the name of, God. Transcendent peace
And silence did await upon these thoughts
That were a frequent comfort to my youth.

The whole is too long to quote. It is one of the most elaborate and closely argued passages on science in English poetry. It concludes with a tribute to the abstract symbolism of mathematics from a poet whose task led him to toil with images derived directly from human experience, and, since they were derived from human experience, were necessarily incomplete:

Mighty is the charm
Of these abstractions to a mind beset
With images, and haunted by herself,
And specially delightful unto me
Was that clear synthesis built up aloft
So gracefully; even then when it appeared
Not more than a mere plaything, or a toy
To sense embodied: not the thing it is
In verity, an independent world,
Created out of pure intelligence.

The sincerity of the whole passage is unquestionable, and it is obviously the result of much personal reflection. The lucid and complete symbolism of mathematics attracted him after his own trafficking with the cloudy and imperfect symbols derived from human experience.

In the most profound episode in the whole of *The Prelude* it is to mathematics that Wordsworth returned. The moment can be found in Book X of the earlier version of *The Prelude,* where Wordsworth described how he reached a stage of moral despair from his distress at England's declaration of war on revolutionary France:

> Thus I fared
> Dragging all passions, notions, shapes of faith
> Like culprits to the bar, suspiciously
> Calling the mind to question in plain day
> Her titles and her honours, now believing,
> Now disbelieving, endlessly perplex'd
> With impulse, motive, right and wrong, the ground
> Of moral obligation, what the rule
> And what the sanction, till, demanding *proof*
> And seeking it in everything, I lost
> All feeling of conviction, and, in fine,
> Sick, wearied out with contrarieties,
> Yielded up moral questions in despair.[3]

According to the earliest version of *The Prelude,* written only a few years after the experience, it was at this stage in his mental dilemma and despair that Wordsworth confessed how he turned to mathematics:

> And for my future studies, as the sole
> Employment of the enquiring faculty,
> Turn'd towards mathematics, and their clear
> And solid evidence.

By 1850 this passage had been much revised and the reference to "mathematics" had disappeared, but it is there in the version closest to the event.

Apart from these personal references to mathematics, Book V of *The Prelude* describes a dream following on Wordsworth's reading of Cervantes. Here he gave, as it were in a symbol, the place of science and imagination, or vision perhaps it should be called, in human life. He described how, in his dream, an Arab showed him a stone and a shell: in the stone he symbolised science and in the shell, the arts, particularly the art of poetry:

> the Arab told me that the stone
> (To give it in the language of the dream)
> Was 'Euclid's Elements'; and 'This,' said he,
> 'Is something of more worth,' and at the word
> Stretched forth the shell, so beautiful in shape,

[3] Book X, l. 889, etc.

> In colour so resplendent, with command
> That I should hold it to my ear.

In this passage Wordsworth seems to suggest, as he had done elsewhere, that there are separate functions for science and the arts to fulfil:

> The one that held acquaintance with the stars,
> And wedded soul to soul in purest bond
> Of reason, undisturbed by space or time.

The other,

> with power
> To exhilarate the spirit, and to soothe
> Through every clime, the heart of human kind.[4]

Thus in all that concerns science as an investigation of nature, and particularly in mathematics, Wordsworth showed much sympathy and not a little understanding.

There was another side of the problem. Wordsworth saw, with some clarity, the coming of the machine age, and his admiration of mathematics and of science as a method of investigating the mysteries of the universe made him in no way diminish his hostility to the increase of industrialisation in England, with all the social consequences that he deplored. It might almost be said that he was sympathetic to science but hostile to technology. With a little excessive simplification one might say that he was for mathematics, but against the factory and the steam-engine.

In the preface to *Lyrical Ballads*, there is a passage added to the preface of 1800 for the edition of 1802, in which Wordsworth reasserted his desire to discover means of co-operation between science and the arts. It is one of the most extensive statements of the kind written by an English poet. Unfortunately its prophecy was not fulfilled but that does not diminish Wordsworth's insight and courage in making it:

"The knowledge both of the Poet and the Man of Science is pleasure; but the knowledge of the one cleaves to us as a necessary part of our existence, our natural and unalienable inheritance; the other is a personal and individual acquisition, slow to come to us, and by no habitual and direct sympathy connecting us with our fellow-beings. The Man of Science seeks truth as a remote and unknown benefactor; he cherishes and loves it in his solitude: the Poet, singing a song in

[4] Book V, the last of the passages quoted ends at line 109.

which all human beings join with him, rejoices in the presence of truth as our visible friend and hourly companion. Poetry is the breath and finer spirit of all knowledge: it is the impassioned expression which is in the countenance of all Science. Emphatically may it be said of the Poet, as Shakespeare hath said of man, 'that he looks before and after.' He is the rock of defence for human nature; an upholder and preserver, carrying everywhere with him relationship and love. In spite of difference of soil and climate, of language and manners, of laws, and customs: in spite of things silently gone out of mind, and things violently destroyed; the Poet binds together by passion and knowledge the vast empire of human society, as it is spread over the whole earth, and over all time. The objects of the Poet's thoughts are everywhere; though the eyes and senses of man are, it is true, his favourite guides, yet he will follow wheresoever he can find an atmosphere of sensation in which to move his wings. Poetry is the first and last of all knowledge—it is as immortal as the heart of man. If the labours of Men of science should ever create any material revolution, direct or indirect, in our condition, and in the impressions which we habitually receive, the Poet will sleep then no more than at present; he will be ready to follow the steps of the Man of Science, not only in those general indirect effects, but he will be at his side, carrying sensation into the midst of the objects of the science itself. The remotest discoveries of the Chemist, the Botanist, or Mineralogist, will be as proper objects of the Poet's art as any upon which it can be employed, if the time should ever come when these things shall be familiar to us, and the relations under which they are contemplated by the followers of these respective sciences shall be manifestly and palpably material to us as enjoying and suffering beings. If the time should ever come when what is now called Science, thus familiarised to men shall be ready to put on, as it were, a form of flesh and blood, the Poet will lend his divine spirit to aid the transfiguration, and will welcome the Being thus produced, as a dear and genuine inmate of the household of man."

In estimating the influence of science on Wordsworth, as it varies from one period to another, it may be remembered that from about 1800, and particularly in the years that immediately follow, Wordsworth was in touch with Sir Humphry Davy, then still a young man, but already a chemist of brilliant achievement.[5] The interest in Davy began with Coleridge but he had conveyed his enthusiasm to Wordsworth. In a letter to Davy of February 3, 1801, Coleridge had set out a proposal for starting a Chemical Laboratory with Calvert and gave his reasons why he thought Wordsworth would join in the enterprise: "because he feels it more necessary for him to have some intellectual pursuit less closely connected with deep passion than poetry and is of course desirous, too, not to be so wholly

[5] I am indebted to Dr. Helen Darbishire for the references that follow.

ignorant of knowledge, so exceedingly important." The years of his admiration for Davy may thus be regarded as the period when his esteem for science was at its highest.

While a claim can thus be made for Wordsworth's interest in science, it has to be modified by the intrusion of other ideas particularly in his later work. In those later years he became more orthodox in his approach to Christianity and this, strengthened by Coleridge's opposition to a mechanical view of the universe, led him in the sonnet series *Cave of Staffa*, 1833 to speak up for religion as opposed to science. Professor Douglas Bush quotes the references,[6] and notes that "we hear of 'the almighty hand' of 'the sovereign Architect,' and of the presumption that would assign 'Mechanic laws to agency divine.' In *At Sea off the Isle of Man* (1833), he feels wistful regret for the imaginative and poetical age in which nature was impelled, not 'by laws inanimate,' but by active and visible powers of will and passion . . . He goes on in the next sonnet to ask if we should regret that science has torn the veil from old fables, and answers that man's reason must still face mysteries which only religious faith can overleap."

It would be unjust to summarise Wordsworth's view from these later pieces and this Professor Bush readily admits. What after all are important, are not Wordsworth's views in his old age, when he was poetically weary, but his views in the period when poetically he was at the height of his creation. It was then that he placed a higher value on science than at any other period in his life. Apart from an increased acceptance of formal Christianity there hardened in him an understandable fear of technology and of the ungracious materialism of the society which the industrial revolution had produced.

Even in the days when he praised science he also insisted on the existence of intuitive experience and the mystical wisdom. Partly from his reading of Rousseau, but with confirmation from his own experience, he placed a value on feeling and on sentiment which could find no room in scientific interpretations of the universe. The ugly, urban and mechanised civilisation of the industrial age, with its emphasis on economic problems and mere commercial success, filled him with a deep fear. He seemed to see the resources of the imagination in wonder and myth being blurred out of existence in the routine drudgery of the smoky, factory towns. Further, he dreaded that nature herself would be disfigured by the penetrative activities of a technological society:

> Great God! I'd rather be
> A Pagan suckled in a creed outworn;

[6] *Science and English Poetry*, 1950, p. 97.

> So might I, standing on this pleasant lea,
> Have glimpses that would make me less forlorn;
> Have sight of Proteus rising from the sea;
> Or hear Old Triton blow his wreathéd horn.

Technology meant the loss of the civilisation that led to man's direct contact with nature on which so much of his conception of the civilised life was based. It meant the railroads in the Lakes and many other changes, the dangers of which he understood. At times they seemed as evil to him as did the Reform Bill itself, and from one of Mrs. Wordsworth's letters we know that he feared the Reform Bill more than a current threat of cholera in the Lakes.

Even his fear of technology and of the eruption of the harsh features of the industrial age into the scenes of nature which he loved did not blind him to the possibilities of human development that lay in scientific and technological progress. It would be asserting too much to say that this balanced view is present consistently but it is there, as for instance in the 'Steamboats, Viaducts and Railways' in *Itinerary Poems* of 1833.[7]

> Motions and Means, on land and sea at war
> With old poetic feeling, not for this,
> Shall ye, by Poets even, be judged amiss!
> Nor shall your presence, howsoe'er it mar
> The loveliness of Nature, prove a bar
> To the Mind's gaining that prophetic sense
> Of future change, that point of vision, whence
> May be discovered what in soul ye are.
> In spite of all that beauty may disown
> In your harsh features, Nature doth embrace
> Her lawful offspring in Man's art; and Time,
> Pleased with your triumphs o'er his brother Space
> Accepts from your bold hands the proffered crown
> Of hope, and smiles on you with cheer sublime.

Miss Darbishire tells me that there is a copy of this sonnet in Wordsworth's hand in the Library at St. John's College, Cambridge, dated November 11, 1844, in which he made a significant change in the last line. Instead of "and smiles on you" he wrote "and welcomes you with cheer sublime." Wordsworth must be given credit for this, whatever he may have said elsewhere against railways.

Apart altogether from these passages on technology it is clear that in the period when Wordsworth's creative power was at its height he thought about science and its importance more possibly than any major poet of the period. If the systematic study of

[7] I am again indebted to Miss Helen Darbishire for this reference.

135

growth and development is a scientific interest then *The Prelude* is more perhaps than any great poem in the language a scientific poem. It marks the nearest point to which art, still legitimately employing its own methods, can approach the mental sciences. If psychology is a science, then the subtler analysis of different states of consciousness again constitutes *The Prelude* as a scientific poem. It renders additional evidence for the affirmation that it is the great modern poem in the language.

Wordsworth was, further, concerned between the difference between the modes of thought that lead to poetry and to scientific exploration. Miss Helen Darbishire calls my attention to a Fenwick note written on "This lawn a carpet all alive" which Wordsworth composed in 1829. The note reads: "Some are of opinion that the habit of analysing, decomposing, and anatomising, is inevitably unfavourable to the perception of beauty. People are led into this mistake by overlooking the fact that such processes being to a certain extent within the reach of a limited intellect, we are apt to ascribe to them that insensibility of which they are in truth the effect and not the cause. Admiration and love, to which all knowledge truly vital must tend, are felt by men of real genius in proportion as their discoveries in natural Philosophy are enlarged; and the beauty in form of a plant or an animal is not made less but more apparent as a whole by more accurate insight into its constituent properties and powers. A Savant who is not also a poet in soul and a religionist in heart is a feeble and unhappy creature."

Wordsworth saw that the sciences and the arts each had their own function to fulfil. He had in his moments of keenest enlightenment a reverence for science, particularly for mathematics but also through Coleridge and Davy for chemistry. In his own work he had a profound understanding of that approach to the human mind later to be defined as psychology. Above all of his contemporaries he had responded to the problems and possibilities of science in his time.

jerome h. buckley

DOUBT AND FAITH IN
TENNYSON'S *IN MEMORIAM*

Though it was to serve a whole generation as a sort of Victorian *Essay on Man, In Memoriam* drew its primary strength from the poet's most intimate subjective experience. It is much more, of course, than a chapter in autobiography, and Tennyson did not wish it to be read as such. The "I," the self of the poem, he explained, "is not always the author speaking of himself, but the voice of the human race speaking through him." [1] But such universality as the "I" attains is incidental to the deeply personal analysis; the self is representative only insofar as it must learn to accept the conditions of a general humanity and the circumstances of a particular culture. Whatever its public overtone, *In Memoriam* was written to satisfy a private need, and as a whole it occupies a place in Tennyson's own development comparable to that of *The Prelude* in the career of Wordsworth. Like *The Prelude*, which appeared posthumously in the same year,[2] it describes the loss of hope and the recovery of assent, the reassertion of the dedicated spirit; it grounds a new faith on the persistence of the remembered past; and it freely reorders literal facts to achieve its psychological pattern, to illustrate "the growth of a poet's mind" or, as Tennyson

Reprinted by permission of the publishers from Jerome Hamilton Buckley's *Tennyson: The Growth of A Poet*, Cambridge, Mass.: Copyright 1960, Harvard University Press, by the President and Fellows of Harvard College.

[1] *Memoir*, I, 305.
[2] Tennyson sometimes felt that his poem, too, if it were to appear at all, would be posthumously published. In 1847 he wrote to his aunt concerning the elegies, which he was still revising: "Perhaps they will not see the light till I have ceased to be."

JEROME H. BUCKLEY

called it, "the way of the soul." Yet, despite the calculated arrange-
ment of its parts, *In Memoriam* is far less systematic a chronicle
than *The Prelude,* and far less epical in formal intention. Of its
many critics, T. S. Eliot has been, I think, the most acute in perceiving the mode of its composition and the novelty of its design.
"In Memoriam," he writes, "is the whole poem. It is unique: it is
a long poem made by putting together lyrics, which have only the
unity and continuity of a diary, the concentrated diary of a man
confessing himself. It is a diary of which we have to read every
word." [3]

    . . . Hallam is the one recurrent "object" of *In Memoriam* as a
whole, the single entity to which the diverse moods directly or in-
directly relate, and ultimately even the "objective," or at least part
of it, toward which the spirit aspires. But the composing poet
himself is the real "subject," and the quality of his changing sensibility, rather than the affirmed fact of Hallam's merit, constitutes
the central interest of the poem. Hallam is the symbol of life—life
which the final faith believes indestructible but which the first grief
sees only to have been suddenly and inexplicably removed from
its human context. Hallam's passing brings death into the poet's
world, and death in its many connotations,[4] as the survivor must
learn to accept or transcend it, becomes at the outset Tennyson's
essential theme.

    . . . As *In Memoriam* develops, the conventions of the artificial
pastoral fuse more and more with the elements of a real pastoral.

---

[3] T. S. Eliot, *Essays Ancient and Modern,* p. 183. Other critics have, of
course, been concerned with other aspects of the poem. A. C. Bradley's
Commentary (London, 1901; rev. ed., 1930) remains the best running
gloss on *In Memoriam,* its order, syntax, and often cryptic allusions.
Eleanor Bustin Mattes has studied the intellectual influences on the
elegy in her *In Memoriam: The Way of A Soul* (New York, 1951).
Graham Hough comments on the conflict between science and religion
in "The Natural Theology of *In Memoriam,*" *Review of English Studies,*
XXIII (1947), pp. 244-256; and Basil Willey reviews the problem—
rather more sympathetically—in *More Nineteenth Century Studies: A
Group of Honest Doubters* (New York, 1956), pp. 79-105. Interesting
appraisals of the scientific content will also be found in A. N. Whitehead's *Science and the Modern World* (New York, 1925) and in Georg
Roppen's *Evolution and Poetic Belief* (Oslo, 1956). E. D. H. Johnson,
on the other hand, has taken a fresh and rewarding approach to the
poem as the record of an aesthetic development, in his Essay: *"In
Memoriam:* The Way of the Poet," *Victorian Studies,* II (1958), pp.
139-148. And John D. Rosenberg writes perceptively of the relation between the intellectual argument and the symbolic structure in "The Two
Kingdoms of *In Memoriam,*" *Journal of English and German Philology,*
LVIII (1959), pp. 228-240.
[4] On the literary connotations of death, see Kenneth Burke, "Thanatopsis
for Critics, a Brief Thesaurus of Deaths and Dyings," *Essays in Criticism,*
II (1952), pp. 369-375.

The "meadows breathing of the past / And woodlands holy to the dead" assume definite outlines, and each tree or flower is drawn from observation with a careful and literal truth to nature. Though recalled with deep nostalgia, the old life at Somersby is presented in concrete sensuous detail; the witch-elms checker the flat lawn in sharp patterns of light and shade; the air is cool in "the ambrosial dark," and the distant landscape winks through the heat; in the morning comes the sound of the scythe against the damp grass, and at evening

> We heard behind the woodbine veil
> The milk that bubbled in the pail,
> And buzzings of the honeyed hours.

The idyllic mode, which dictates the pastoral artifices, helps shape these fond sad recollections of a life in harmony with its natural setting. Yet the poet is not to be deceived either by his selective memory or by his conscious control of "measured language." There is very little of the pathetic fallacy in the elegies. The nature that seems to die on the fateful September day of Hallam's death must in any case suffer decay with the coming of autumn. For nature, seen in her vast impersonality, cares nothing for man. If on a small scale she has provided the genial background of a pastoral idyl, as the agent of evolutionary change she is uncompromisingly "red in tooth and claw" and quite indifferent to every human yearning for beauty, order, and permanence. With affection and characteristic precision, Tennyson perceives the burning red maple and the spiced carnation and the night moths "with ermine capes / and woolly breasts and beaded eyes"; but all the while his imagination and intellect are haunted by the concepts of a science too large and too abstract to engage his personal sympathies.

In the postulates of the new knowledge, the "I" finds no reassurance of the value of either life or art. He has followed with concern the nebular hypothesis of the astronomers, and he has been early in his acceptance of the doctrine of uniformitarian change propounded by Lyell and the advanced geologists; but he is unable to discover evidence of purpose in the dark "worlds of space" or human value in the "Aeonian hills." He dreams of an ordered pastoral nature, a lost Eden, or of a far-off future time when the complete design of creation may again stand revealed; but he at once recognizes his dream as the projection of subjective desire, which may indeed have no correspondence with reality:

> So runs my dream: but what am I?
> An infant crying in the night:

JEROME H. BUCKLEY

> An infant crying for the light:
> And with no language but a cry.

The naked "cry" that rings through the bleakest of the elegies is so poignant that many readers have felt it the most compelling voice in the poem. Tennyson, however, whose aesthetic judgment always demands pattern and control, cannot but repudiate the confusion that, in destroying his perspective, has

> made me that delirious man
> Whose fancy fuses old and new,
> And flashes into false and true,
> And mingles all without a plan.

If the universe itself, he insists, lacks planned continuity, then the macrocosm must be simply the product of an aesthetic madness, a chaos of

> Fantastic beauty; such as lurks
> In some wild Poet, when he works
> Without a conscience or an aim.

Ultimately, in the final lyrics, he comes to regard "knowledge" itself, if "cut from love and faith," as the expression of a similar delirium, "some wild Pallas from the brain / Of demons." But by then the "reverence" he has acquired protects him from the menace of such knowledge; and faith, transcending disorder and denial, allows him at least an intimation of aesthetic wholeness:

> I see in part
> That all, as in some piece of art
> Is toil coöperant to an end.

. . . Whatever the disorder of its original composition, *In Memoriam* is thus meant to escape the error of wildness, delirium, and mere subjective rhapsody; it is even, according to Tennyson's own rather ponderous description of its total design, to be read as "a kind of *Divina Commedia,* ending with happiness." [5]

But the happy ending is not, as in Dante, foreseen with certainty. The intellectual commitment of the early lyrics is to science rather than to theology. The poet assumes, perhaps too readily, that all real knowledge is scientific or at least empirical;[6] of the "larger hope"

[5] *Memoir,* I, 304.
[6] Like Huxley and most of the Victorian scientists, Tennyson thinks of science as entirely inductive and empirical; he has no inkling of the extent to which later science will be deductive and conceptual.

140

which seems essential to his will to live, he is quite persuaded that he "cannot know," since "knowledge is of things we see." He is driven, therefore, to ask whether the unseen God, to whom he lifts his lame hands of faith, can coexist with an amoral nature, the "scientific" view of which he endorses as proven and obviously accurate:

> Are God and Nature then at strife,
>   That Nature lends such evil dreams?
>   So careful of the type she seems,
> So careless of the single life?

The question, which could not have arisen in quite the same terms before Tennyson's time, foreshadows the precise problem that was to confront John Stuart Mill in "Nature," the first of his *Three Essays on Religion*. But Tennyson saw more clearly than Mill the ineffectuality of any attempt at a logical answer. The question merely prompts a more fearful one; if the testimony of "scarped cliff and quarried stone" proves Nature careless even of the type (she cries, "I care for nothing, all shall go"), must man, too, with all his bright illusions and high idealisms, perish as no more than another trial and error of the evolutionary process?

> And he, shall he,

> Man, her last work, who seem'd so fair,
>   Such splendid purpose in his eyes,
>   Who roll'd the psalm to wintry skies,
> Who built him fanes of fruitless prayer,

> Who trusted God was love indeed
>   And love Creation's final law—
>   Tho' Nature, red in tooth and claw
> With ravine, shriek'd against his creed—

> Who loved, who suffer'd countless ills,
>   Who battle for the True, the just,
>   Be blown about the desert dust,
> Or seal'd within the iron hills?

It is irrelevant to object that *In Memoriam*, published nine years before *The Origin of Species* and more than twenty before *The Descent of Man*, is not proto-Darwinian insofar as it does not present the doctrine of natural selection and transmutation. For the elegist is concerned with the purpose and quality of human life rather than the means by which mankind reached its present state. His great question arises out of the precise intellectual at-

141

mosphere in which the Darwinian hypothesis was to be born, and it anticipates the serious debate that Darwinism in particular and Victorian science in general would provoke. Man, "who *seemed* so fair" under the older idealistic dispensation, now seems debased by a monistic naturalism which denies the soul and insists, with a dogged literalness that "The spirit does but mean the breath." The fundamental conflict of the poem thus turns on an epistemological problem: the extent to which the old appearance did correspond with the reality, or to which the new "knowledge" (or "science") does give an adequate account of the human condition. The poet professes a deep devotion to knowledge and looks forward to its wide extension:

> Who loves not Knowledge? Who shall rail
> Against her beauty? May she mix
> With men and prosper! Who shall fix
> Her pillars? Let her work prevail.

But he demands that knowledge "know her place," submit to the guidance of wisdom, learn that "reverence" must interpret and supplement the known and the knowable:

> Let knowledge grow from more to more,
> But more of reverence in us dwell;
> That mind and soul according well,
> May make one music as before.

When it lacks due reverence for the claims of the soul, knowledge forfeits its right to command the allegiance or respect of mankind; having regained his assent, the poet rather truculently declares suicide preferable to life in a world of "magnetic mockeries":

> Let Science prove we are, and then
> What matters Science unto men,
> At least to me? I would not stay.

He does not, of course, at the last believe knowledge capable of such proof; for he has once again warmed to the same "heat of inward evidence" that conquered the cold reason in "The Two Voices"; he has found life's necessary sanction quite beyond the things we see, altogether beyond knowing.

Concern with the mode of perception and the reality of the perceiving self turns the essential "action" of *In Memoriam* toward the inner experience. As in Tennyson's earliest verse, the dream and the vision are called upon to explore and at last to validate the wavering personality. In the night of despair, "Nature lends such evil dreams" to the frail ego; and in hours of hope "So runs my dream, but what am I?" Dreaming, the poet wanders across a wasteland and through a dark city, where all men scoff at his sorrow, until "an angel of the night" reaches out a reassuring hand. Half-waking, he tries to recall the features of the dead Hallam, but these "mix with hollow masks of night" and the nightmare images of Dante's hell:

> Cloud-towers by ghostly masons wrought,
>   A gulf that ever shuts and gapes,
>   A hand that points, and palled shapes
> In shadowy thoroughfares of thought;
>
> And crowds that stream from yawning doors,
>   And shoals of pucker'd faces drive;
>   Dark bulks that tumble half alive,
> And lazy lengths on boundless shores.

Only when "the nerve of sense is numb" and the self yields to the calm of the hushed summer night does the moment of full apprehension come, the "epiphany" that reveals the continuous life for which his whole heart hungers; as he reads Hallam's letters, the past suddenly asserts its persistence and its infinite extension:

> And strangely on the silence broke
>   The silent-speaking words, and strange
>   Was love's dumb cry defying change
> To test his worth; and strangely spoke
>
> The faith, the vigour, bold to dwell
>   On doubts that drive the coward back,
>   And keen thro' wordy snares to track
> Suggestion to her inmost cell.
>
> So word by word, and line by line,
>   The dead man touch'd me from the past,
>   And all at once it seem'd at last
> His living soul was flash'd on mine,
>
> And mine in his was wound, and whirl'd
>   About empyreal heights of thought,
>   And came on that which is, and caught
> The deep pulsations of the world,
>
> Aeonian music measuring out
>   The steps of Time—the shocks of Chance—
>   The blows of Death. . . .[7]

[7] Editions after 1880 were revised so that "His living soul" read "The living soul," and "mine in his" became "mine in this." The change was apparently intended to facilitate the transition from the awareness of the individual dead man to the perception of the One, the ultimate reality.

Eventually the trance is "stricken thro' with doubt"; the appearances of the world in all its "doubtful dusk" obscure the vision, and the poet returns to awareness of simple physical sensation. Yet he brings with him renewed purpose and composure; his experience has given him the certitude that "science" could not establish and therefore cannot destroy.

Though unable to sustain his vision, the "I" of the poem finds in his mystical insight the surest warrant for spiritual recovery. Tennyson, as we have seen, had been familiar with such "spots of time" from his childhood, and there was, of course, ample literary precedent for his use of "mystical" materials. In the Confessions of St. Augustine—to cite but one striking example—he might have found a remarkably similar passage recounting the ascent of the mind by degrees from the physical and transitory to the unchangeable until "with the flash of a trembling glance, it arrived at *that which is*." [8] Yet he was perplexed as always by the difficulty of communicating what was essentially private and, in sensuous terms, incommunicable. The poet accordingly, having described his trance, at once recognizes an inadequacy in the description:

> Vague words! but ah, how hard to frame
> In matter-moulded forms of speech,
> Or ev'n for intellect to reach
> Thro' memory that which I became.

The mystical vision is assuredly the sanction of his faith, but he does not choose to seek fulfillment in a sustained and conscious pursuit of the mystic's isolation. Having found faith, he must assume his place in society and "take what fruit may be / Of sorrow under human skies." And as poet, aware of his mission, he must work in his fallible yet inexhaustible medium, the "matter-moulded forms of speech."

But whether or not it defies translation into poetic language, the trance has for the poet a profound religious implication. Lifted through and beyond self-consciousness, his individual spirit attains a brief communion with universal Spirit; "what I am" for the moment beholds "What is." Yet Tennyson at no time insists that his private vision is representative or even that some way of "mysti-

[8] Confessions, Book VII, chap. xvii, Sec. 23, *Confessions and Enchiridion*, trans. and ed. Albert C. Outler, (Philadelphia, 1955), p. 151. Tennyson's trance is compared to St. Augustine's vision by Percy H. Osmond, *The Mystical Poets of the English Church* (London, 1919), pp. 309-310. The passage in the Confessions continues: "But I was not able to sustain my gaze. My weakness was dashed back, and I lapsed again into my accustomed ways." The ecstatic experience, in other words, took place some time before Augustine's conversion and had no direct relation to his decision to become a Christian.

cism" is open to all others. He assumes only that each man will feel the necessity of believing where he cannot prove; and only insofar as he makes this assumption does he think of his voice in the poem as "the voice of the human race speaking through him." For his own part, he rejects the standard "proofs" of God's existence, especially Paley's argument from design, which the Cambridge Apostles had attacked and which a later evolutionary science seemed further to discredit:

> That which we dare invoke to bless;
>   Our dearest faith; our ghastliest doubt;
>   He, They, One, All; within, without;
> The Power in darkness whom we guess;
>
> I found him not in world or sun,
>   Or eagle's wing, or insect's eye;
>   Nor thro' the questions men may try,
> The petty cobwebs we have spun.

By intuition alone, the cry of his believing heart, can he answer the negations of an apparently "Godless" nature. His faith, which thus rests on the premise of feeling, resembles that of Pascal, who likewise trusted the reasons of the heart which reason could not know. Its source, like the ground of Newman's assent, is psychological rather than logical, the will of the whole man rather a postulate of the rational faculty. And in its development, it is frequently not far removed from Kierkegaardian "existentialism," which similarly balances the demands of the inner life against the claims of nineteenth-century "knowledge."

In his *Concluding Unscientific Postscript*, which may serve as an unexpected yet oddly apposite gloss on the faith of *In Memoriam*, Kierkegaard describes his own inability to find God in the design of the objective world:

> I contemplate the order of nature in the hope of finding God, and I see omnipotence and wisdom; but I also see much else that disturbs my mind and excites anxiety. The sum of all this is an objective uncertainty. But it is for this very reason that the inwardness becomes as intense as it is, for it embraces this objective uncertainty with the entire passion of the infinite.

And to Kierkegaard *"an objective uncertainty held fast in an appropriation-process of the most passionate inwardness is the truth,* the highest truth attainable for an *existing* individual." [9] Such truth

[9] Søren Kierkegaard, *Concluding Unscientific Postscript*, trans. David F. Swenson and Walter Lowrie (Princeton, 1944), p. 182; these passages are reprinted with an excellent brief introduction by Henry D. Aiken, *The Age of Ideology* (New York, 1956), p. 239. I have quoted from the 1944 edition with the kind permission of Princeton University Press.

is apparently close to the faith that lives in "honest doubt," doubt that the physical order can in itself provide spiritual certainty. In a prose paraphrase of his poetic statement, Tennyson affirms the position even more emphatically than the philosopher:

> God *is* love, transcendent, all-pervading! We do not get *this* faith from nature or the world. If we look at Nature alone, full of perfection and imperfection, she tells us that God is disease, murder and rapine. We get this faith from ourselves, from what is highest within us. . . .[10]

Believing that all "retreat to eternity *via* recollection is barred by the fact of sin," [11] Kierkegaard questions the possibility of a complete mystical communion. Yet his faith requires "the moment of passion" comparable to the trance experience of *In Memoriam*, for "it is only momentarily that the particular individual is able to realize existentially a unity of the infinite and the finite which transcends existence." [12] Through passionate feeling, he maintains, and not by logical processes, the individual man may unify his life and achieve the dignity of selfhood. True self-awareness, as *The Sickness unto Death* tells us,[13] is born, paradoxically, of man's despair, the possibility of which is his "advantage over the beast," since in the deepest despair the soul faces its fear of imminent annihilation, "struggles with death" but comes to know the agonizing life-in-death, the torment of "not to be able to die" as prelude to acceptance of its indestructible obligation. Having also "fought with Death" and reached the level of total or metaphysical anxiety, the poet likewise finds his acute self-consciousness an essential element in his final self-realization. Such similarities are inevitable; for Tennyson, though he differs sharply from the philosopher in his estimate of the aesthetic and moral components of life, is ultimately, according to Kierkegaard's definition, "the subjective thinker": he is one who "seeks to understand the abstract determination of being human in terms of this particular existing human being." [14]

Fortified by his personal intuition, the elegist may at last give his sorrow positive resolution. He may assimilate the apparent

---

[10] *Memoir*, I, 314.
[11] Kierkegaard, paraphrased by Howard Albert Johnson, "The Diety in Time," pamphlet published by the College of Preachers, Washington Cathedral, Washington, D.C., reprinted from *Theology Today*, January 1945. Cf. Tennyson's comment on the mists of sin and the far planet, quoted above, Chap. IV.
[12] *Concluding Unscientific Postscript*, p. 176.
[13] See the *Sickness unto Death*, trans. Walter Lowrie (New York, 1954), pp. 148-154.
[14] *Concluding Unscientific Postscript*, p. 315.

confusions of history; he may trust that, though all political institutions are shaken in "the night of fear" and "the great Aeon sinks
in blood," "social truth" nonetheless shall not be utterly destroyed;
for

> The love that rose on stronger wings,
>   Unpalsied when he met with Death,
>   Is comrade of the lesser faith
> That sees the course of human things.

Subjectively reappraised, natural evolution itself may now be seen
as the dimly understood analogue of a possible spiritual progress;
and God, whom faith has apprehended, may be construed as the
origin and the end of all change, the "one far-off divine event,/To
which the whole creation moves." Though the prologue addresses
the Son of God as the principle of immortal Love, and thus as the
warranty of the worth of human love, *In Memoriam* is seldom
specifically Christian. Tennyson goes behind the dogmas of his
own broad Anglicanism to discover the availability of any religious
faith at all and finally to establish subjective experience as sufficient ground for a full assent to the reality of God and the value
of the human enterprise. His poem accordingly is not a defense of
any formal creed but an apology for a general "Faith beyond the
forms of Faith." And as such it is at once universal in its implication and directly relevant to a Victorian England which was finding all dogmatic positions increasingly vulnerable. . . .

*   *   *

r. b. heilman

HAWTHORNE'S "THE BIRTHMARK": SCIENCE AS RELIGION

Hawthorne's "The Birthmark" has been called, not inappropriately, a parable. The "truth" which it aims to set forth can be disengaged from the narrative: in a rational attempt to "perfect" nature man may destroy the organic life from which the imperfection is inseparable. But, as Messrs. Brooks and Warren have made clear, it is necessary to guard against an oversimplification of what the story says, to guard particularly against converting even a parabolic drama into melodrama. Aylmer, the overweening scientist, resembles less the villain than the tragic hero: in his catastrophic attempt to improve on human actuality there is not only pride and a deficient sense of reality but also disinterested aspiration. The story does not advocate total resignation or a flat acquiescence in the immediate state of affairs. Despite its firm expository conclusion, "The Birthmark" hardly advocates at all; it enters the neighborhood of greatness because it has a great theme, but is not tempted into pat answers. The theme which Hawthorne explores may be defined as the problem of mediating between irrational passivity and a hyperrational reorganization of life. Failure in this problem, as in others, may coincide with urgent good will; this is the formulation of the tragic actor which Hawthorne adopts, in contrast with the tragic structure in which an evil or perverted will is joined to saving qualities such as the capacity for repentance. But Hawthorne makes a more precise definition of the tragic error—one which is worth a brief examination.

This definition is made implicitly in the language of the story—

Copyright, 1949, by the Duke University Press. Reprinted from the *South Atlantic Quarterly*, October, 1949.

language which may be either literal or figurative but in either case has influential overtones. What we find recurrently in "The Birthmark," and therefore insistently asking to be taken into account, is the terminology and imagery of religion. Specifically religious problems are not overtly introduced into the story, but the language of religion is there so unfailingly that, like iterative imagery in drama and poetry, it must be closely inspected if a final reading of the story is to be complete. What it does is create a story that transcends the parabolic: the foreground parable concerns man's relations with nature, but the immanent story is about man's conceptions of evil. The further we trace the implications of language, the less simple we discover Hawthorne's tale to be.

The scientific progress of Aylmer's day, we are told, "seemed to open paths into the region of *miracle*"; scientists are called *votaries;* Aylmer may have shared their "*faith* in man's ultimate control over Nature." The subjects of their study are called *secrets,* but also, repeatedly, *mysteries;* at the end, the "*mysterious* symbol had passed away," but it had been inseparable from the very "*mystery* of life." When Georgiana's and Aylmer's union has been virtually identified with the scientific effort to remove the birthmark, Georgiana thinks of Aylmer's devotion to her—to the perfected her— as "*holy* love." What is made clear by such terms, which function precisely like poetic images, is that science itself has become religion, able to provide an ultimate account of reality and therefore to exact complete human dedication. It has become religion not only for Aylmer but also for Georgiana—". . . she *prayed* that, for a single moment, she might satisfy his highest and deepest conception." Indeed, her taking of Aylmer's final potion, which is to effect her transformation, is recorded in terms which make it virtually a Christian act. The drink is "bright enough to be the draught of *immortality*"; to Georgiana it is "like water from a *heavenly* fountain," and it will allay "a feverish thirst that had parched me for many days." Since Biblical language makes frequent use of metaphors of thirst to express spiritual yearnings, it is difficult not to read in such a passage a reminiscence of John 4:14—". . . whosoever drinketh of the waters that I shall give him shall never thirst; but the water that I shall give him shall be in him a well of water springing up into everlasting life."

The question, of course, is whether Georgiana's draught is really heavenly and has the power to allay the thirst that from the soul doth rise; whether, in other words, the auspices under which she drinks are spiritual principles. The irony of her illusion is subtly carried on by her blunt command, "Give me the goblet." At one level the analogy with communion is amplified; but *goblet* also has a metaphorical value, and we are inevitably reminded of the cup which is an ordeal: ". . . the cup which my Father hath given me, shall I not drink it?" Georgiana has overcome her dread and has come to conceive of herself, at least in part, as a sacrifice. The end is the secular salvation of mortal man.

The cup has been given by Aylmer. The language-pattern of the story indicates that in the religion of science Aylmer is less priest than God. The votaries believed, Hawthorne records, that the scientist would "lay his hands on the *secret of creative force* and perhaps *make new worlds* for himself." The word *wonders* is used repeatedly to describe what Aylmer and other scientists achieved. Aylmer, though he speaks jokingly, does apply the term *sorcerer* to himself; a laboratory exploit of his is *magical;* he is confident that he can "draw a *magic* circle around her within which no evil might intrude." He could make, he intimates, "an *immortal* nostrum"; he has created an "elixir of *immortality*"; the potion which he prepares for Georgiana may be the draught "of *immortal* happiness or misery." Aylmer has given to the problems offered by the birthmark such deep thought that he feels almost able "to *create* a being less perfect" than Georgiana. He is sure that he can make her cheek *faultless.* And then he makes an illusion which contributes importantly to this part of the meaning: "Even Pygmalion, when his sculptured woman assumed life, felt not greater ecstasy than mine will be." Formally, Aylmer rarely fails to exhibit a consciousness of human limitations; but still he cannot discipline that part of himself which aspires to infinite power. At the conclusion of the experiment he exclaims spontaneously, "By *Heaven!* it is well nigh gone!" What is this Heaven? Has a superhuman power aided him? Or has his power itself seemed to go beyond the terrestrial? A minute later he lets "the light of *natural* day" enter the room, and Aminadob, "the *earthly* mass," chuckles grossly. It is as though Aylmer has descended for a moment into another kind of reality from that which is proper to him. Indeed, he distinguishes two kinds of force which he declares have been at work: "Matter and spirit—*earth and heaven*—have both done their part in this!" But the question is whether Aylmer really accepts the dualism to which his words give expression.

In fact, we have almost a parody of the Father who gives the bitter cup to drink. Aylmer, as we have seen, is virtually translated into the godhead: His "*sorcerer's* book," Georgiana insists to him, "has made me *worship* you more than ever." The confusion of values has spread to Georgiana. Aylmer's own confusion is shown further in his paradoxical inclination to adore as well as create: "the spectral hand wrote mortality where he would fain have *worshiped.*" Yet later, in a context which shows that his evaluation is moral, he assures her, "You are fit for heaven without tasting death!" Perhaps, then, she ought to be almost suitable for adoration, and the hand itself should seem a negligible flaw. Yet over it Aylmer is almost hysterical, while, as we shall see, he is blind to more serious flaws closer to home.

That Aylmer is a confused man has always been plain to readers of the story. But, when we examine it in detail, we discover that the language of the story defines his confusion very precisely—defines it as the mistaking of science for religion. The essential story, I have said, is about man's conception of evil: Aylmer does not, in the long run, regard evil as real. Without actually denying its reality, Aylmer in effect simplifies and attenuates it by treating it as manageable, subject to human control, indeed removable. Aylmer's religion reverses the Christian sense of the reality of evil—a reality which can ultimately be dealt with only by divine grace. Aylmer is a romantic perfectibilitarian, who suffers from a dangerous fastidiousness in the presence of complex actuality. "You are perfect!" he assures Georgiana—as she is dying. He believes in perfectibility without retaining the modifying concept of damnability. Man's confidence in his ability to deal with evil by some physical or psychological or social surgery makes him an earthly god: in his presumption he proposes to establish a heaven on earth. Thus, like Aylmer, man becomes committed to a hyperrational—that is, a shallowly grounded—reorganization of life. Hawthorne brilliantly summarizes the metaphysics of the scientific religion in Aylmer's explication of the series of steps in his rehabilitation of Georgiana. He tells her, "I have already administered agents powerful enough to change your entire physical system. Only one thing remains to be tried." ". . . to change your entire physical system" is, in this cosmology, the equivalent of regeneration or conversion. Aylmer's faith becomes, in effect: improve the body, and you save the soul.

Hawthorne repeatedly underlines the error of Aylmer's ways. His confusion of values shows in the fact that his husbandly love can have strength only "by intertwining itself with his love of science." The birthmark which he proposes to remove is "fairy," "mysterious," "magic"—terms which indicate how much more is at stake than Aylmer suspects at his most acute. He accepts uncritically Georgiana's assurance that from his hand she is willing "to take a dose of poison," an ironic anticipation of the way in which his elixir actually does work. He demands complete "trust" and is angry when, following him into the laboratory, she throws "the blight of that fatal birthmark over my labors"—his own word, *blight*, having a summary accuracy of which he is ironically innocent. Aylmer accepts entirely his wife's passionate exclamation that if the birthmark is not removed "we shall both go mad!" What the reader must see in this madness is a simple inability to accept the facts of life. It is precisely this inability of which Hawthorne, throughout the story, keeps reminding us, almost overwhelmingly.

Hawthorne could hardly have found a better symbol than the birthmark, which speaks of the imperfection born with man, with man as a race. Here is original sin in fine imaginative form. Aylmer does not altogether fail to see what is involved; he is not crudely stupid; but his sense of power leads him to undervalue the penalties of life. His tragedy is that he lacks the tragic sense; he is, we may say, a characteristic modern, the exponent of an age which has deified science and regards it as an irresistibly utopianizing force. His tragic flaw is to fail to see the tragic flaw in humanity. Hawthorne never lets the reader forget the deep significance of the "human hand" which scars Georgiana. He comments ironically on the lovers who hoped to see "one living specimen of ideal loveliness without the semblance of a flaw," a suggestion of a common attitude for which Aylmer speaks. The birthmark is a "symbol of imperfection," "the spectral hand that wrote mortality," the "sole token of human imperfection." This "fatal flaw of humanity"—the terms are virtually Christian—implies that all the productions of nature are "temporary and finite" and that "their perfection must be wrought by toil and pain." For spiritual discipline Aylmer wants to substitute magic—not quite pushbutton magic perhaps, but still a shortcut, a kind of prestidigitation. It is not that he is ignorant in a gross way; he sees much, but his premises stop him at the threshold of wisdom. He recognizes that the blemish on Georgiana's face is a "mark of earthly imperfection"; he even selects it "as the symbol of his wife's liability to sin, sorrow, decay, and death." The frequency of images of death in the story is a thematic reminder of the reality from which Aylmer doggedly turns away. Although here he actually puts his finger upon the realities which the mature man must come to terms with, his faith leads him to feel, as we have seen, "that he could draw a magic circle round her within which no evil might intrude." Evil is manageable: the symbol itself has become the reality.

What we finally come to is the problem of spirit, and the test of Aylmer's creed is the kind of spiritual values it embodies. We hear repeatedly about Aylmer's spirit and his interest in the spiritual. He had "attempted to fathom," we learn, "the very process by which Nature assimilates all her precious influences from earth and air, and from the *spiritual* world, to create and foster man, her masterpiece." Aminadab represents "man's physical nature"; in Aylmer we see "the *spiritual* element." Georgiana is almost convinced "that her husband possessed sway over the *spiritual* world." As she reads his record of experiments, the author, apparently speaking for her, comments: "He handled physical details as if there were nothing beyond them; yet *spiritualized* them all, and redeemed himself from materialism by his strong and eager aspiration towards the *infinite*. In his grasp the veriest clod of earth assumed a *soul*." His failures are those of "the *spirit* burdened with clay and working in matter"; "his *spirit* was ever on the march, ever ascending"—the spirit, one is tempted to say, of progress. But as a result of this spiritual yearning of his, another's "angelic spirit" leaves on its "heavenward flight."

At the end Hawthorne, distinguishing "mortal" and "celestial," reaffirms a dualism which he has insisted upon throughout the story and which, as various words of theirs make clear, is formally assented to also by Georgiana and Aylmer. But the first defect of Aylmer's religion, as the drama makes clear, is that in practice he does not accept dualism at all: for him, spirit is not distinct from matter but is the perfecting of matter. The material stigma that shocks him he is said, just once, to regard as symbol; but his efforts at amelioration are directed wholly at the symbol, not at its antecedent substance. Aylmer is actually symptom-doctoring and is unaware that the locus of the disease is elsewhere. His creed is secular and monistic. All the talk about spirit is an ironic commentary upon his essential lack of insight into real problems of spirit.

The story specifies what level of spiritual comprehension Aylmer does reach. He aspires, and his aspiration is presented with a good deal of sympathy, as is just; as between aspiration and passivity, the choice is, in the main, clear; but a judgment must be made between one kind of aspiration and another. So the question becomes: how, and toward what, does Aylmer actually aspire? Does he, for instance, aspire toward better insight? Toward charity? Toward wisdom? Or is it not rather that his aspiration is inextricably involved with the exercise of power? "There is no taint of imperfection on thy spirit," he tells Georgiana. Why? Because Georgiana has just indicated an unreserved willingness to accept his potion; her faith in him is total. He is not content with her perfection of "spirit." For him, immense knowledge is a means of doing things, of achieving physical, visible ends. We see in him no evidence of concern with the quality of his own life, or perception, or thought.

In this man of science divine discontent is with others; as Georgiana puts it, his love "would accept nothing less than perfection nor miserably make itself contented with an earthlier nature than he had dreamed of." It is of course Georgiana who shall be "all perfect." The romantic scientist has no thought of the problem of perfecting himself; indeed, his spiritual perception is very close to that of uplift and do-good-ism. He begs the real problem of spirit

153

and is fanatical about the shortcomings of the world. Hawthorne is very acute in analyzing further the especial quality of Aylmer's outward-bound perfectionism and in discerning in it a core of intense fastidiousness. This hypersensitivity rushes in, indeed, at the very moment at which Aylmer fleetingly achieves a kind of wholeness of response to Georgiana, an acceptance of her which implies a spiritual modification of himself. "Yet once, by a strange and unaccountable impulse, he pressed it [the birthmark] with his lips." Here is virtually a redefinition of his love. But immediately his fastidiousness reasserts itself and gives the parting tone to the action: "His *spirit* recoiled, however, in the very act. . . ." That is his spirit: a primary awareness of the flaws of others and of the demand which they appear to make for remedy from without.

The heir of Prometheus kills his beneficiary, not by conferring a single blessing, but by endeavoring to eradicate the imperfections humanity is heir to. Upon this aspiration to divinity Hawthorne comments in his account of Aylmer's library, of the works of "these antique naturalists" who "perhaps imagined themselves to have acquired from the investigation of Nature a power above Nature, and from physics a sway over the spiritual world." Hawthorne has already remarked that the "great creative Mother . . . is yet severely careful to keep her own secrets." What Hawthorne has done, really, is to blueprint the course of science in modern imagination, to dramatize its persuasive faith in its omnipotence, and thus its taking on the colors of religion.

This very formulation commits Hawthorne to a critique—a critique which he makes by disclosing the false spirituality of Aylmer. It is the false spirituality of power conjoined with fastidiousness, of physical improvement, of external remedy, of *ad hoc* prescriptions, of reform: Aylmer's surgery is a fine symbol for a familiar code. Yet the code would have only an innocuous life in a museum-case if it did not gain converts. Thus we have Georgiana's very important role in the story: she is less the innocent victim than the fascinated sharer in magic who conspires in her own doom. Georgiana, the woman killed with kindness by the man who would be god, is really humanity—with its share of the heroic, its common sense, which enables it to question heroes, and yet its capacity for being beguiled, for combining good intention, devotion, and destructive delusion. In the marriage of science and humanity we see the inevitably catastrophic interaction of a mechanical perfectionism and the "birthmark of mortality." Science has no way of coming to terms with human imperfection, and humanity, tutored by science, can no longer accept its liability to sin and death.

Ironically, it is Georgiana who cuts off, or at least helps cut off, a final path of spiritual rectification for Aylmer. "Do not *repent*," she says, "that . . . you have rejected the best earth could offer." Not only is Aylmer's definition of "the best" inadequate, but he is encouraged in a hardening of spirit which precludes his entering upon a reconsideration of values. His religion offers no way of dealing with his pride. And his pride—with its intense demand that the world submit itself to his limited criteria—gives us another definition of the spiritual defect of this man who is so convinced that spirit is his concern. When Georgiana confesses her desire to worship him more fully, he scarcely bothers to be deprecatory: "Ah, wait for this one success, . . . then *worship* me if you will. I shall deem myself hardly unworthy of it." These are the ultimate marks of his moral infatuation.

The critical problem in "The Birthmark" has to do with the kind of mistake Aylmer makes. Hawthorne's language tells us, subtly but insistently, that Aylmer has apotheosized science; and the images and drama together define the spiritual shortcoming of this new revelation—its belief in the eradicability of evil, its Faustian proneness to love power, its incapacity to bring about renunciation or self-examination, its pride. I once thought that Hawthorne had stopped short of the proper goal of the story by not including the next phase of Aylmer's experience—the phase in which, if the tragic view of Aylmer were to prevail, Aylmer would entertain the Furies. But the summation of Aylmer's defects is that he cannot see the Furies. The story stops where it must.

edward h. davidson

POE: A CRITICAL STUDY

[A selection from Chapter 8, "*Eureka*."] . . . In the strict terms of "science," *Eureka* is hardly a scientific treatise at all, but, like other imaginative projections of man's knowledge of the world, such as Lucretius' *De rerum natura* or Goethe's *Faust,* it is a poetic frame on which a great body of scientific information is hung. We must, therefore, first understand its basic "science" before we can undertake to discover its other philosophic and imaginative contexts.

The book is concerned with three scientific problems relating to the physical universe: first, the concept of creation (or, how did matter become what it appears to be?); socond, the nature of matter (or, what is matter and how is the observed physical universe energized?); and third, the prospect for the natural world (or, toward what end is the everchanging universe moving?).[1] Around these three points Poe's argument is set forth and joined.

The preamble to *Eureka* consists of a whimsical attack on Aristotelian, Baconian, utilitarian, inductive logic which would abandon the guiding hypothesis as a means of investigation and substitute the collection of sense data as facts. Yet, by contrast,

Reprinted by permission of the Belknap Press and Harvard U. Press from *Poe: A Critical Study* by Edward H. Davidson, Cambridge, Mass.: © 1957 by the President and Fellows of Harvard College.
[1] In his way Poe conformed to the design Emerson had set in the chapter entitled "Spirit" in *Nature* (1836): What is matter? whence did it come? wherto is it going? See Emerson, *Complete Works* (Centenary Edition, Boston and New York, 1903), I, 61-65. It seems unlikely that Poe was in any way aware of Emerson's epoch-making book published twelve years before his own essay; yet the line of similarity is apparent: both were attempting, poetically and rationally at once, to bring back to philosophy and even to the daily lives of men, what presumptuous natural science and positivism had come to regard as their province alone.

Poe could not rest comfortably on the deductive method: as a choice between the two, he considers the intuition as the surer way to truth and cites Kepler's discoveries as examples of the way scientific advancement has been made through mystical insights into the laws of nature: "Yes!—these vital laws Kepler *guessed*— that is to say, he *imagined* them." [2] . . .

*   *   *

II

It would be both easy and difficult to say exactly where Poe had obtained his ideas for *Eureka*. Many of these ideas were in the common and popular currency of scientific thought which, like the scientific thought of any time, is a bewildering compound of popular science, of the still-surviving science of a past age, and of the diverse blends which men make of their religious faith and their assumptions of what science is or ought to be. Poe's science is also a religion—not the religion of any formal churches but the religion of what a few men thought would be a scientific hypothesis concerning God at a time in Western thought just before the impact of Darwinian evolutionary ideas. *Eureka* might in one term be regarded as a treatise in "scientific religion" at a moment in intellectual history when the ordered universe of the eighteenth century was still a self-explanatory fact, when the Deity could obviously be conceived as the original and the still-continuing force in His universe, and when man—his history reaching back only to the starting-point of recorded time—was a creature that existed as the highest order of beings in a universe which had been designed expressly for his pleasure and perfection.

The basic hypothesis to account for that universe is, in *Eureka,* a machine. It is a mechanism which is very like the cosmological system of Newton, Locke, and the eighteenth-century empiricists —with those happy variants introduced by Poe himself in order to make the universe an "unknown known" or a poem. Poe conceives of the universe as matter, motion, and force in a succession of instantaneous configurations of matter. He acknowledges Newton's law as a description of the presently observed condition of things, but he seeks to go beyond the Newtonian formulation in order to posit a law not only for the observed condition but for the origin of matter: *"Every atom, of every body, attracts every other atom, both of its own and of every other body, with a force which varies inversely as the squares of the distances between the attracting and attracted atom . . . ; the general result being a tendency of all, with a similar force, to a general centre."* [3] Then

[2] *The Complete Works of Edgar Allan Poe*, edited by James A. Harrison (17 vols.; New York, 1902), XVI, 197.
[3] *The Complete Works of Edgar Allan Poe*, XVI, 215, 221.

EDWARD H. DAVIDSON

he appended the theory of Laplace as a further proof for the origin of the material universe in some generating principle or thought: matter was radiated from a source into nebula; the particles of the nebula were themselves dispersed into a steadily increasing complexity and heterogeneity. The process can be expressed by the following formula:

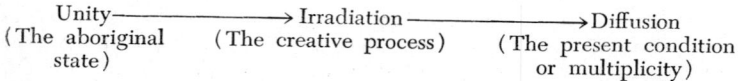

$$\text{Unity} \longrightarrow \text{Irradiation} \longrightarrow \text{Diffusion}$$

(The aboriginal state)   (The creative process)   (The present condition or multiplicity)

At some moment in God's historical time this process will be reversed: the force of dispersion will be withdrawn; the force of attraction, basic to all organic and inorganic life and even to human consciousness, will become sufficiently powerful to overcome the force of disunity and dispersion, and all those infinitely various forms will move back to their original state of homogeneity; the whole universe will once more be in its primal "concentricity" or unity.

Like his age, Poe found another support for his theory of unity in heterogeneity or animism in mechanism. The discoveries in electricity from the age of Franklin onward had argued the presence of a primal energy or an "ether" inhabiting all the spaces of the universe and dispersed even between the infinitely minute particles of observed matter. This ether, sometimes confused with electricity, was the means of transmitting light and energy from the sun, of holding atoms in the physically observed forms, and even of transferring sense data from one mind to another. Electricity was, therefore, the force which seemed to function in the universe as the clearest physical demonstration of "spirit" or the animating and diffusive power of God. We might now consider how the observed forms of the world, man's place in the world, and even man's thought could be explained according to the then current theories of electrical energy.[4]

Matter, once dispersed throughout the universe, now exists in

[4] Poe relied for further proofs of his cosmological system on such electrical and magnetic theories of his time as Sir John Herschel's four determinations: (1) Electricity is not limited to a few substances but is found in all; (2) magnetic and electrical phenomena conform to the same principles of inverse squares as does gravitation; that is, the force of electrical energy increases as the square of its distance from its source; (3) electricity, according to Volta, is generated by contact between different substances; and (4) there is a direct relationship between electrical and nervous phenomena. These principles supplied Poe with a set of laws and, when they could not function satisfactorily as laws, of analogies which explained not only the constitution of matter but the interaction of matter and mind.

158

gradations; some of these distinctions between kinds and degrees of matter man at present knows and assigns to scientific and logical organizations; others are so remote or "pure" as to be beyond his comprehension. The reason why matter is in these various gradations is the "electrical principle" which governs the form all substances assume. Matter is never in a state of rest; its motion is, however, not merely an observed fact or a logical, causal shift of constituent parts. The direction of motion is an act of mind expressing itself through the agency of the electrical energy that animates all things. Motion cannot therefore be called "thought," for the electrical force which is the energizing of thought is long antecedent to that thought and that action. Behind all observed matter and behind all thought is a primal electrical force; thinking is the conscious paralleling of an individual thought with that universal direction. Behind even thought is unity. What man terms "thinking" is merely his instinctive, inevitable conformity to an elemental principle which is the one principle animating all motion and matter. Matter and mind are one in the total design. Thought in man is the same as the mechanism of the universe.

What, then, is the condition of man, and why does man seem to be the one being who is somehow disfigured and out of place in the cosmic design?

Man encompasses both spirit and substance and consists of two forms of "bodies": one is a rudimentary or simply physical existence; the other is a variable component which governs man's conformity (even though man himself may be unaware of this condition) to the ultimate configurations of matter and motion as they existed once in the primal order of God. Throughout the passage of time or the corrosive action of the dispersive force in the human realm, man has become more and more separated from his long-ago conformity to the unity of matter, motion, life, and spirit; he has become incapable of perceiving more than a mere fraction of what exists. Only, as it were, by working back from disunity through dispersion to unity in thought can man ever penetrate the small circle of his present existence and reach the aboriginal concept which is the unity of the universe.

Man's mind and being are not alone in this tendency; all forms and all created matter conform to the law of "simplicity" or the law of unity from which everything has come and to which everything will inevitably return. In support of this thesis of "simplicity," Poe borrowed a rule of Keplerian physics which had stated, in effect, that atoms are drawn toward each other and thus eventually toward some coherent design or unity. Just so, Poe reasoned, the human mind, itself a form lodged in the universe, tends toward "concentrality" and in continually expressing its "tendency always to return to unity." By the very nature of this tendency or struggle, the material world is incomplete or abnormal: man's mind, necessarily in conformity with the known laws of matter, is also functioning in diversity, in multiplicity, in crude approximations to the true nature of things. And, just as the atoms and the material forms "struggle back" to the center, so too does the human mind move toward the primal order of final being. But this struggle is difficult: so far as it can ever go toward ultimate completion, the mind is permitted, in its present state, only rare flashes of brilliant and fragmentary illumination, such as at moments of scientific discovery or of poetic insight, into the absolute reality which lies behind this illusory structure of the material world. . . .

❄   ❄   ❄

. . . Poe's science and metaphysics, positing matter and mind as originating in a central Idea and then undergoing dispersion throughout space and time, argued that the material universe was not fixed or rooted in "common sense." Quite the contrary: in *Eureka* the world assumed the form of a chimera whose every moment might exhibit some new condition of things which had almost no relevance to an antecedent condition. What Poe did was to set up a rational, empirical order of things as those things are assumed to exist in common sense and in sensory experience—and then posit a concurrent order of things-as-ideas existing in a totality of experience beyond empiricism and abstract logic. There was, there must be, the "unknown" in human thought toward the comprehension of which man is moving, else there would have been no change in the past intellectual history of man. In the end, we do rely on the experience of our sense impressions—and we do not. Poe's denial of the methodological value of either inductive or deductive logic and his positing of the superior capacity of the intuitional faculty cut straight through the Lockean or positivist philosophy of knowledge and left him with a "mechanistic animism." True, he involved himself in so many contradictions that *Eureka* can be accounted only as "imaginative metaphysics" at best; yet, as we shall see, its imaginative approach to problems of thought may have transgressed logic but pointed the way toward a poetically conceptual idea of man and his mind.

. . . Poe was speaking for the urgency of his age which had, for more than a century, committed itself to a mechanistic universe —yet it was a universe which had God or an animating intelligence in it. It was a unity with every sign and behavior of multiplicity; it was a world of absolute fixity and predictability which was nonetheless undergoing a continuous process toward the consummation of a grand design. *Eureka* was the positing of an invariable machine

160

—and it was a protest against everything mechanistic and empirical. . . .

[A] major problem which is undertaken in *Eureka* . . . is the question of art and the artist. Poe was seeking some way of avoiding the admission that there was, after all, a final rift between science and art and between the world of things and the artist. He conjured up the known pluralisms of the universe—scientific and philosophic—and then posited an ultimate monism. So too art must be, in this term, regarded as but another extension and demonstration of "the plot of God" and the artist as a god-player. Poe's argument may be one more example of the forlorn hope of establishing any relationship between the data of experience transmitted into the life of practical affairs and those transmitted into art. As Hume long ago pointed out, philosophic and artistic doctrine fails to justify the practice of daily life. Nevertheless, whatever fallacy he may have invited, Poe set forth a dialectic of the autonomy of art and of expressive symbolism. We might now consider some of the implications of that urgent demand that somehow the artist does belong in the universe and that what he communicated is not just word, line, or tonality. . . .

        ❃   ❃   ❃

The . . . problem of the artist was the relation of the work of art not only to its own time-concept or range of expression but to the variable time-views of critics and viewers in its own time and in the time to come. Following the analogy which Poe used in other relations between empirical science and critical theory, we can see the implication of the idea of dispersion of force: just as the world ages and becomes more chaotic, so the older art becomes, the more it must somehow project a vision of the lost unity. In "Al Aaraaf" Poe had an early glimpse of this view of the lost centrality of things; in *Eureka* he tried to expand the whole concept in order to demonstrate that, while empirical science and the rational mind of man drive toward diffusion and the comprehension of itself in particles, the imagination is impelled toward a unitary determination. And the older the time, the wider the separation between the two. In their origin, science and art were one; in the dispersion of man's faculties and his knowledge, the two have become an intellectual and metaphysical universe apart.

This bifurcation of man's original insight into two ways of thought, the one empirical and the other imaginative, while it brought a remarkable sharpening of the factual and discursive, nonetheless caused a virtual atrophy of the imaginative insight, or else, in the passage of time, relegated poetic exercise to a mere plaything. Scientific inquiry becomes easier with advancing times;

161

imaginative and artistic discourse becomes more difficult, if not virtually impossible. The reason is not only that the struggle toward a unitary idea becomes increasingly difficult with the onrush of the dispersive tendency toward multiplicity, but the language problem becomes more onerous. The romantic writer like Poe felt an almost desperate necessity to recapture the lost sense of the oneness of things and to vivify language as a means of re-creation of man's aboriginal insight. In Romantic terms, men once spoke poetry; and, as Emerson stated, the farther we go back in time, the language of prose more closely approached the precise images which only imaginative discourse can render. But the passage of time slowly extracts clear meaning from language until men in a later time, not themselves knowing the meaning of words and discourse, must have the meaning reattached to the language for them.

Men have lost their capacity for image-making; they have similarly lost their ability to understand images: the relationship, once so clear in their minds, between the object and its stimulus, has long been reduced to a monontonously repeated sound. Therefore, in the latter ages of man, the artist or writer must undertake the burden of rediscovering and then making the relevances for his fellowmen. The later the time, the more terrible this burden becomes. With Poe we have almost a formulation of the theory of modern symbolism: namely, the artist must recast and make relevant the long-separated dualism of man's mind; he must bridge between the chaotic, particularized world of empirical data and the instinctive, cognitive awareness that mind and matter cohere in a disclosed design. Poe as a symbolist was among the first to formulate a theory—and *Eureka,* itself an extended symbol, is the central statement—that art is man's one instrument for making some order out of the infinitude of empirical formlessness. He also understood the perilous dichotomy which is the paradox of the symbolist method: symbolism is the way of the mind and the imagination to make coherent an infinite variety of impressions, ideas, and forms which might otherwise remain totally disordered; yet the order which the imagination enforces is only that order alone which is in the picture or the poem; "reality" is as chaotic and fractured as ever; only the word, the metaphor, the tonality, the imposed coherence make a design out of what still is, empirically, shapelessness. Art and science are not one; they are not so much at war as they are worlds apart in their ways of understanding and inquiry; they may both drive toward that "one," but in the present order of created things, they only suggest the gap which has been widening ever since man entered the realm of logical positivism and relegated poetry and myth and even the arts to superstition or to mere entertainment.

What, in the end, Poe was forced to acknowledge was that, in order to remain "pure," art had to disavow any connection with science, with the world as it is, with the forlorn hope that it can in any way direct the lives of men. *Eureka* was one more in the considerable line of Romantic protests against common sense and against art as morality; it affirmed that the work of art is like the creative act of God: a special, a private autonomy, a unique disclosure of idea and fact, word and idea. After the poem or the artwork had been made, the maker was absolved from any further responsibility; it ceased to be his as soon as he had made it; he was not, as was God, granted the power to explain himself. Nor would his readers or viewers be given the right to find him in it. Criticism and philosophy met at this point at which the "personality" of the thinker and maker was of no consequence, for the work of art had a life of its own long after it had left its maker's hands. By investigating the abstract laws of nature one might find the teleological being called God; by studying the poem one might find, not the poet, but "the rationale of verse" or the method which poetry, or art, allows in seeking the meaning of time and man, history and art (for art rests on its precedence), man and the total abstract design of the universe. The "meaning" could never be finally stated; the "way" was always through the imperfect range of discourse, metaphor, analogy, symbol. But if the artist could somehow establish a provisional set of relevances and then, as it were, grant his symbolic order the right to have a life of its own, as Poe did in "The Raven" and in "The Fall of the House of Usher," to name only two of a dozen, then art opened a further range of expression and understanding beyond the limits which empirical data insisted were all that existed. Poe therefore wrote *Eureka*, supposedly a scientific treatise, in order to demonstrate that knowledge was not science but intuition, that the artist must free himself from the moral and from the empirical, and that the artist must admit to himself that he can pursue his "forlorn demon" alone or only in terms of the history of his art.

※　　※　　※

[A selection from Chapter 4, "Death, Eros, and Horror."] Death and horror would seem to be associated, and indeed they must be in any investigation of the mind and art of Poe. But we must now consider the theme of horror as something apart and as available for inquiry for its own sake. We must also consider this theme, as we have the topic of death, as contained in both the poetry and the short stories, though our emphasis will of necessity fall on the poetry. Yet it was such a theme as that of death or horror which binds Poe's story-writing career to his poetic experience and writing; by only slightly shifting the emphasis and the rhetorical devices he could write "tales of horror" just as ably as he had written poems of horror, and then come back, in his later life, to write poems of death and horror again. One might easily draw a line from the very early "Tamerlane" through "The Fall of the House of Usher" to "The Raven": all of them were studies of stages in consciousness when the real world slipped away or disintegrated and the mind found itself fronting the "horror" of its own loneliness and loss.

First of all, we might define the Poesque version of horror as that region or mysterious middle ground where the normal, rational faculties of thinking and choice have, for reasons beyond knowing, been suspended; ethical and religious beliefs are still the portion of men, but are powerless to function. All power of choice and all sense of direction have been lost; in fact, they have been so long lost that the nightmare world of presumed reality obeys no laws of reason or stability. It is a highly complex metaphysical condition wherein the constants of heaven and hell are fixed at their opposite polarity, but between them is the vast region wherein the human will is situated and is powerless to effect any variation of its own existence. It is a realm where the will cannot exist, not because it never had an existence but because it somehow lost its power to function. It is a world like that in "The City in the Sea": moral man once lived in that long-ago world, but now everything is shadowy and atrophied. In such a horror world men are moral mutes or paralytics; they are like Roderick Usher, the "Last of the Visigoths," at the very end of a long line of ethically directed ancestors. Horror is, then, the urgent need for moral knowledge and direction—and its total lack. The characters in such a situation can only dream of a condition which once existed but which they would never be able to follow, even if they were able to recapture it. They are like the creatures in Poe's most complete allegorical presentations, those in the apocalyptic visions like "The Conversation of Eiros and Charmion" (1839) and "The Colloquy of Monos and Una" (1841): they are the victims of an Apocalypse which has had no perceptible reason for being.

Yet even the lack or the negation of a moral principle had to be based on some system of good and evil. A Christian view, such as Hawthorne propounded, conceived that sin entered the world with man and remains with man forever, while nature exists outside either in a dualism with man or in an implacable state of indifference to him. The naturalism of a Melville or Mark Twain, to draw a brief contrast, found the basis for evil not in man but in the primal order of nature and at the center of the universe itself: man is thereby lodged in a universe of evil, and his tragedy is that he alone of all forms of life can both know and strive to meliorate his condition. This naturalism, as it was with Twain, can be driven far enough to exonerate man of all blame or consequence for the rigidly deterministic order. . . .

III

Horror was . . . not only a philosophy or a method of explaining the mystery of the universe; it was also "psychology" or a method of inquiring into special states of mind. It was a means to externalize, in vivid physical objects, inner states of being and a method of portraying the mind's awareness of itself. These "objects" of horror were not themselves necessarily horrible; they were what they were because a mind saw them and was even destroyed by them. In one way this was Poe's contribution to the dark subliminal literature of a later time: he demonstrated that states of consciousness are not simply isolated conditions of madness but are somehow intimately and intricately related to the physical world around it. Poe's fault (to hasten ahead of our exposition for a moment) was that, once he had found a vivid externalization for a condition of inner consciousness—a crack in the wall, a black cat, a portrait, an insistent heartbeat—the physical exemplification assumed command; and in the succeeding narrative, whether in poem or in short story, the objectification was out of all proportion to the inner condition. One might say that the symbol ran away with the idea; Poe was content to let the convulsive dance of objectified forms enact the drama. Thus rhetoric and landscape conveyed the agony.

Taken altogether, these conditions of consciousness which Poe exposed did not suggest that Poe was revealing himself or aspects of his own inner being but was actually detailing certain stages and varieties of what might be termed the "Romantic consciousness." Horror was therefore Poe's insight into Romantic self-consciousness—into the tendency of the Romantic mind to consider that its own psychic response to life and to the world was a sufficient subject for life. The tendency need not have ended in "horror"; it did end in the capacity of the Romantic mind both to create and to be almost simultaneously scrutinizing itself at the moment of creative activity. We might explore some of these conditions of consciousness as they are contained in certain of Poe's poems and short stories.

One obvious quality of the protagonist or "I" in these discourses was its inhuman arrogance and self-exaltation. This was the frame

EDWARD H. DAVIDSON

within which the Romantic ego functioned: it had to expunge its weaker, grosser self, to descend into a private hell, to suffer self-loss, and to rise again; it was Goethe's Werther, Carlyle's Teufels-drockh, Byron's Manfred, and Shelley's Prometheus, all of them primal explorations of the self becoming aware of and making peace with its unique self and experience.[5] Poe's "I" is different from them all in one significant way: while he may be endowed with extraordinary learning and may have the power to accomplish vast aims, he can never weep like Werther, curse like Teufelsdrockh, rage like Manfred, or suffer like Prometheus. He is not the Romantic hero-god; he is only a little man. He is the Romantic hero reduced to the limited vision of commonplace men, and yet he is required, certainly according to all the literary and philosophic antecedents of which Poe was aware, to live and die in a hell or heaven which is totally beyond his comprehension. Only on rare occasions are this hero's sufferings magically alleviated by his knowledge of vortices in the Scandanavian maelstrom or by the timely arrival of the rescuing army to release him from the swinging knife of the inquisition.

What marks Poe's studies of a man caught in some inner or outer horror is that, for all the sufferings the protagonist must undergo, the fictive "I" never learns anything. The anguish is wasted because the sufferer comes out of the action precisely the same as he went into it. Nothing has really occurred "inside"; there was no inner consciousness to begin with, and the pilgrimage of the questing self had been wrought entirely in terms of the scene, the natural objects in easy accord and attendance, and the incantatory spell-weaving which somehow reduced the tangible world to a mere logarithm. The symbolic projection took precedence and triumphed over what it was originally designed to prefigure and represent. Therefore, nothing could happen to the mind caught in the terror of an event; everything must happen to the outside world which is made to envision the agony. All the while the mind remains unmoved. . . .

*　　*　　*

These tales were Poe's rationalizations of horror; that is, the principle of horror itself seems to imply that the horrific is that which suddenly interrupts or shatters the rational order of the universe; however completely that order is restored, the human

[5] The works referred to are Goethe's *The Sorrows of Young Werther*; Carlyle's *Sartor Resartus;* Byron's *Manfred;* and Shelley's *Prometheus Unbound.* The protagonists of these works illustrate the type of Romantic hero who sets up the force of his own personality in rebellion against some powerful divine or social order. [Ed.]

mind forced to endure that "apocalypse" or shock will be forever dislocated or maddened. The young man in "The Raven" will never recover his "soul" or his acceptance of the coherence of things after his terrible insight, not only into his own madness, but into the madness of the universe itself. The young man in "The Pit and the Pendulum" was able to maintain his sanity by the power of his will to escape the swinging knife-blade just long enough to be fortuitously rescued from a private psychic world which every moment threatened him with insanity and annihilation. These and other inquiries into the dark world of the mind suggest that Poe, however much his horror was a rather simple externalization of inner states of being, was demonstrating that horror itself or various phases of loss of self might be ways into farther and deeper understanding. Horror, madness, and death are man's avenues into the ultimate rationale of existence of which our own mortal existence is but a crude fragment. Man in his earthly habit lives on the virtually unquestioned assumption that he can predict and understand nearly every event that occurs in his own life and in the diurnal motions of the planets; Poe, however much his rhetoric may have been apocalyptic and frenzied and his narrative struggling to be *outré*, was nevertheless writing a series of quite moral poems and tales concerning the evidence everywhere before man's eyes of the total disunity and incoherence of his own life which is an infinitesimal part of the universal "plot of God." Man must, however, be terrified or driven to comprehend that what seems to be fractured is actually a segment of the universal design and what appears to be madness may be "divinest sense."

*   *   *

hyatt howe waggoner

ROBERT FROST: THE STRATEGIC RETREAT

Man is, and yet is not, involved in the flux of nature and time. He is a creature, subject to nature's necessities and limitations; but he is also a free spirit who knows the brevity of his years and by this knowledge transcends the temporal by some capacity within himself.—REINHOLD NIEBUHR *in* The Nature and Destiny of Man

1 Storm Fear

Robert Frost remarked a few years ago that he was not the "Platonist" Robinson was,[1] thus shrewdly suggesting the essential temperamental difference between himself and the poet with whom he must always be compared. Robinson's longing for truth and meaning was perhaps bound to be frustrated, given his time and place and temperament; bound to be frustrated at any time or any place, says Mr. Frost, acknowledging his "tendency to scoff" at "literary tears" shed over man's plight. It is easy, then, to classify Robinson as a frustrated idealist and Frost as a satisfied, perhaps a complacent, realist, using those terms in their popular sense; easy, and for some purposes no doubt useful, but there are other approaches more revealing.

For Mr. Frost, too, has persistently felt and written about man's need for more certainty than is required for merely practical purposes. "The artist in me cries out for design," he has said;[2] yet he has not restrained his inclination to scoff. He *rejects* myth and metaphysics; the blind do not reject color. His philosophy of the

From Hyatt Howe Waggoner's *The Heel of Elohim: Science and Values in Modern American Poetry*, copyright 1950 by the University of Oklahoma Press.
[1] Quoted in Lawrance Thompson, *Fire and Ice* (New York, 1942), 192.
[2] Unless otherwise identified, all quotations from Mr. Frost are from his poetry.

limited may finally come to seem, as it has recently been fashionable to point out, a limitation in his work, but it is not a naïve philosophy. It is based on a willful, a consciously designed and elaborately guarded rejection. He has made a strategic retreat from a world with which he has acknowledged a lover's quarrel.

There is a difference, Mr. Frost has remarked, between a flight and a retreat. The one step backward that he has taken to save himself from going down with the avalanche may be characterized not as a flight but as a seeking, or it may be thought of simply as a calculated strategy. In any case it is the dominant note in the poetry from *A Boy's Will* to *A Masque of Mercy*. The note is struck in the most youthful poems. "Into My Own," the first poem in *A Boy's Will*, is both Emersonian (one goes apart to discover the true self) and Frostian in a way that Emerson would have had difficulty in understanding (one is haunted by the dark trees, one actually embraces the doom without calling it by a different name in the next sentence). The difference from the Emersonian way is crucial—partly because there is so such of Emerson in Frost. Emerson's strategy, as he admitted in *Nature*, had been to embrace idealism as a way of transforming the unpleasant facts that made the young men sad; he admitted the facts, particularly in the late *Conduct of Life*, but his usual way was to follow the admission with a denial, or at least to change the subject quickly.

Not so the youthful Frost. His time of year is the fall, his time of day the night. He writes no poems about spring. The early poems of *A Boy's Will*—though they often betray that groping for an idiom and an attitude characteristic of youthful poetry, though they do not always have what we have come to recognize as the true Frost ring, though they are often within a tradition we have come not to admire—yet recognize the lifelong problem and suggest the lifelong answer. "My November Guest" avows "the love of bare November days." Despite its remnants of nineteenth-century poetic diction, its "o'er," "do blow," and the like, it suggests the later Frost by announcing the presence of that neutral universe which Emerson had thought to exorcize with his "ideal theory." "Storm Fear" states the result: we must "save ourselves unaided." (Robinson had felt it impossible to save ourselves unaided; Frost called him a Platonist.) When the young poet looks, in "Vantage Point," at the homes of men, he sees, just beyond, the graves of men. "Now Close the Windows" recognizes that "it will be long ere the earliest bird." "In Hardwood Groves" urges acceptance of the world as it is, little as the heart may like it; "Reluctance" shows the heart still seeking, unwilling to accept the end of a season. During a line storm the young man thinks of "the sea's return," the ages before man, the "ancient lands," a thought that brings its own desolation. But the poet has already decided to counter hate with love, to embrace with one arm the better to strike with the other: "The fact is the sweetest dream that labor knows."

Here then in the earliest poems are the provocation and the essence of the strategic response: a diminished world, and acceptance without approval. The situation to which acceptance without approval was the response was of course, in the largest sense, "our world" as Mr. Frost saw it. He saw it then and he sees it now as "diminished" even while he scoffs at the victims of the modern temper. What chiefly diminished it, is too clear to need further demonstration of the kind I once supplied in an earlier study of the poet.[3] There are too many direct and indirect references to science as the antagonist and too many clear statements on the matter—Mr. Frost's poetry is nearer to the poetry of statement than to symbolism—to leave anyone acquainted with the poetry in doubt. But the nature of the issue should be noted.

Man longs for reasons, ultimately for a Reason; but science, which seems to be our only dependable knowledge, gives none. And contemporary thought, taking its cue from science, denies the possibility of there being any. The old reasons, though possibly specious, kept off the dark. Like Hemingway's universal symbol of the old man who wanted to stay in a clean, well-lighted place, Frost has yearned for light. But what the heart demands, the mind, in our time, cannot supply. Science has given us light of a kind, but it has taken away the light we most desire, leaving us only a "flickering, human pathetic light" that we strive to "maintain against the night." Time and space have been enlarged until we are diminished into nothing. (So that we are in the same plight as the men of the Middle Ages, who were dwarfed by God; all ages are the same for the soul.[4]) "Space ails us moderns: we are sick with space." We have "taken artificial light Against the ancient sovereignty of night," but it is not bright enough to keep us unaware of "the heartless and enormous Outer Black." The literate farmer argued that science "cheapened speed," but the poet replied that "A good cheap anti-dark is now the need." In our day science holds "the ministry of fear"; our science "unnerves" us:

> He thought if he could have his space all curved. . . .
> His science wouldn't get him so unnerved.

The darkness is complete, being both interstellar and philosophic: as Job said to God in *A Masque of Reason*,

[3] In *American Literature*, Vol. XIII, No. 3 (November, 1941), 207-23.
[4] See "The Lesson for Today."

> We don't know where we are, or who we are
> Don't know one another; don't know You;
> Don't know what time it is . . . .
> It comes down to a doubt about the wisdom
> of having children—after having had them.

As science brings more light of fact, it increases the darkness of the understanding. It looked to the young Frost, as it looks to him now, as if

> . . . a night of dark intent
> Was coming, and not only a night, an age.

II *The Response*

The heart of man is terrified by the dark, but his mind can do something—not enough, but something—to discipline the heart. What I have called Frost's strategy is precisely the response of the mind to a situation at which the heart rebels. From the earliest to the latest poems we may observe the maneuver developing until it becomes the poet's characteristic stance.

North of Boston, the poet's second volume, is made up almost entirely of long narrative and dramatic poems on New England characters, but when the poet returned, in *Mountain Interval,* to the lyric, he returned to the theme which had been present only as a mood in the character studies. "Oven Bird" determines the key of *Mountain Interval;* it phrases the crucial question: the question is "what to make of a diminished thing." Both "Hyla Brook" and "In the Home Stretch" suggest the elements of an answer: there are no ends and beginnings, only middles; don't remember too much, don't look too far; "We love the things we love for what they are." And "The Exposed Nest" and "Out, Out—" further emphasize the attitude: the way to take the diminished thing is not to care too much, to turn back to one's affairs.

New Hampshire, the fourth volume, continues the strain with increased emphasis. Many of the poems develop the theme of the limitation of man's knowledge. "Some may know what they seek in school and church," but the poet is content to hold in his hand the meteoric fragment which is, he feels, "the one world . . . I am like to compass." The certainty man would like to pin his faith to has been sought in vain: "We've looked and looked, but after all where are we?" Using the figure of the telescope, "The Star Splitter" humorously and "I Will Sing You One O" seriously deny the usefulness of science in man's quest for certainty. Fragmentary blue must suffice those for whom a view of Heaven has become impossible. Now and then clear days come even in New England to whet our desire for a more perfect blue, but one had best not count on them. Once truth seemed to glimmer as a pebble at the bottom of a well, then something. . . . The poet hopes he will go after the knowledge "beyond the bounds of life" when he is free to. Meanwhile, there is a life to live and the way to live it is not to cling too tightly, to learn to let go with the mind ("Wild Grapes"), to accept the end of a season ("Nothing Gold Can Stay"), to learn that the phoebes are not weeping for the burned house on the deserted farm ("The Need of Being Versed in Country Things").

West Running Brook saw the poet at the height of his powers, and several of the finest lyrics in the volume are on the theme which it is my present concern to trace. "Once by the Pacific" foresees a dark night ahead for the soul. "The Peaceful Shepherd" suggests a willingness to forget the crown, the scales, and the cross, since we may know them by their fruits. "A Winter Eden" offers us the only kind of Eden we are likely to know; we had better make the most of it, though

> An hour of winter day might seem too short
> To make it worth life's while to wake and sport.

And in one of the loveliest lyrics in all his verse the poet insists on what should have been clear to everyone, though it has not been to those who have thought of his strategy as a flight from "reality": "I have been one acquainted with the night."

Two poems in *West Running Brook* state afresh the reason for the strategy. When he looks up by chance at the constellations, the poet is reminded that there is no revelation in nature; and in "The Bear" he expounds humorously on man's pathetic attempts to reach certainty: like a caged bear, man seeks restlessly in science and philosophy for the absolutes which neither can provide; neither telescope nor microscope. Plato nor Aristotle can answer the questions we most want answered. In Emersonian fashion the poem scoffs at the claims of reason, but its failure to mention the alternative of intuition marks the poet's difference from the master. Man simply goes on swaying futilely back and forth from cheek to cheek—that is, when he is not pacing with equal futility back and forth from telescope to microscope and back to telescope. "All revelation" may have been ours, as the poet says in a later poem, but it is not the kind we seem to know how to use. It is discernible anyway only to those whose eyes are turned in the right direction, only, in short, to those who have mastered the defensive strategy.

An ever increasing proportion of the poems in the later volumes, especially in *A Further Range, A Witness Tree,* and *Steeple Bush,* reiterate and amplify the complex of attitudes which I have been tracing. Several of the poems devoted to it—"Desert Places" and

"Come In," for example—are among the very finest the poet has ever written. But without commenting further on individual poems, I want to summarize the several aspects of the challenge and the strategic response and turn to their final significance in all of the poetry.

The dark, the doom, the not knowing can be accepted by the mind, but the heart rebels. When the light flickers and the gloom increases, the mind takes a quick step back to "common sense," to "matter of fact," and continues to accept a life that sometimes looks "sinister-grave." The mind accepts time's tearing down what has been built up, the inhuman perspectives of geology and astronomy, the loneliness and cold of "the long night." The mind counters the heart's fear by suggesting that "it's knowing what to do with things that counts." Though man can see neither out far nor in deep, and though his attempts to interpret his most certain knowledge result only in a futile turning "from force to matter and back to force," yet man has his defenses:

> The Infinite's being so wide
> Is the reason the Powers provide
> For my inner defense my hide.

With defenses intact—and mental as well as biological forces have contrived them—the poet can afford to stand "freely face to face All night with universal space." He can feel the loneliness that comes on in desert places (a loneliness that "will be more lonely ere it will be less"), recognize that the stars have "no expression, nothing to express," yet remain unfrightened. He has learned not to care when he tramples the autumn leaves in the mud, thus hastening the end of a season; and if he even takes a sort of pleasure in the trampling, perhaps it is because fear sometimes makes us destroy what we love.

> Perhaps I have put forth too much strength and
> been too fierce from fear.
> I have safely trodden underfoot the leaves of
> another year.

The poet long ago decided that the "discipline man needed most Was to learn submission to unreason." He has adopted an attitude of pragmatic acquiescence, a variety of positivism that would suggest the position of the logical positivists, were it not that the poet's laughter is directed at science even more often than it is at metaphysics. Having achieved his difficult renunciation, Mr. Frost is able in his poetry to practice what Mr. Eliot has hoped to learn: "to care and not to care." The achievement has been the result of the unremitting effort of a lifetime. To trace this effort is to realize how accurate the poet is when he says in a late poem:

> I have been so instinctively thorough
> About my crevice and burrow.

III Denials and Affirmations

Mr. Frost is a man of many denials. His personal manner, his conservative political position, the harshness with which he usually judges his contemporaries—these and more aspects of a cultivated hardness need not concern us here. But his denials, as we have already seen, are not limited to things political, social, and personal, nor do they all set him off from his time. On the contrary, his denial of the value of systematic reason is quite in keeping with the temper of an age which fears the tyranny of words and has ceased studying philosophy. And his denial of the value of theology,[5] side by side with his acceptance of the religious spirit as a natural part of man, strikes a purely contemporary, though not an advanced contemporary, note. Only men go in for metaphysics and theology; "You don't catch women trying to be Plato." In his humorous and inconclusive poem on the problem of evil, the poet treats Job's wife more sympathetically than he does Job, just as in some of the early character studies, he showed more sympathy for the women than for the men. Women have never been much concerned with Truth "in the abstract high singular."

But it is chiefly the two denials that he makes with regard to science that concern us here. First, what science reveals is neither so new nor so important as its more excited devotees suppose. The "sun of science" may actually have risen, as John Burroughs put it, but the shadows have not receded and the day is not perceptibly different in the ways that count most. "The truths we keep coming back and back to" are still with us, and though "thought cleaves the interstellar gloom," it is not to admit any light that much alters our condition. In psychology as in the other sciences, what is taken to be completely new is frequently as old as the Greeks:

> The already known had once more been confirmed
> By psychological experiment.[6]

[5] By which I mean the rational clarification and systematization of religious doctrines, insights, or revelations, but by which the general public today—including, it would seem, Mr. Frost—means the rationalization of superstition, an activity at best useless and at worst pernicious. See A Masque of Reason, "The Fear of God," "Innate Helium," "Skeptic," and "Etherealizing."

[6] A more striking illustration of this attitude was Mr. Frost's contention, in a conversation with me some years ago, that the essence of Einsteinian relativity, all that is philosophically important in the theory, is contained in Emerson's "Uriel." See my article in American Literature cited in N. 3 above.

News of the expanding universe is usually referred to humorously in the poems: "The world's size has no more to do with us Than has the universe's." In short, whatever the Truth may be, whatever the nature of the Secret that "sits in the middle and knows, While we dance round in a ring and suppose," at least the poet "will not have it systematic."

Second, Mr. Frost has denied as firmly as ever Hawthorne or Thoreau did that science will usher in a Utopia. "Science ought to know," of course, since it knows everything else, but the millenium which is so near now ("It is almost the year 2000"), this "end de luxe" promised us, seems more likely to be a "bursting rapture" provided by atomic physics than what the devotees of "scientism" have imagined. As life comes to be more and more dominated by science, pure and applied ("But now 'twas there as elsewhere, any gain Was made by getting science on the brain"), it becomes increasingly questionable whether or not the change should be called "progress." "Scientism" is Mr. Frost's word for an uncritical attitude toward science, and it says all that needs to be said on the subject.

Balancing these denials are three major affirmations in Mr. Frost's poetry. There is, first, faith in the pragmatic intelligence. Because we have intelligence,

> We will not be put off the final goal
> We have it hidden in us to attain.

The tree fallen across the road only stimulates our ingenuity; we will find a way around. The world was obviously not planned for man's convenience or comfort, but, though nature often appears to be actively hostile,

> She may know cove and cape,
> But she does not know mankind
> If by any change of shape,
> She hopes to cut off mind.

Of the many expressions of faith in the pragmatic intelligence, perhaps "Riders" is the most memorable. "What is this talked of mystery of birth But being mounted bareback on the earth?"

> The surest thing there is is we are riders
> And though none too successful at it, guiders,
> Through everything presented, land and tide
> And now the very air, of what we ride.

The intelligence that is helpless to find answers to ultimate questions is not easily thwarted in practical affairs: "We have ideas yet we haven't tried."

The second affirmation is everywhere in the poems implied, and perhaps less frequently stated than the first only because it is so basic and, to the poet, so obvious: it is the right of the individual to go his own way. The presence in Mr. Frost's work of a kind of individualism very like Emerson's has several times been commented on and need not be stressed here. Like the author of "Uriel," which in *A Masque of Reason* he called "the greatest Western poem yet," Mr. Frost bids us to "a one-man revolution" and warns that we're "too unseparate." "Steal away and steal away. Don't join too many gangs."

The third affirmation completes the other two and is the necessary logical basis of the mood of acceptance that the poet has been able to protect by staying close to his strategic burrow. I think it can most accurately be called a recognition of the naturalness of life and mind. Surely it is neither "optimism" nor religious faith in any ordinary sense, as so many of the poet's critics would have it. Lawrance Thompson, in his book on the poetry, has written that "Sitting by a Bush" is "motivated by a strong religious faith," yet what the poem asserts is only that what is called elsewhere the "innate helium" of the religious spirit is as native to us as our breath; the *fact* of life is the basis of our faith. Though this poem comes closer than any other to supplying an argument for those who want to believe that the poet is some sort of Christian, it does not come even as close to the historic faith as the vaguest sort of Protestant modernism, which the poet has blasted in *A Masque of Reason* in the *tendency* passage. True, the contrast between Watsonian behaviorism and other forms of materialism in our day, on the one hand, and Mr. Frost's recognition of the reality and even the "naturalness" of life and mind, on the other, makes it possible to apply the term "idealistic" to the poet's outlook; but the difference between that outlook and the outlook of any historic religion is so great that to call any of the poems religious without a preliminary definition of terms can only lead to confusion. If we are to be clear about what "Sitting by a Bush," for instance, asserts, we can only return to the poem itself and insist that it be attended to: life began "When dust really took in the sun" and religious faith began with it—both, it is implied, being natural products of the earth's processes. This is more nearly the assertion of a fact, or what is taken to be a fact, than of a faith.

A fuller statement of the same attitude is found in "West Running Brook." Beginning and ending as it does with the brook itself, the downward flow which suggests the degradation of energy, science's second law of thermodynamics, it asserts the *naturalness* of the eddy which the current flings back upon itself. The ripple seems to be defying the current, but a hidden rock explains it. Moving ever upward against the stream, it is analogous to life maintaining itself in

> The universal cataract of death
> That spends to nothingness—and unresisted,
> Save by some strange resistance in itself. . . .
> Our life runs down in sending up the clock.
> The brook runs down in sending up our life.
> The sun runs down in sending up the brook.
> And there is something sending up the sun.
> It is this backward motion toward the source,
> Against the stream, that most we see ourselves in,
> It is from this in nature we are from.

We have here of course a figure comparable to Bergson's fountain, though significantly in Frost's poem the downward rush creates the ripple while in Bergson's metaphor the upward surge, the *élan vital,* is the primary force. Although it is possible to acknowledge the likeness between Frost and Bergson that Mr. Thompson points out,[7] what seems to me more prominent and significant is the difference between the outlooks of the two. Mr. Frost's ideas are not apt ever to serve as the cornerstone of any church.[8]

Just how irrelevant to the religious attitude and religious needs Mr. Frost's outlook finally is when traced to its most general expression may be better suggested by his often implied, occasionally asserted faith that the universe is somewhat more for us than against, else "our hold on the planet wouldn't have so increased." This is, of course, a denial of some of the more extreme of the conclusions sometimes drawn from the "alien universe" concept, a denial that life is a "disease of matter," that man is a doomed biological accident. Yet the denial of such ideas as these does not in itself make one religious, and one may hold such ideas and be in a manner religious, as we shall see in the case of Robinson Jeffers. To say that the universe is more for us than against us is simply to assert a naturalism that includes biology rather than one which is based exclusively on physics. Religions are not built on such affirmations as this.

IV *The Craft as Expression*

The strategic retreat is as apparent in Mr. Frost's idiom as it is in the attitudes expressed in his poems. The symbols most characteristic of his poetry, commonly drawn from country sights and sounds,

[7] *Fire and Ice,* 197.
[8] See T. S. Eliot, *The Rock* (New York, 1934), 22.

are symbols of diminution, of deprivation, of retreat and acceptance. The closing of the windows, the falling of the leaves, the unmelodious late-summer song of the ovenbird, darkness, cold, the flickering light, the deserted house, the abandoned farm, the lost opportunity, the steeple bush which marks the end of a pasture's usefulness for farming, the backward step to avoid disaster, storm fear and home burial, bare trees, the sweet beckoning call of the hermit thrush in the dark evergreen woods at evening—these are the stuff of the poems. Anyone who should care to count and classify all the symbols in Mr. Frost's poems would find, I think, that a significant majority of them are the ones I have named or their like, and that they convey a mood of disciplined acceptance. Like Joseph Conrad's major symbol in "The Heart of Darkness," the poet's darkness is that of a naturalist whose heart rebels at the ring of iron but whose mind is occupied in trying to make the situation acceptable. (It is significant, however, that the poet's use of darkness parallels only two of the levels of meaning of the symbol in Conrad's story, the level suggested by Marlowe's reference to "jewels flashing in the night of time" and that suggested by the jungle. Conrad's story seems to me far more complex than any Frost poem.) Notable, too, is the number of times the poet draws on the concepts, terminology, and facts of science, especially of astronomy and geology, for his figures, almost always with one of two effects: either to suggest the nature of "the heartless and enormous outer black" or to disparage, humorously, those who take science so seriously as either to pin all their hopes on it or to be utterly distressed by it. In short, the poet's favorite symbols are as eloquent as is a prose paraphrase of his poems of an attitude of reluctant acceptance of a diminished world.

So, too, his characteristic devices of understatement, humor, and plainness. When understatement is not simply a device for humor, it is a guarded way of saying things, a way characteristic not only of Yankees but of anyone who does not wish to feel or say too much. Mr. Frost is chiefly a lyric poet, but like the ovenbird which he has honored, he has been able to continue singing long after others have ceased because he knows "in singing not to sing." Understatement, interestingly enough one of the favorite literary devices of our day, is as much a defensive gesture in Mr. Frost's work as it is in that of Ernest Hemingway.

Humor is Mr. Frost's way of taking an unpleasant reality. He has noted that there are only two ways to take the world, "tragic or comic." His humor is as much a reaction to perceived tragedy as are the "literary tears," as he calls them, of different temperaments, of, say, a Robinson or an Eliot. If his acknowledged tendency to scoff makes him seem at times insensitive, we should not be misled by it into thinking that he is at heart simply a jolly fellow or that the intention of his poems is to be funny. Though some poems like "Departmental" exist chiefly as poetic jokes, the great bulk of the poetry exhibits humor functioning as a conscious thickening of the skin, a careful strengthening of the "inner defense."

The plainness of speech in Mr. Frost's poems, like his unlaced tennis shoes and his rumpled hair, is not only an expression of his personality—and all mature personalities are in part consciously contrived, are, in no pejorative sense, poses, maneuvers, strategies, masks—it is also a stylistic expression of the conviction that "the fact is the sweetest dream that labor knows." Earlier, more illusioned poets tended to transform or transcend facts, to heighten style, to aspire to the sublime. Mr. Frost prefers the horizontal analogy and the low-pressure, conversational phrase. That his early experiments in this type of poetry constituted one of the most significant poetic advances of the early twentieth century does not in any way diminish the pertinence of the observation that his special way of saying things is in the nature of a retreat both from a too florid, and so defenseless, poetry and from a too trusting, and so likewise defenseless, view of the world.

v "The Armful"

If Robert Frost has refused to "come in" to the dark which he has so constantly and clearly perceived, it is not because he has perceived without understanding, but because he has preferred the way of hardening himself to an unpleasant reality to that of either succumbing to it or, as he would have it, deluding himself about it. One of the most perfect symbols to suggest his whole strategy may be found in "The Armful." Trying to carry many ill-assorted parcels, trying to keep them all somehow precariously in balance, but realizing that despite his best efforts some will fall, the poet *stoops* to prevent the fall—and *prevent* is used in the poem in the older sense of *to anticipate*. The strategy has been to try to anticipate the inevitable. If such a policy entails a stooping posture, it likewise lessens the destruction of life's various and conflicting values. So, too, Emerson, with his ambiguous dualistic monism, his spontaneity of fate, and his deification of the whole course of things, tried to soften the fall from Christian supernaturalism to scientific naturalism. Mr. Frost's position is, in many more respects than I have found it possible to mention, basically Emersonian. Like Emerson's, it is the result of the effort of a sturdy and cheerful temperament to adjust itself to an unpleasantly changed reality.

But it is the modifications which Mr. Frost has made in Emersonianism, modifications forced by his perception of a "stormy stormy world," rather than the Emersonianism itself, which are

179

interesting. Endeavoring not to be "resentful of man's condition," he has followed a different path from that of Robinson, in whom also one may discern Emersonian elements. Unlike Robinson, who thought life not worth while if man were deprived of the Light, he has made what light he has do; and unlike Mr. Eliot, who has refused to stoop to prevent the dropping of values, who has gladly dropped a great many values indeed the better to cling to the highest, he has balanced the load and tightened his grip. Adopting the dusk as his special time of day as morning was Thoreau's, he has been able to say that, as gloom was wasted on a character in one of his poems, so

> It is on me by night or day,
> Who have, as I suppose, ahead
> The darkest of it still to dread.

Mr. Frost has saved himself from Robinson's melancholy, Eliot's pious despair, and Crane's agony by not asking for a Purpose or a Law, by not attempting to redeem or regenerate the natural, by not listening for the sounding heel of Elohim, by cracking a joke and listening instead for an ovenbird; in short, by accepting a diminished thing. His strategic retreat has prevented both conquest and rout, as planned retreats are apt to do. His grand maneuver is his answer to Lord Russell's question, "How, in such an alien and inhuman world, can so powerless a creature as Man preserve his aspirations untarnished?"

PART THREE

Anthology of Selected Literature

john donne

TRADITION AND THE NEW PHILOSOPHY

from AN ANATOMY OF THE WORLD
WHEREIN
BY OCCASION OF THE UNTIMELY DEATH OF
MISTRESS ELIZABETH DRURY, THE FRAILTY AND THE
DECAY OF THIS WHOLE WORLD IS REPRESENTED

The First Anniversary

When that rich soul which to her heaven   *The entry*
     is gone,   *into the*
Whom all do celebrate, who know they   *work.*
     have one,
(For who is sure he hath a soul, unless
It see, and judge, and follow worthiness,
And by deeds praise it? he who doth not this,
May lodge an inmate soul, but 'tis not his.)
When that queen ended here her progress time,
And, as to her standing house, to heaven did climb,
Where loth to make the saints attend her long,
She's now a part both of the quire, and song,   10
This world, in that great earthquake languishèd;
For in a common bath of tears it bled,
Which drew the strongest vital spirits out:
But succored then with a perplexèd doubt,
Whether the world did lose, or gain in this,
(Because since now no other way there is,
But goodness, to see her, whom all would see,
All must endeavor to be good as she)
This great consumption to a fever turned   19
And so the world had fits; it joyed, it mourned;

And, as men think that agues physic are,
And th'ague being spent, give over care,
So thou sick world, mistak'st thyself to be
Well, when alas, thou'rt in a lethargy. . . .

[*Donne makes the death of Elizabeth Drury symbolic of the death of virtue in the first fall of man.
Man's condition of sin is revealed always in the impossibility of real and enduring physical health.
Donne then anatomizes man's condition in terms of
birth, his relationships with women, his size, and the
length of his days.*]

        ❁   ❁   ❁

This man, whom God did woo, and loth to attend
Till man came up, did down to man descend,
This man, so great, that all that is, is his,
Oh what a trifle, and poor thing he is!   170
If man were anything, he's nothing now:
Help, or at least some time to waste, allow
To his other wants, yet when he did depart
With her whom we lament, he lost his heart.
She, of whom th' ancients seemed to prophesy,
When they called virtues by the name of *she;*
She in whom virtue was so much refined,
That for allay unto so pure a mind
She took the weaker sex; she that could drive
The poisonous tincture, and the stain of *Eve,*   180
Out of her thoughts, and deeds; and purify
All, by a true religious alchemy;
She, she is dead; she's dead: when thou knowest this,
Thou knowest how poor a trifling thing man is.
And learn'st thus much by our Anatomy,
The heart being perished, no part can be free.
And that except thou feed (not banquet) on
The supernatural food, religion,
Thy better growth grows witherèd, and scant;
Be more than man, or thou'rt less than an ant.
Then, as mankind, so is the world's whole frame
Quite out of joint, almost created lame: 192
For, before God had made up all the rest,
Corruption entered, and depraved the best.
It seized the angels, and then first of all
The world did in her cradle take a fall,
And turned her brains, and took a general maim,

Wronging each joint of th' universal frame.
The noblest part, man, felt it first; and
    then
Both beasts and plants, cursed in the
    curse of man.

*Decay of
nature in
other parts.*

So did the world from the first hour decay,   201
That evening was beginning of the day,
And now the springs and summers which we see,
Like sons of women after fifty be.
And new philosophy calls all in doubt,[1]
The element of fire is quite put out,[2]
The sun is lost, and th' earth,[3] and no man's wit
Can well direct him where to look for it.
And freely men confess that this world's spent,
When in the planets and the firmament   210
They seek so many new;[4] then see that this
Is crumbled out again to his atomies.
'Tis all in pieces, all coherence gone;
All just supply, and all relation:
Prince, subject, father, son, are things forgot,
For every man alone thinks he hath got
To be a phoenix, and that then can be
None of that kind, of which he is, but he.
This is the world's condition now, and now
She that should all parts to reunion bow,   **220**
She that had all magnetic force alone,
To draw, and fasten sundered parts in one;
She whom wise nature had invented then
When she observed that every sort of men
Did in their voyage in this world's sea stray,
And needed a new compass for their way;
She that was best, and first original
Of all fair copies, and the general
Steward to fate; she whose rich eyes, and breast
Gilt the West Indies, and perfumed the East;
Whose having breathed in this world, did bestow   231
Spice on those Isles, and bade them still smell so,
And that rich Indy which doth gold inter,

[1] *new . . . doubt:* The new philosophies of Copernicus, Kepler and Galileo had called in doubt the medieval cosmography.
[2] *element . . . out:* Fire, one of nature's four elements according to the ancients, was thought to surround the earth between the air and the moon.
[3] *sun . . . earth:* Medieval thinkers believed that the sun went around the earth, but the new scientists discredited this view.
[4] *seek . . . new:* Donne refers here to the telescope.

JOHN DONNE

Is but as single money, coined from her:
She to whom this world must itself refer,
As suburbs, or the microcosm of her,
She, she is dead; she's dead: when thou know'st this,
Thou know'st how lame a cripple this world is.
And learn'st thus much by our Anatomy,
That this world's general sickness doth not lie   240
In any humor, or one certain part;
But as thou sawest it rotten at the heart,
Thou seest a hectic fever hath got hold
Of the whole substance, not to be controlled,
And that thou hast but one way, not to admit
The world's infection, to be none of it.
For the world's subtlest immaterial parts
Feel this consuming wound, and age's darts.
For the world's beauty is decayed or   *Disformity*
 gone,   *of parts.*
Beauty, that's color, and proportion.
We think the heavens enjoy their spherical,   251
Their round proportion embracing all;
But yet their various and perplexèd course,
Observed in divers ages, doth enforce
Men to find out so many eccentric parts,
Such divers downright lines, such overthwarts,[5]
As disproportion that pure form: it tears
The firmament in eight and forty shares,[6]
And in these constellations then arise
New stars, and old do vanish from our eyes: 260
As though heav'n suffered earthquakes, peace, or
 war,
When new towers rise, and old demolished are.
They have impaled within a zodiac
The freeborn sun, and keep twelve signs awake
To watch his steps; the Goat and Crab control,
And fright him back, who else to either pole
(Did not these tropics fetter him) might run:
For his course is not round; nor can the sun
Perfect a circle, or maintain his way
One inch direct; but where he rose today   270
He comes no more, but with a cozening line,
Steals by that point, and so is serpentine:
And seeming weary with his reeling thus,

[5] *overthwarts:* Transverse thrusts or displacements.
[6] *eight . . . shares:* Ptolemy propounded the view that the stars were divided into forty-eight constellations.

186

He means to sleep, being now fall'n nearer us.
So, of the stars, which boast that they do run
In circle still, none ends where he begun.
All their proportion's lame, it sinks, it swells.
For of meridians, and parallels,
Man hath weaved out a net, and this net thrown
Upon the heavens, and now they are his own.   280
Loth to go up the hill, or labor thus
To go to heaven, we make heaven come to us.
We spur, we rein the stars, and in their race
They're diversely content t' obey our pace.
But keeps the earth her round proportion still?
Doth not a Teneriffe, or higher hill
Rise so high like a rock, that one might think
The floating moon would shipwreck there, and sink?
Seas are so deep, that whales being struck today,
Perchance tomorrow, scarce at middle way   290
Of their wished journey's end, the bottom, die.
And men, to sound depths, so much line untie,
As one might justly think that there would rise
At end thereof, one of th' Antipodes:
If under all, a vault infernal be,
(Which sure is spacious, except that we
Invent another torment, that there must
Millions into a strait hot room be thrust)
Then solidness, and roundness have no place.
Are these but warts, and pockholes in the face   300
Of th' earth? Think so: but yet confess, in this
The world's proportion disfigured is:
That those two legs whereon it doth rely,
Reward and punishment, are bent awry.

*   *   *

. . . and, blessed maid,
   . . . Accept this tribute, and his first year's rent,
Who till his dark short taper's end be spent,
As oft as thy feast sees this widowed earth,
Will yearly celebrate thy second birth,   450
That is, thy death; for though the soul of man
Be got when man is made, 'tis born but then
When man doth die; our body's as the womb,
And, as a midwife, death directs it home.
And you her creatures, whom she works upon,
And have your salt, and best concoction
From her example, and her virtue, if you

In reverence to her, do think it due,
That no one should her praises thus rehearse,
As matter fit for chronicle, not verse;   460
Vouchsafe to call to mind that God did make
A last, and lasting'st piece, a song. He spake
To *Moses* to deliver unto all,
That song, because he knew they would let fall
The Law, the Prophets, and the History,
But keep the song still in their memory:
Such an opinion (in due measure) made
Me this great office boldly to invade:
Nor could incomprehensibleness deter
Me, from thus trying to emprison her,   470
Which when I saw that a strict grave could do,
I saw not why verse might not do so too.
Verse hath a middle nature: heaven keeps souls,
The grave keeps bodies, verse the fame enrolls.

from HOLY SONNETS

v

I am a little world made cunningly
Of elements, and an angelic sprite;
But black sin hath betrayed to endless night
My world's both parts, and, oh, both parts must die.
You which beyond that heaven which was most high
Have found new spheres, and of new lands can write,
Pour new seas in mine eyes, that so I might
Drown my world with my weeping earnestly,
Or wash it if it must be drowned no more:
But oh it must be burnt! alas the fire   10
Of lust and envy have burnt it heretofore,
And made it fouler; let their flames retire,
And burn me, O Lord, with a fiery zeal
Of Thee and Thy house, which doth in eating heal.

A VALEDICTION: OF WEEPING

Let me pour forth
My tears before thy face, whilst I stay here,
For thy face coins them, and thy stamp they bear,
And by this mintage they are something worth,
For thus they be
Pregnant of thee;
Fruits of much grief they are, emblems of more;
When a tear falls, that thou falls which it bore,

So thou and I are nothing then, when on a diverse
    shore.
              On a round ball 10
A workman that hath copies by, can lay
An Europe, Afric, and an Asia,
And quickly make that, which was nothing, *All;*[1]
          So doth each tear,
          Which thee doth wear,
A globe, yea world by that impression grow,[2]
Till thy tears mixed with mine do overflow
This world, by waters sent from thee, my heaven
    dissolvèd so.
          O more than moon,
Draw not up seas to drown me in thy sphere, 20
Weep me not dead, in thine arms, but forbear
To teach the sea, what it may do too soon;
          Let not the wind
          Example find,
To do me more harm, than it purposeth;
Since thou and I sigh one another's breath,
Whoe'er sighs most, is cruelest, and hastes the
    other's death.

[1] *All:* a globe which is an exact representation of the world.
[2] Each tear becomes an exact representation of his mistress.

189

john milton

SCIENTIFIC KNOWLEDGE
IN A BIBLICAL SCHEME

from *PARADISE LOST*

Book 1

The Argument. This first book proposes, first in brief, the whole
subject, man's disobedience, and the loss thereupon of Paradise,
wherein he was placed; then touches the prime cause of his fall, the
Serpent, or rather Satan in the Serpent, who revolting from God,
and drawing to his side many legions of angels, was by the command of God driven out of heaven with all his crew into the great
deep. Which action passed over, the poem hastes into the midst of
things, presenting Satan with his angels now fallen into hell, described here not in the center (for heaven and earth may be supposed as yet not made, certainly not yet accursed) but in a place of
utter darkness, fitliest called Chaos. Here Satan with his angels lying on the burning lake, thunderstruck and astonished, after a certain space recovers, as from confusion, calls up him who next in
order and dignity lay by him; they confer of their miserable fall.
Satan awakens all his legions, who lay till then in the same manner
confounded; they rise, their numbers, array of battle, their chief
leaders named, according to the idols known afterwards in Canaan
and the countries adjoining. To these Satan directs his speech, com-
forts them with hope yet of regaining heaven, but tells them lastly
of a new world and new kind of creature to be created, according
to an ancient prophecy or report in heaven; for that angels were
long before this visible creation was the opinion of many ancient
Fathers. To find out the truth of this prophecy, and what to determine thereon, he refers to a full council. What his associates thence

attempt. Pandemonium, the palace of Satan, rises, suddenly built
out of the deep; the infernal peers there sit in council.

Of man's first disobedience, and the fruit
Of that forbidden tree whose mortal taste
Brought death into the world and all our woe,
With loss of Eden, till one greater Man[1]
Restore us, and regain the blissful seat,   5
Sing, Heavenly Muse,[2] that on the secret top
Of Oreb, or of Sinai, didst inspire
That shepherd [3] who first taught the chosen seed
In the beginning how the heavens and earth
Rose out of Chaos: or, if Sion hill   10
Delight thee more, and Siloa's brook, that flowed
Fast by the oracle of God,[4] I thence
Invoke thy aid to my adventurous song,
That with no middle flight intends to soar
Above the Aonian mount,[5] while it pursues   15
Things unattempted yet in prose or rime.
And chiefly thou, O Spirit,[6] that dost prefer
Before all temples the upright heart and pure,
Instruct me, for thou know'st; thou from the first
Wast present, and with mighty wings outspread   20
Dovelike sat'st brooding on the vast abyss,
And mad'st it pregnant: what in me is dark
Illumine, what is low raise and support;
That, to the highth of this great argument,
I may assert Eternal Providence   25
And justify the ways of God to men.
    Say first, for heaven hides nothing from thy view
Nor the deep tract of hell, say first what cause
Moved our grand parents, in that happy state,
Favored of heaven so highly, to fall off   30
From their Creator, and transgress his will
For one restraint, lords of the world besides.
Who first seduced them to that foul revolt?
The infernal Serpent; he is was whose guile,
Stirred up with envy and revenge, deceived   35

---

[1] Christ [All Footnotes are editorial.]
[2] Urania was the Muse of astronomy and was thus the Muse of heavenly wisdom.
[3] Moses
[4] The Temple of Jerusalem stood near the spring of Siloam.
[5] Mt. Helicon, which the Greeks believed were sacred to the Muses.
[6] The Holy Ghost.

The mother of mankind, what time[7] his pride
Had cast him out from heaven, with all his host
Of rebel angels, by whose aid aspiring
To set himself in glory above his peers,
He trusted to have equaled the Most High,   40
If he opposed, and with ambitious aim
Against the throne and monarchy of God,
Raised impious war in heaven and battle proud,
With vain attempt. Him the Almighty Power
Hurled headlong flaming from the ethereal sky,   45
With hideous ruin and combustion, down
To bottomless perdition, there to dwell
In adamantine chains and penal fire,
Who durst defy the Omnipotent to arms.
    Nine times the space that measures day and night   50
To mortal men, he with his horrid crew
Lay vanquished, rolling in the fiery gulf,
Confounded, though immortal. But his doom
Reserved him to more wrath; for now the thought
Both of lost happiness and lasting pain   55
Torments him: round he throws his baleful eyes,
That witnessed huge affliction and dismay,
Mixed with obdurate pride and steadfast hate.
At once, as far as angel's ken, he views
The dismal situation waste and wild.   60
A dungeon horrible, on all sides round,
As one great furnace flamed; yet from those flames
No light; but rather darkness visible
Served only to discover sights of woe,
Regions of sorrow, doleful shades, where peace   65
And rest can never dwell, hope never comes
That comes to all, but torture without end
Still urges, and a fiery deluge, fed
With ever-burning sulphur unconsumed.
Such place eternal justice had prepared   70
For those rebellious; here their prison ordained
In utter darkness, and their portion set
As far removed from God and light of heaven
As from the center thrice to the utmost pole.[8]
Oh, how unlike the place from whence they fell!   75
There the companions of his fall, o'erwhelmed
With floods and whirlwinds of tempestuous fire,
He soon discerns, and weltering by his side

[7] When
[8] The outermost Ptolemaic sphere of the universe.

One next himself in power, and next in crime,
Long after known in Palestine, and named   80
Beëlzebub. To whom the arch-enemy,
And thence in heaven called Satan, with bold words
Breaking the horrid silence, thus began:
   "If thou beest he—but oh, how fallen! how changed
From him who in the happy realms of light,   85
Clothed with transcendent brightness, didst outshine
Myriads, though bright!—if he whom mutual league,
United thoughts and counsels, equal hope
And hazard in the glorious enterprise
Joined with me once, now misery hath joined   90
In equal ruin; into what pit thou seest
From what highth fallen: so much the stronger proved
He with his thunder: and till then who knew
The force of those dire arms? Yet not for those,
Nor what the potent Victor in his rage   95
Can else inflict, do I repent or change,
Though changed in outward luster, that fixed mind
And high disdain, from sense of injured merit,
That with the Mightiest raised me to contend,
And to the fierce contention brought along   100
Innumerable force of spirits armed
That durst dislike his reign, and, me preferring,
His utmost power with adverse power opposed
In dubious battle on the plains of heaven,
And shook his throne. What though the field be lost?   105
All is not lost; the unconquerable will,
And study of revenge, immortal hate,
And courage never to submit or yield:
And what is else not to be overcome[9]
That glory never shall his wrath or might   110
Extort from me. To bow and sue for grace
With suppliant knee, and deify his power
Who, from the terror of this arm, so late
Doubted his empire—that were low indeed;
That were an ignominy and shame beneath   115
This downfall; since by fate the strength of gods
And the empyreal [10] substance cannot fail;
Since, through experience of this great event,
In arms not worse, in foresight much advanced,
We may with more successful hope resolve   120
To wage by force or guile eternal war,

[9] The only way left to prove he is not overcome.
[10] Sublime

JOHN MILTON

> Irreconcilable to our grand Foe,
> Who now triúmphs, and in the excess of joy
> Sole reigning holds the tyranny of heaven."   124

❋   ❋   ❋

Book VII

The Argument—Raphael at the request of Adam relates how and wherefore this world was first created; that God, after the expelling of Satan and his Angels out of Heaven, declar'd his pleasure to create another World and other Creatures to dwell therein; sends his Son with Glory and attendance of Angels to perform the work of Creation in six days: the Angels celebrate with Hymns the performance thereof, and his reascension into Heaven.

> . . . On heav'nly ground they stood, and from the shore[1]   210
> They view'd the vast immeasurable Abyss
> Outrageous as a Sea, dark, wasteful, wild,
> Up from the bottom turn'd by furious winds
> And surging waves, as Mountains to assault
> Heav'n's highth, and with the Centre mix the Pole.   215
>   Silence, ye troubl'd waves, and thou Deep, peace,
> Said then th' Omnific Word, your discord end:
>   Nor stay'd, but on the Wings of Cherubim
> Uplifted, in Paternal Glory rode
> Far into *Chaos,* and the World unborn;   220
> For *Chaos* heard his voice: him all his Train
> Follow'd in bright procession to behold
> Creation, and the wonders of his might.
> Then stay'd the fervid Wheels, and in his hand
> He took the golden Compasses, prepar'd [2]   225
> In God's Eternal store, to circumscribe
> This Universe, and all created things:
> One foot he centred, and the other turn'd
> Round through the vast profundity obscure,
> And said, thus far extend, thus far thy bounds,   230
> This be thy just Circumference, O World.

[1] Milton here attempts to reconcile the pagan Greek accounts of creation (especially Anaximander's theory of the separating out of opposites from the Boundless) and the Judaic-Christian account in *Genesis.*

[2] The poet describes God in anthropomorphic terms, a God who places the immovable leg of His compass on Earth and with the other leg draws a circle which bounds in all creation. This is in keeping with the Aristotelian-Ptolemaic cosmology, which believed in the earth as the center of the universe. Consult George W. Whiting, "The Golden Compasses in *Paradise Lost*," *Notes and Queries,* CLXXII (1937), 294-295.

Thus God the Heav'n created, thus the Earth,
Matter unform'd and void: Darkness profound [3]
Cover'd th' Abyss: but on the wat'ry calm
His brooding wings the Spirit of God outspread,   235
And vital virtue infus'd, and vital warmth
Throughout the fluid Mass, but downward purg'd
The black tartareous cold Infernal dregs
Adverse to life; then founded, then conglob'd
Like things to like, the rest to several place   240
Disparted, and between spun out the Air,
And Earth self-balanc't on her Centre hung.
          Let there be Light, said God, and forthwith Light
Ethereal, first of things, quintessence pure
Sprung from the Deep, and from her Native East   245
To journey through the airy gloom began,
Spher'd in a radiant Cloud, for yet the Sun
Was not; shee in a cloudy Tabernacle
Sojourn'd the while. God saw the Light was good;
And light from darkness by the Hemisphere   250
Divided: Light the Day, and Darkness Night
He nam'd. Thus was the first Day Ev'n and Morn: . . .
          Again, God said, let there be Firmament[4]
Amid the Waters, and let it divide
The Waters from the Waters: and God made
The Firmament, expanse of liquid, pure,
Transparent, Elemental Air, diffus'd   265
In circuit to the uttermost convex
Of this great Round:[5] partition firm and sure,
The Waters underneath from those above
Dividing: for as Earth, so he the World [6]
Built on circumfluous Waters calm, in wide   270
Crystálline Ocean, and the loud misrule
Of *Chaos* far remov'd, lest fierce extremes
Contiguous might distemper the whole frame:
And Heav'n he nam'd the Firmament: So Ev'n
And Morning *Chorus* sung the second Day.   275

[2] Again Milton tries to harmonize Christian and early Greek accounts of creation. In this instance he is probably referring not to Anaximander's theory but to Plato's in the *Timaeus*.
[4] The firmament is a crust or shell which separates the created waters of the created universe from the "uncreated" and timeless "waters" of Chaos or the Boundless. This is another reference to Anaximander's idea of a timeless and uncreated primordial unity (Chaos or, as he called it, the Boundless) out of which God created an ordered or limited universe.
[5] "Round" means all creation.
[6] "World" means universe (all creation), not merely the Earth.

JOHN MILTON

The Earth was form'd, but in the Womb as yet
Of Waters, Embryon immature involv'd,
Appear'd not: over all the fact of Earth
Main Ocean flow'd, not idle, but with warm
Prolific humour soft'ning all her Globe,[7]   280
Fermented the great Mother to conceive,
Satiate with genial moisture, when God said
Be gather'd now ye Waters under Heav'n
Into one place, and let dry Land appear.

*   *   *

Book VIII

The Argument—Adam inquires concerning celestial Motions, is
doubtfully answer'd, and exhorted to search rather things more
worthy of knowledge: Adam assents, and still desirous to detain
Raphael, relates to him what he remember'd since his own Creation, his placing in Paradise, his talk with God concerning solitude
and fit society, his first meeting and Nuptials with Eve, his discourse with the Angel thereupon; who after admonitions repeated
departs.

To ask or search I blame thee not, for Heav'n
Is as the Book of God before thee set,
Wherein to read his wond'rous Works, and learn
His Seasons, Hours, or Days, or Months, or Years;
This to attain, whether Heav'n move or Earth,   70
Imports not, if thou reck'n right; the rest
From Man or Angel the great Architect
Did wisely to conceal, and not divulge
His secrets to be scann'd by them who ought
Rather admire; or if they list to try   75
Conjecture, he his Fabric of the Heav'ns
Hath left to thir disputes, perhaps to move
His laughter at thir quaint Opinions wide[1]
Hereafter, when they come to model Heav'n
And calculate the Stars, how they will wield   80
The mighty frame, how build, unbuild, contrive

[7] Once again Milton attempts to synthesize the Christian account of
genesis with the pagan accounts of the sexual genesis of the universe,
especially Ovid's (*Metamorphosis,* I) and Lucretius' (*De Rerum Natura,* V).
[1] God laughs when He reviews the complex system of eccentric circles
and epicycles devised by such astronomers as Ptolemy to explain planetary motion. God's humor is provoked by the contrast between the
simplicity of His plan and the complexity of the plans suggested by
Ptolemy and others.

To save appearances, how gird the Sphere
With Centric and Eccentric scribbl'd o'er,
Cycle and Epicycle, Orb in Orb:
Already by thy reasoning this I guess,   85
Who art to lead thy offspring, and supposest
That bodies bright and greater should not serve
The less not bright, nor Heav'n such journeys run,
Earth sitting still, when she alone receives
The benefit: consider first, that Great   90
Or Bright infers not Excellence: the Earth
Though, in comparison of Heav'n, so small,
Nor glistering, may of solid good contain
More plenty than the Sun that barren shines,
Whose virtue on itself works no effect,   95
But in the fruitful Earth; there first receiv'd
His beams, unactive else, thir vigor find.
Yet not to Earth are those bright Luminaries
Officious, but to thee Earth's habitant.
And for the Heav'n's wide Circuit, let it speak   100
The Maker's high magnificence, who built
So spacious, and his Line stretcht out so far;
That Man may know he dwells not in his own;
An Edifice too large for him to fill,
Lodg'd in a small partition, and the rest   105
Ordain'd for uses to his Lord best known.
The swiftness of those Circles áttribute,
Though numberless, to his Omnipotence,
That to corporeal substances could add
Speed almost Spiritual; mee thou think'st not slow,   110
Who since the Morning hour set out from Heav'n
Where God resides, and ere mid-day arriv'd
In *Eden*, distance inexpressible
By Numbers that have name. But this I urge,
Admitting Motion in the Heav'ns, to show   115
Invalid that which thee to doubt it mov'd;
Not that I so affirm, though so it seem
To thee who hast thy dwelling here on Earth.
God to remove his ways from human sense,
Plac'd Heav'n from Earth so far, that earthly sight,   120
If it presume, might err in things too high,
And no advantage gain. What if the Sun[2]

---

[2] Milton suggests that the Copernican system might be the correct explanation of planetary motion; however, man's obligation is not to pry into these secrets (cf. lines 167-178), but rather to serve and fear God.

197

Be Centre to the World, and other Stars
By his attractive virtue and their own[3]
Incited, dance about him various rounds?   125
Thir wandring course now high, now low, then hid,
Progressive, retrograde, or standing still,
In six thou seest, and what if sev'nth to these
The Planet Earth, so steadfast though she seem,
Insensibly three different Motions move? [4]   130
Which else to several Spheres thou must ascribe,
Mov'd contrary with thwart obliquities,
Or save the Sun his labour, and that swift
Nocturnal and Diurnal rhomb supos'd,[5]
Invisible else above all Stars, the Wheel   135
Of Day and Night; which needs not thy belief,
If Earth industrious of herself fetch Day
Travelling East, and with her part averse
From the Sun's beam meet Night, her other part
Still luminous by his ray. What if that light   140
Sent from her through the wide transpicuous air,
To the terrestrial Moon be as a Star[6]
Enlight'ning her by Day, as she by Night
This Earth? reciprocal, if Land be there,
Fields and Inhabitants: Her spots thou seest   145
As Clouds, and Clouds may rain, and Rain produce
Fruits in her sof'n'd Soil, for some to eat
Allotted there; and other Suns perhaps
With thir attendant Moons thou wilt descry[7]
Communicating Male and Female Light,   150
Which two great Sexes animate the World,
Stor'd in each Orb perhaps with some that live.
For such vast room in Nature unpossest
By living Soul, desert and desolate,
Only to shine, yet scarce to cóntribute   155

[3] Here, Milton anticipates Newton's law of gravitation. By using Gilbert's findings on magnetism, Milton describes the power of the sun to move other planets about it by magnetic attraction.
[4] The three motions of the earth are rotation, revolution in its own orbit, and the imperceptible revolution of its poles which causes equinoxes.
[5] This refers to the *primum mobile* which Ptolemy hypothesized containing all the seven planets and all the fixed stars. This was Ptolemy's attempt to explain the daily rotation of the seven spheres and the fixed stars.
[6] In this context, "terrestrial" means inhabited.
[7] In this context, "moons" means other planets. Milton is speculating on the possibility of a plurality of worlds.

Each Orb a glimpse of Light, convey'd so far
Down to this habitable, which returns
Light back to them, is obvious to dispute.[8]
But whether thus these things, or whether not,
Whether the Sun predominant in Heav'n   160
Rise on the Earth, or Earth rise on the Sun,
Hee from the East his flaming road begin,
Or Shee from West her silent course advance
With inoffensive pace that spinning sleeps
On her soft Axle, while she paces Ev'n,   165
And bears thee soft with the smooth Air along,
Solicit not thy thoughts with matters hid,
Leave them to God above, him serve and fear;
Of other Creatures, as him pleases best,
Wherever plac't, let him dispose: joy thou   170
In what he gives to thee, this Paradise
And thy fair *Eve:* Heav'n is for thee too high
To know what passes there; be lowly wise:
Think only what concerns thee and thy being;
Dream not of other Worlds, what Creatures there 175
Live, in what state, condition or degree,
Contented that thus far hath been reveal'd
Not of Earth only but of highest Heav'n.
    To whom thus *Adam* clear'd of doubt, repli'd.
How fully hast thou satisfi'd me, pure   180
Intelligence of Heav'n, Angel serene,
And freed from intricacies, taught to live
The easiest way, nor with perplexing thoughts
To interrupt the sweet of Life, from which
God hath bid dwell far off all anxious cares,   185
And not molest us, unless we ourselves
Seek them with wand'ring thoughts, and notions vain.
But apt the Mind or Fancy is to rove[9]
Uncheckt, and of her roving is no end;
Till warn'd, or by experience taught, she learn 190
That not to know at large of things remote
From use, obscure and subtle, but to know
That which before us lies in daily life,

[8] In this context "obvious to dispute" means open to dispute. In his
Seventh Prolusion Milton poses the idea that all the stars (lights) in the
heavens were created only for sinful man's pleasure and illumination.
[9] Milton is implying that reason does not contradict faith. What seems
to be reason here is actually Fancy—or man's imagination—which op-
poses faith. Reason's function is to check or restrain unbridled imagination; this is a basic belief of Puritanism.

JOHN MILTON

> Is the prime Wisdom; what is more is fume,
> Or emptiness, or fond impertinence,[10]   195
> And renders us in things that most concern
> Unpractis'd, unprepar'd, and still to seek.

❉   ❉   ❉

[10] In this context, "fond impertinence" means trivial or irrelevant speculations which please man's fancy (imagination).

alexander pope

THE WORLD AS AN ORDERED MACHINE

from AN ESSAY ON MAN

Epistle 1

I. Say first, of God above, or man below,
What can we reason, but from what we know?
Of man, what see we but his station here,
From which to reason, or to which refer   20
Through worlds unnumbered though the God be known,
'Tis ours to trace him only in our own.
He, who through vast immensity can pierce,
See worlds on worlds compose one universe,
Observe how system into system runs,
What other planets circle other suns,
What varied being peoples every star,
May tell why Heaven has made us as we are.
But of this frame[1] the bearings, and the ties,
The strong connections, nice dependencies,   30
Gradations just, has thy pervading soul
Looked through? or can a part contain the whole?
    Is the great chain, that draws all to agree,
And drawn supports, upheld by God, or thee?

VII. Far as creation's ample range extends,
The scale of sensual, mental powers ascends:
Mark how it mounts, to man's imperial race,
From the green myriads in the peopled grass: 210
What modes of sight betwixt each wide extreme,

---

[1] "This frame" is the ordered universe described in Leibniz's theory
of Pre-established Harmony. [All Footnotes are editorial.]

The mole's dim curtain, and the lynx's beam:
Of smell, the headlong lioness between,
And hound sagacious on the tainted green:
Of hearing, from the life that fills the flood,
To that which warbles through the vernal wood:
The spider's touch, how exquisitely fine!
Feels at each thread, and lives along the line:
In the nice bee,[2] what sense so subtly true
From poisonous herbs extracts the healing dew?   220
How instinct varies in the groveling swine,
Compared, half-reasoning elephant, with thine!
'Twixt that, and reason, what a nice barrier,
Forever separate, yet forever near!
Remembrance and reflection how allied;
What thin partitions sense from thought divide:
And middle natures, how they long to join,
Yet never pass th' insuperable line!
Without this just gradation, could they be
Subjected, these to those, or all to thee?   230
The powers of all subdued by thee alone,
Is not thy reason all these powers in one?

VIII. See, through this air, this ocean, and this earth,
All matter quick, and bursting into birth.
Above, how high progressive life may go!
Around, how wide! how deep extend below!
Vast chain of being! which from God began,
Natures ethereal, human, angel, man,
Beast, bird, fish, insect, what no eye can see,
No glass can reach; from Infinite to thee,   240
From thee to nothing.—On superior powers
Were we to press, inferior might on ours:
Or in the full creation leave a void,
Where, one step broken, the great scale's destroyed:
From nature's chain whatever link you strike,
Tenth or ten-thousandth, breaks the chain alike.
    And, if each system in gradation roll
Alike essential to th' amazing whole,
The least confusion but in one, not all
That system only, but the whole must fall.   250
Let earth unbalanced from her orbit fly,
Planets and suns run lawless through the sky;
Let ruling angels from their spheres be hurled,
Being on being wrecked, and world on world;

---

[2] In this context "nice bee" means wise bee.

Heaven's whole foundations to their center nod,
And nature tremble to the throne of God.
All this dread order break—from whom? for thee?
Vile worm!—O madness! Pride! Impiety!

IX. What if the foot, ordained the dust to tread,
Or hand, to toil, aspired to be the head? 260
What if the head, the eye, or ear repined
To serve mere engines to the ruling mind?
Just as absurd for any part to claim
To be another, in this general frame:
Just as absurd, to mourn the tasks or pains,
The great directing mind of all ordains.
All are but parts of one stupendous whole,
Whose body nature is, and God the soul;
That, changed through all, and yet in all the same;
Great in the earth, as in th' ethereal frame; 270
Warms in the sun, refreshes in the breeze,
Glows in the stars, and blossoms in the trees,
Lives through all life, extends through all extent,
Spreads undivided, operates unspent;
Breathes in our soul, informs our mortal part
As full, as perfect, in a hair as heart:
As full, as perfect, in vile man that mourns,
As the rapt Seraph that adores and burns:
To him no high, no low, no great, no small;
He fills, he bounds, connects, and equals all. 280

X. Cease then, nor order imperfection name:
Our proper bliss depends on what we blame.
Know thy own point: This kind, this due degree
Of blindness, weakness, Heaven bestows on thee.
Submit.—In this, or any other sphere,
Secure to be as blessed as thou canst bear:
Safe in the hand of one disposing power,
Or in the natal, or the mortal hour.
All nature is but art, unknown to thee;
All chance, direction, which thou canst not see; 290
All discord, harmony not understood;
All partial evil, universal good:
And, spite of pride, in erring reason's spite,
One truth is clear, *Whatever is, is right*.

EPISTLE 2

Know then thyself, presume not God to scan,
The proper study of mankind is man.

Placed on this isthmus of a middle state,
A being darkly wise and rudely great:
With too much knowledge for the skeptic side,
With too much weakness for the stoic's pride,
He hangs between; in doubt to act, or rest;
In doubt to deem himself a god, or beast;
In doubt his mind or body to prefer;
Born but to die, and reasoning but to err;   10
Alike in ignorance, his reason such,
Whether he thinks too little, or too much:
Chaos of thought and passion, all confused;
Still by himself abused, or disabused;
Created half to rise, and half to fall;
Great lord of all things, yet a prey to all;
Sole judge of truth, in endless error hurled:
The glory, jest, and riddle of the world! . . .
  Go, wondrous creature; mount where science guides,
Go, measure earth, weigh air, and state the tides;   20
Instruct the planets in what orbs to run,
Correct old Time, and regulate the sun;[1]
Go, soar with Plato to th' empyreal sphere,[2]
To the first good, first perfect, and first fair;
Or tread the mazy round his followers trod,
And quitting sense call imitating God;
As eastern priests in giddy circles run,[3]
And turn their heads to imitate the sun.
Go, teach Eternal Wisdom how to rule—
Then drop into thyself, and be a fool!   30
  Superior beings, when of late they saw
A mortal man unfold all nature's law,
Admired such wisdom in an earthly shape,
And showed a Newton, as we show an ape.
  Could he, whose rules the rapid comet bind,
Describe or fix one movement of his mind?
Who saw its fires here rise, and there descend,
Explain his own beginning or his end?

[1] In the eighteenth century European countries began to adopt the new Gregorian calendar to account for the twelve days lost through the inaccuracies of the old Julian calendar.
[2] Pope refers to the Platonic world of pure ideas that transcends the world of matter. Pope is also referring to the ninth sphere in Ptolemy's system of the universe. Since this ninth sphere was the outermost sphere, its motion (first motion or *primum mobile*) set all the innermost spheres (planets and stars) in motion.
[3] This refers to the Oriental whirling dervishes or Moslem monks "whose worship rites include dancing, howling, or whirling" (Cf. *Dict. of Mythology* by Jobes).

Alas! what wonder! Man's superior part
Unchecked may rise, and climb from art to art;   40
But when his own great work is but begun,
What reason weaves, by passion is undone.
   Trace science, then, with modesty thy guide;
First strip off all her equipage of pride;
Deduct what is but vanity or dress,
Or learning's luxury, or idleness,
Or tricks to show the stretch of human brain,
Mere curious pleasure, or ingenious pain;
Expunge the whole, or lop th' excrescent parts
Of all our vices have created arts;   50
Then see how little the remaining sum,
Which served the past, and must the times to come!

       ❁   ❁   ❁

jonathan swift

MECHANISTIC THINKING
REDUCED TO ABSURDITY

[A selection from *Gulliver's Travels*, Part III, "A Voyage to Laputa."] Chapter II—*The Humours and Dispositions of the Laputians described. An Account of their Learning. Of the King and his Court. The Author's Reception there. The Inhabitants subject to Fears and Disquietudes. An Account of the Women.*

At my alighting I was surrounded by a Crowd of People, but those who stood nearest seemed to be of better Quality. They beheld me with all the Marks and Circumstances of Wonder; neither indeed was I much in their Debt; having never till then seen a Race of Mortals so singular in their Shapes, Habits, and Countenances. Their Heads were all reclined to the Right, or the Left; one of their Eyes turned inward, and the other directly up to the Zenith.[1] Their outward Garments were adorned with the Figures of Suns, Moons, and Stars, interwoven with those of Fiddles, Flutes, Harps, Trumpets, Harpsicords, and many more Instruments of Musick, unknown to us in *Europe*. I observed here and there many in the Habit of Servants, with a blown Bladder fastned like a Flail to the End of a short Stick, which they carried in their Hands. In each Bladder was a small Quantity of dried Pease, or little Pebbles, (as I was afterwards informed.) With these Bladders they now and then flapped the Mouths and Ears of those who stood near them, of which Practice I could not then conceive the Meaning. It seems, the Minds of these People are so taken up with intense Speculations, that they neither can speak, or attend to the Discourses of others, without being rouzed by some external Taction upon the Organs of Speech and Hearing; for which Reason, those Persons who are able to af-

[1] *Zenith:* A point in the heavens directly overhead. (Footnotes editorial.)

ford it, always keep a *Flapper*, (the Original is *Climenole*) in their Family, as one of their Domesticks; nor ever walk abroad or make Visits without him. And the Business of this Officer is, when two or more Persons are in Company, gently to strike with his Bladder the Mouth of him who is to speak, and the Right Ear of him or them to whom the Speaker addresseth himself. This *Flapper* is likewise employed diligently to attend his Master in his Walks, and upon Occasion to give him a soft Flap on his Eyes; because he is always so wrapped up in Cogitation, that he is in manifest Danger of falling down every Precipice, and bouncing his Head against every Post; and in the Streets, of jostling others, or being jostled himself into the Kennel.[2]

It was necessary to give the Reader this Information, without which he would be at the same Loss with me, to understand the Proceedings of these People, as they conducted me up the Stairs to the Top of the Island, and from thence to the Royal Palace. While we were ascending, they forgot several Times what they were about, and left me to my self, till their Memories were again rouzed by their *Flappers;* for they appeared altogether unmoved by the Sight of my foreign Habit and Countenance, and by the Shouts of the Vulgar, whose Thoughts and Minds were more disengaged.

At last we entered the Palace, and proceeded into the Chamber of Presence; where I saw the King seated on his Throne, attended on each Side by Persons of prime Quality. Before the Throne, was a large Table filled with Globes and Spheres, and Mathematical Instruments of all Kinds. His Majesty took not the least Notice of us, although our Entrance were not without sufficient Noise, by the Concourse of all Persons belonging to the Court. But, he was then deep in a Problem, and we attended at least an Hour, before he could solve it. There stood by him on each Side, a young Page, with Flaps in their Hands; and when they saw he was at Leisure, one of them gently struck his Mouth, and the other his Right Ear; at which he started like one awaked on the sudden, and looking towards me, and the Company I was in, recollected the Occasion of our coming, whereof he had been informed before. He spoke some Words; whereupon immediately a young Man with a Flap came up to my Side, and flapt me gently on the Right Ear; but I made Signs as well as I could, that I had no Occasion for such an Instrument; which as I afterwards found, gave his Majesty and the whole Court a very mean Opinion of my Understanding. The King,[3] as far as I could conjecture, asked me several Questions, and

[2] *Kennel:* Gutter.
[3] This probably refers to George I, the English King from Germany, who, while he pretended to be a patron of the arts and sciences, was himself uncultured, and knew very little English.

I addressed my self to him in all the Languages I had. When it was found, that I could neither understand nor be understood, I was conducted by his Order to an Apartment in his Palace, (this Prince being distinguished above all his Predecessors for his Hospitality to Strangers,) where two Servants were appointed to attend me. My Dinner was brought, and four Persons of Quality, whom I remembered to have seen very near the King's Person, did me the Honour to dine with me. We had two Courses, of three Dishes each. In the first Course, there was a Shoulder of Mutton, cut into an Æquilateral Triangle; a Piece of Beef into a Rhomboides; and a Pudding into a Cycloid. The second Course was two Ducks, trussed up into the Form of Fiddles; Sausages and Puddings resembling Flutes and Haut-boys,[4] and a Breast of Veal in the Shape of a Harp. The Servants cut our Bread into Cones, Cylinders, Parallelograms, and several other Mathematical Figures.

While we were at Dinner, I made bold to ask the Names of several Things in their Language; and those noble Persons, by the Assistance of their *Flappers,* delighted to give me Answers, hoping to raise my Admiration of their great Abilities, if I could be brought to converse with them. I was soon able to call for Bread, and Drink, or whatever else I wanted.

After Dinner my Company withdrew, and a Person was sent to me by the King's Order, attended by a *Flapper.* He brought with him Pen, Ink, and Paper, and three or four Books; giving me to understand by Signs, that he was sent to teach me the Language. We sat together four Hours, in which Time I wrote down a great Number of Words in Columns, with the Translations over against them. I likewise made a Shift to learn several short Sentences. For my Tutor would order one of my Servants to fetch something, to turn about, to make a Bow, to sit, or stand, or walk, and the like. Then I took down the Sentence in Writing. He shewed me also in one of his Books, the Figures of the Sun, Moon, and Stars, the Zodiack, the Tropics and Polar Circles, together with the Denominations of many Figures of Planes and Solids. He gave me the Names and Descriptions of all the Musical Instruments, and the general Terms of Art in playing on each of them. After he had left me, I placed all my Words with their Interpretations in alphabetical Order. And thus in a few Days, by the Help of a very faithful Memory, I got some Insight into their Language.

The Word, which I interpret the *Flying* or *Floating Island,* is in the Original *Laputa;* whereof I could never learn the true Etymology. *Lap* in the old obsolete Language signifieth *High,* and *Untuh* a *Governor;* from which they say by Corruption was derived *Laputa* from *Lapuntuh.* But I do not approve of this Derivation,

_____
[4] *Haut-boys:* Oboes.

which seems to be a little strained. I ventured to offer to the Learned among them a Conjecture of my own, that *Laputa* was *quasi Lap outed; Lap* signifying properly the dancing of the Sun Beams in the Sea; and *outed* a Wing, which however I shall not obtrude, but submit to the judicious Reader.[5]

Those to whom the King had entrusted me, observing how ill I was clad, ordered a Taylor to come next Morning, and take my Measure for a Suit of Cloths. This Operator did his Office after a different Manner from those of his Trade in *Europe*. He first took my Altitude by a Quadrant, and then with Rule and Compasses, described the Dimensions and Out-Lines of my whole Body; all which he entred upon Paper, and in six Days brought my Cloths very ill made, and quite out of Shape, by happening to mistake a Figure in the Calculation. But my Comfort was, that I observed such Accidents very frequent, and little regarded.

During my Confinement for want of Cloaths, and by an Indisposition that held me some Days longer, I much enlarged my Dictionary; and when I went next to Court, was able to understand many Things the King spoke, and to return him some Kind of Answers. His Majesty had given Orders, that the Island should move North-East and by East, to the vertical Point over *Lagado*, the Metropolis of the whole Kingdom, below upon the firm Earth. It was about Ninety Leagues distant, and our Voyage lasted four Days and an Half. I was not in the least sensible of the progressive Motion made in the Air by the Island. On the second Morning, about Eleven o'Clock, the King himself in Person, attended by his Nobility, Courtiers, and Officers, having prepared all their Musical Instruments, played on them for three Hours without Intermission; so that I was quite stunned with the Noise; neither could I possibly guess the Meaning, till my Tutor informed me. He said, that the People of their Island had their Ears adapted to hear the Musick of the Spheres, which always played at certain Periods; and the Court was now prepared to bear their Part in whatever Instrument they most excelled.

In our Journey towards *Lagado* the Capital City, his Majesty ordered that the Island should stop over certain Towns and Villages, from whence he might receive the Petitions of his Subjects. And to this Purpose, several Packthreads were let down with small Weights at the Bottom. On these Packthreads the People strung their Petitions, which mounted up directly like the Scraps of Paper fastned by School-boys at the End of the String that holds their

[5] The most probable derivation of *Laputa* is the Spanish *la puta*, "the whore," which accurately defines a people who refuse to recognize the true physical nature of man. Gulliver, with his characteristic ingenuousness, fails to consider this possibility.

Kite. Sometimes we received Wine and Victuals from below, which were drawn up by Pullies.

The Knowledge I had in Mathematicks gave me great Assistance in acquiring their Phraseology, which depended much upon that Science and Musick; and in the latter I was not unskilled. Their Ideas are perpetually conversant in Lines and Figures. If they would, for Example, praise the Beauty of a Woman, or any other Animal, they describe it by Rhombs, Circles, Parallelograms, Ellipses and other Geometrical Terms; or else by Words of Art drawn from Musick, needless here to repeat. I observed in the King's Kitchen all Sorts of Mathematical and Musical Instruments, after the Figures of which they cut up the Joynts that were served to his Majesty's Table.

Their Houses are very ill built, the Walls bevil, without one right Angle in any Apartment; and this Defect ariseth from the Contempt they bear for practical Geometry; which they despise as vulgar and mechanick, those Instructions they give being too refined for the Intellectuals of their Workmen; which occasions perpetual Mistakes. And although they are dextrous enough upon a Piece of Paper, in the Management of the Rule, the Pencil, and the Divider, yet in the common Actions and Behaviour of Life, I have not seen a more clumsy, awkward, and unhandy People, nor so slow and perplexed in their Conceptions upon all other Subjects, except those of Mathematicks and Musick. They are very bad Reasoners, and vehemently given to Opposition, unless when they happen to be of the right Opinion, which is seldom their Case. Imagination, Fancy, and Invention, they are wholly Strangers to, nor have any Words in their Language by which those Ideas can be expressed; the whole Compass of their Thoughts and Mind, being shut up within the two forementioned Sciences.

Most of them, and especially those who deal in the Astronomical Part, have great Faith in judicial Astrology, although they are ashamed to own it publickly. But, what I chiefly admired, and thought altogether unaccountable, was the strong Disposition I observed in them towards News and Politicks; perpetually enquiring into publick Affairs, giving their Judgments in Matters of State; and passionately disputing every Inch of a Party Opinion. I have indeed observed the same Disposition among most of the Mathematicians I have known in *Europe;* although I could never discover the least Analogy between the two Sciences; unless those People suppose, that because the smallest Circle hath as many Degrees as the largest, therefore the Regulation and Management of the World require no more Abilities than the handling and turning of a Globe. But, I rather take this Quality to spring from a very common Infirmity of human Nature, inclining us to be more curious and conceited in Matters where we have least Concern, and for which we are least adapted either by Study or Nature.

These People are under continual Disquietudes, never enjoying a Minute's Peace of Mind; and their Disturbances proceed from Causes which very little affect the rest of Mortals. Their Apprehensions[6] arise from several Changes they dread in the Celestial Bodies. For instance; that the Earth by the continual Approaches of the Sun towards it, must in Course of Time be absorbed or swallowed up. That the Face of the Sun will by Degrees be encrusted with its own Effluvia, and give no more Light to the World. That, the Earth very narrowly escaped a Brush from the Tail of the last Comet which would have infallibly reduced it to Ashes; and that the next, which they have calculated for One and Thirty Years hence, will probably destroy us. For, if in its Perihelion it should approach within a certain Degree of the Sun, (as by their Calculations they have Reason to dread) it will conceive a Degree of Heat ten Thousand Times more intense than that of red hot glowing Iron; and in its Absence from the Sun, carry a blazing Tail Ten Hundred Thousand and Fourteen Miles long; through which if the Earth should pass at the Distance of one Hundred Thousand Miles from the *Nucleus,* or main Body of the Comet, it must in its Passage be set on Fire, and reduced to Ashes. That the Sun daily spending its Rays without any Nutriment to supply them, will at last be wholly consumed and annihilated; which must be attended with the Destruction of this Earth, and of all the Planets that receive their Light from it.

They are so perpetually alarmed with the Apprehensions of these and the like impending Dangers, that they can neither sleep quietly in their Beds, nor have any Relish for the common Pleasures or Amusements of Life. When they meet an Acquaintance in the Morning, the first Question is about the Sun's Health; how he looked at his Setting and Rising, and what Hopes they have to avoid the Stroak of the approaching Comet. This Conversation they are apt to run into with the same Temper that Boys discover, in delighting to hear terrible Stories of Sprites and Hobgoblins, which they greedily listen to, and dare not go to Bed for fear.

The Women of the Island have Abundance of Vivacity; they contemn their Husbands, and are exceedingly fond of Strangers, whereof there is always a considerable Number from the Continent below, attending at Court, either upon Affairs of the several Towns and Corporations, or their own particular Occasions; but are

---

[6] The list of apprehensions which follows satirizes scientific beliefs prevalent in Swift's own time. See "The Scientific Background of Swift's Voyage to Laputa" in *Science and Imagination* by Marjorie Hope Nicolson.

much despised, because they want the same Endowments. Among these the Ladies chuse their Gallants: But the Vexation is, that they act with too much Ease and Security; for the Husband is always so rapt in Speculation, that the Mistress and Lover may proceed to the greatest Familiarities before his Face, if he be but provided with Paper and Implements, and without his *Flapper* at his Side.

The Wives and Daughters lament their Confinement to the Island, although I think it the most delicious Spot of Ground in the World; and although they live here in the greatest Plenty and Magnificence, and are allowed to do whatever they please: They long to see the World, and take the Diversions of the Metropolis, which they are not allowed to do without a particular Licence from the King; and this is not easy to be obtained, because the People of Quality have found by frequent Experience, how hard it is to persuade their Women to return from below. I was told, that a great Court Lady, who had several Children, is married to the prime Minister, the richest Subject in the Kingdom, a very graceful Person, extremely fond of her, and lives in the finest Palace of the Island, went down to *Lagado*, on the Pretence of Health, there hid her self for several Months, till the King sent a Warrant to search for her; and she was found in an obscure Eating-House all in Rags, having pawned her Cloths to maintain an old deformed Footman, who beat her every Day, and in whose Company she was taken much against her Will. And although her Husband received her with all possible Kindness, and without the least Reproach; she soon after contrived to steal down again with all her Jewels, to the same Gallant, and hath not been heard of since.

This may perhaps pass with the Reader rather for an *European* or *English Story*, than for one of a Country so remote. But he may please to consider, that the Caprices of Womankind are not limited by any Climate or Nation; and that they are much more uniform than can be easily imagined.

In about a Month's Time I had made a tolerable Proficiency in their Language, and was able to answer most of the King's Questions, when I had the Honour to attend him. His Majesty discovered not the least Curiosity to enquire into the Laws, Government, History, Religion, or Manners of the Countries where I had been; but confined his Questions to the State of Mathematicks, and received the Account I gave him, with great Contempt and Indifference, though often rouzed by his *Flapper* on each Side.

Chapter v. *The Author permitted to see the grand Academy of* Lagado. *The Academy largely described. The Arts wherein the Professors employ themselves.*

This Academy is not an entire single Building, but a Continuation of several Houses on both Sides of a Street; which growing waste, was purchased and applyed to that Use.

I was received very kindly by the Warden, and went for many Days to the Academy. Every Room hath in it one or more Projectors; and I believe I could not be in fewer than five Hundred Rooms.

The first Man I saw was of a meagre Aspect, with sooty Hands and Face, his Hair and Beard long, ragged and singed in several Places. His Clothes, Shirt, and Skin were all of the same Colour. He had been Eight Years upon a Project for extracting Sun-Beams out of Cucumbers, which were to be put into Vials hermetically sealed, and let out to warm the Air in raw inclement Summers.[1] He told me, he did not doubt in Eight Years more, that he should be able to supply Governors Gardens with Sun-shine at a reasonable Rate; but he complained that his Stock was low, and intreated me to give him something as an Encouragement to Ingenuity, especially since this had been a very dear Season for Cucumbers. I made him a small Present, for my Lord had furnished me with Money on purpose, because he knew their Practice of begging from all who go to see them.

I went into another Chamber, but was ready to hasten back, being almost overcome with a horrible Stink. My Conductor pressed me forward, conjuring me in a Whisper to give no Offence, which would be highly resented; and therefore I durst not so much as stop my Nose. The Projector of this Cell was the most ancient Student of the Academy. His Face and Beard were of a pale Yellow; his Hands and Clothes dawbed over with Filth. When I was presented to him, he gave me a very close Embrace, (a Compliment I could well have excused). His Employment from his first coming into the Academy, was an Operation to reduce human Excrement to its original Food, by separating the several Parts, removing the Tincture which it receives from the Gall, making the Odour exhale, and scumming off the Saliva. He had a weekly Allowance from the Society, of a Vessel filled with human Ordure, about the Bigness of a *Bristol* Barrel.

I saw another at work to calcine Ice into Gunpowder; who likewise shewed me a Treatise he had written concerning the Malleability of Fire, which he intended to publish.

There was a most ingenious Architect who had contrived a new Method for building Houses, by beginning at the Roof, and working downwards to the Foundation; which he justified to me by

---

[1] The experiments here described satirize experiments attempted or discussed by scientists in Swift's time.

the like Practice of those two prudent Insects the Bee and the Spider.

There was a Man born blind, who had several Apprentices in his own Condition: Their Employment was to mix Colours for Painters, which their Master taught them to distinguish by feeling and smelling. It was indeed my Misfortune to find them at that Time not very perfect in their Lessons; and the Professor himself happened to be generally mistaken: This Artist is much encouraged and esteemed by the whole Fraternity.

In another Apartment I was highly pleased with a Projector, who had found a Device of plowing the Ground with Hogs, to save the Charges of Plows, Cattle, and Labour. The Method is this: In an Acre of Ground you bury at six Inches Distance, and eight deep, a Quantity of Acorns, Dates, Chestnuts, and other Maste or Vegetables whereof these Animals are fondest; then you drive six Hundred or more of them into the Field, where in a few Days they will root up the whole Ground in search of their Food, and make it fit for sowing, at the same time manuring it with their Dung. It is true, upon Experiment they found the Charge and Trouble very great, and they had little or no Crop. However, it is not doubted that this Invention may be capable of great Improvement.

I went into another Room, where the Walls and Ceiling were all hung round with Cobwebs, except a narrow Passage for the Artist to go in and out. At my Entrance he called aloud to me not to disturb his Webs. He lamented the fatal Mistake the World had been so long in of using Silk-Worms, while we had such plenty of domestick Insects, who infinitely excelled the former, because they understood how to weave as well as spin. And he proposed farther, that by employing Spiders, the Charge of dying Silks would be wholly saved; whereof I was fully convinced when he shewed me a vast Number of Flies most beautifully coloured, wherewith he fed his Spiders; assuring us, that the Webs would take a Tincture from them; and as he had them of all Hues, he hoped to fit every Body's Fancy, as soon as he could find proper Food for the Flies, of certain Gums, Oyls, and other glutinous Matter, to give a Strength and Consistence to the Threads.

There was an Astronomer who had undertaken to place a Sun-Dial upon the great Weather-Cock on the Town-House, by adjusting the annual and diurnal Motions of the Earth and Sun, so as to answer and coincide with all accidental Turnings of the Wind.

I was complaining of a small Fit of the Cholick; upon which my Conductor led me into a Room, where a great Physician resided, who was famous for curing that Disease by contrary Operations from the same Instrument. He had a large Pair of Bellows, with a long slender Muzzle of Ivory. This he conveyed eight Inches up the Anus, and drawing in the Wind, he affirmed he could make the Guts as lank as a dried Bladder. But when the Disease was more stubborn and violent, he let in the Muzzle while the Bellows was full of Wind, which he discharged into the Body of the Patient; then withdrew the Instrument to replenish it, clapping his Thumb strongly against the Orifice of the Fundament; and this being repeated three or four Times, the adventitious Wind would rush out, bringing the noxious along with it (like Water put into a Pump) and the Patient recovers. I saw him try both Experiments upon a Dog, but could not discern any Effect from the former. After the latter, the Animal was ready to burst, and made so violent a Discharge, as was very offensive to me and my Companions. The Dog died on the Spot, and we left the Doctor endeavouring to recover him by the same Operation.

I visited many other Apartments, but shall not trouble my Reader with all the Curiosities I observed, being studious of Brevity.

I had hitherto seen only one Side of the Academy, the other being appropriated to the Advancers of speculative Learning; of whom I shall say something when I have mentioned one illustrious Person more, who is called among them *the universal Artist*. He told us, he had been Thirty Years employing his Thoughts for the Improvement of human Life. He had two large Rooms full of wonderful Curiosities, and Fifty Men at work. Some were condensing Air into a dry tangible Substance, by extracting the Nitre, and letting the aqueous or fluid Particles percolate: Others softening Marble for Pillows and Pin-cushions, others petrifying the Hoofs of a living Horse to preserve them from foundring. The Artist himself was at that Time busy upon two great Designs: The first, to sow Land with Chaff, wherein he affirmed the true seminal Virtue to be contained, as he demonstrated by several Experiments which I was not skilful enough to comprehend. The other was, by a certain Composition of Gums, Minerals, and Vegetables outwardly applied, to prevent the Growth of Wool upon two young Lambs; and he hoped in a reasonable Time to propagate the Breed of naked Sheep all over the Kingdom.

We crossed a Walk to the other Part of the Academy, where, as I have already said, the Projectors in speculative Learning resided.

The first Professor I saw was in a very large Room, with Forty Pupils about him. After Salutation, observing me to look earnestly upon a Frame, which took up the greatest Part of both the Length and Breadth of the Room; he said, perhaps I might wonder to see him employed in a Project for improving speculative Knowledge by practical and mechanical Operations. But the World would soon be sensible of its Usefulness; and he flattered himself, that a more noble exalted Thought never sprang in any other Man's Head. Every one knew how laborious the usual Method is of attaining to Arts and Sciences; whereas by his Contrivance, the most ignorant Person at a reasonable Charge, and with a little bodily Labour, may write Books in Philosophy, Poetry, Politicks, Law, Mathematicks and Theology, without the least Assistance from Genius or Study. He then led me to the Frame, about the Sides whereof all his Pupils stood in Ranks. It was Twenty Foot square, placed in the Middle of the Room. The Superficies was composed of several Bits of Wood, about the Bigness of a Dye, but some larger than others. They were all linked together by slender Wires. These Bits of Wood were covered on every Square with Papers pasted on them; and on these Papers were written all the Words of their Language in their several Moods, Tenses, and Declensions, but without any Order. The Professor then desired me to observe, for he was going to set his Engine at work. The Pupils at his Command took each of them hold of an Iron Handle, whereof there were Forty fixed round the Edges of the Frame; and giving them a sudden Turn, the whole Disposition of the Words was entirely changed. He then commanded Six and Thirty of the Lads to read the several Lines softly as they appeared upon the Frame; and where they found three or four Words together that might make Part of a Sentence, they dictated to the four remaining Boys who were Scribes. This Work was repeated three or four Times, and at every Turn the Engine was so contrived, that the Words shifted into new Places, as the square Bits of Wood moved upside down.

Six Hours a-Day the young Students were employed in this Labour; and the Professor shewed me several Volumes in large Folio already collected, of broken Sentences, which he intended to piece together; and out of those rich Materials to give the World a compleat Body of all Arts and Sciences; which however might be still improved, and much expedited, if the Publick would raise a Fund for making and employing five Hundred such Frames in *Lagado,* and oblige the Managers to contribute in common their several Collections.

He assured me, that this Invention had employed all his Thoughts from his Youth; that he had emptied the whole Vocabulary into his Frame, and made the strictest Computation of the general Proportion there is in Books between the Numbers of Particles, Nouns, and Verbs, and other Parts of Speech.

I made my humblest Acknowledgments to this illustrious Person for his great Communicativeness; and promised if ever I had the good Fortune to return to my native Country, that I would do him Justice, as the sole Inventor of this wonderful Machine; the Form and Contrivance of which I desired Leave to delineate upon Paper as in the Figure here annexed. [*The original edition shows a crude sketch of this four-sided contraption for shuffling an alphabet.*] I told him, although it were the Custom of our Learned in *Europe* to steal Inventions from each other, who had thereby at least this Advantage, that it became a Controversy which was the right Owner; yet I would take such Caution, that he should have the Honour entire without a Rival.

We next went to the School of Languages, where three Professors sat in Consultation upon improving that of their own Country.

The first Project was to shorten Discourse by cutting Polysyllables into one, and leaving out Verbs and Participles; because in Reality all things imaginable are but Nouns.

The other, was a Scheme for entirely abolishing all Words what soever: And this was urged as a great Advantage in Point of Health as well as Brevity. For, it is plain, that every Word we speak is in some Degree a Diminution of our Lungs by Corrosion; and consequently contributes to the shortening of our Lives. An Expedient was therefore offered, that since Words are only Names for *Things,* it would be more convenient for all Men to carry about them, such *Things* as were necessary to express the particular Business they are to discourse on. And this Invention would certainly have taken Place, to the great Ease as well as Health of the Subject, if the Women in Conjunction with the Vulgar and Illiterate had not threatned to raise a Rebellion, unless they might be allowed the Liberty to speak with their Tongues, after the Manner of their Forefathers: Such constant irreconcileable Enemies to Science are the common People. However, many of the most Learned and Wise adhere to the new Scheme of expressing themselves by *Things;* which hath only this Inconvenience attending it; that if a Man's Business be very great, and of various Kinds, he must be obliged in Proportion to carry a greater Bundle of *Things* upon his Back, unless he can afford one or two strong Servants to attend him. I have often beheld two of those Sages almost sinking under the Weight of their Packs, like Pedlars among us, who when they met in the Streets, would lay down their Loads, open their Sacks, and hold Conversation for an Hour together; then put up their Implements, help each other to resume their Burthens, and take their Leave.

But, for short Conversations a Man may carry Implements in his Pockets and under his Arms, enough to supply him, and in his House he cannot be at a Loss; therefore the Room where Company meet who practice this Art, is full of all *Things* ready at Hand, requisite to furnish Matter for this Kind of artificial Converse.

Another great Advantage proposed by this Invention, was, that it would serve as an universal Language to be understood in all civilized Nations, whose Goods and Utensils are generally of the same Kind, or nearly resembling, so that their Uses might easily be comprehended. And thus, Embassadors would be qualified to treat with foreign Princes or Ministers of State, to whose Tongues they were utter Strangers.

I was at the Mathematical School, where the Master taught his Pupils after a Method scarce imaginable to us in *Europe.* The Proposition and Demonstration were fairly written on a thin Wafer, with Ink composed of a Cephalick Tincture. This the Student was to swallow upon a fasting Stomach, and for three Days following eat nothing but Bread and Water. As the Wafer digested, the Tincture mounted to his Brain, bearing the Proposition along with it. But the Success hath not hitherto been answerable, partly by some Error in the *Quantum* or Composition, and partly by the Perverseness of Lads; to whom this Bolus is so nauseous, that they generally steal aside, and discharge it upwards before it can operate; neither have they been yet persuaded to use so long an Abstinence as the Prescription requires. . . .

william blake

A MYSTIC'S DENIAL
OF A MECHANICAL WORLD

from AUGURIES OF INNOCENCE
To see a World in a Grain of Sand
And a Heaven in a Wild Flower,
Hold Infinity in the palm of your hand
And Eternity in an hour.

INTRODUCTION to SONGS OF EXPERIENCE
Hear the voice of the Bard!
Who Present, Past, and Future sees;
Whose ears have heard
The Holy Word
That walked among the ancient trees,[1]   5

Calling the lapséd Soul,
And weeping in the evening dew;
That might control
The starry pole,
And fallen, fallen light renew!   10

"O Earth, O Earth, return!
Arise from out the dewy grass;
Night is worn,
And the morn
Rises from the slumberous mass.   15

[1] Genesis iii.8: "And [Adam and Eve] heard the voice of the Lord God walking in the garden in the cool of the day."

219

"Turn away no more;
Why wilt thou turn away?
The starry floor,
The watery shore,
Is given thee till the break of day."   20

MOCK ON, MOCK ON, VOLTAIRE, ROUSSEAU[2]

Mock on, Mock on, Voltaire, Rousseau:
Mock on, Mock on: 'tis all in vain!
You throw the sand against the wind,
And the wind blows it back again.

And every sand becomes a Gem   5
Reflected in the beams divine;
Blown back they blind the mocking Eye,
But still in Israel's paths they shine.

The Atoms of Democritus[3]
And Newton's Particles of light   10
Are sands upon the Red sea shore,
Where Israel's tents do shine so bright.

from MILTON

And did those feet in ancient time
    Walk upon England's mountains green?
And was the holy Lamb of God
    On England's pleasant pastures seen?

And did the Countenance Divine   5
    Shine forth upon our clouded hills?
And was Jerusalem builded here
    Among these dark Satanic mills?

[2] Two 18th century French philosophers, whose influential writings tended to ridicule orthodox religious views. Both Frenchmen took different approaches to a view of the universe ordered by an essentially human concept of reason, rather than by a mysterious divine authority.

[3] The Greek philosopher who first formulated an atomic theory of matter.

Bring me my Bow of burning gold!
   Bring me my Arrows of desire!   10
Bring me my Spear! O clouds, unfold!
   Bring me my Chariot of fire!

I will not cease from Mental Fight,
   Nor shall my Sword sleep in my hand,
Till we have built Jerusalem   15
   In England's green and pleasant Land.

FACT AND FEELING
IN POETIC IMAGINATION

THE TABLES TURNED

Up! up! my Friend, and quit your books;
Or surely you'll grow double:
Up! up! my Friend, and clear your looks;
Why all this toil and trouble?

The sun, above the mountain's head,
A freshening lustre mellow
Through all the long green fields has spread,
His first sweet evening yellow.

Books! 'tis a dull and endless strife:
Come, hear the woodland linnet,   10
How sweet his music! on my life,
There's more of wisdom in it.

And hark! how blithe the throstle sings!
He, too, is no mean preacher:
Come forth into the light of things,
Let Nature be your teacher.

She has a world of ready wealth,
Our minds and hearts to bless—
Spontaneous wisdom breathed by health,
Truth breathed by cheerfulness.   20

One impulse from a vernal wood
May teach you more of man,

Of moral evil and of good,
Than all the sages can.

Sweet is the lore which Nature brings;
Our meddling intellect
Mis-shapes the beauteous forms of things:—
We murder to dissect.

Enough of Science and of Art;
Close up those barren leaves; 30
Come forth, and bring with you a heart
That watches and receives.

LINES

LINES COMPOSED A FEW MILES ABOVE TINTERN ABBEY ON REVISITING THE BANKS OF THE WYE DURING A TOUR. JULY 13, 1798

Five years have past; five summers, with the length
Of five long winters! and again I hear
These waters, rolling from their mountain-springs
With a soft inland murmur.—Once again
Do I behold these steep and lofty cliffs,
That on a wild secluded scene impress
Thoughts of more deep seclusion; and connect
The landscape with the quiet of the sky.
The day is come when I again repose
Here, under this dark sycamore, and view 10
These plots of cottage-ground, these orchard-tufts,
Which at this season, with their unripe fruits,
Are clad in one green hue, and lose themselves
'Mid groves and copses. Once again I see
These hedge-rows, hardly hedge-rows, little lines
Of sportive wood run wild: these pastoral farms,
Green to the very door; and wreaths of smoke
Sent up, in silence, from among the trees!
With some uncertain notice, as might seem
Of vagrant dwellers in the houseless woods, 20
Or of some Hermit's cave, where by his fire
The Hermit sits alone.
                These beauteous forms,
Through a long absence, have not been to me
As is a landscape to a blind man's eye:
But oft, in lonely rooms, and 'mid the din
Of towns and cities, I have owed to them,

In hours of weariness, sensations sweet,
Felt in the blood, and felt along the heart;
And passing even into my purer mind,
With tranquil restoration:—feelings too   30
Of unremembered pleasure; such, perhaps,
As have no slight or trivial influence
On that best portion of a good man's life,
His little, nameless, unremembered, acts
Of kindness and of love. Nor less, I trust,
To them I may have owed another gift,
Of aspect more sublime; that blessed mood,
In which the burthen of the mystery,
In which the heavy and the weary weight
Of all this unintelligible world,   40
Is lightened:—that serene and blessed mood,
In which the affections gently lead us on,—
Until, the breath of this corporeal frame
And even the motion of our human blood
Almost suspended, we are laid asleep
In body, and become a living soul:
While with an eye made quiet by the power
Of harmony, and the deep power of joy,
We see into the life of things.
                                        If this
Be but a vain belief, yet, oh! how oft—   50
In darkness and amid the many shapes
Of joyless daylight; when the fretful stir
Unprofitable, and the fever of the world,
Have hung upon the beatings of my heart—
How oft, in spirit, have I turned to thee,
O sylvan Wye! thou wanderer through the woods,
How often has my spirit turned to thee!

And now, with gleams of half-extinguished thought,
With many recognitions dim and faint,
And somewhat of a sad perplexity,   60
The picture of the mind revives again:
While here I stand, not only with the sense
Of present pleasure, but with pleasing thoughts
That in this moment there is life and food
For future years. And so I dare to hope,
Though changed, no doubt, from what I was when first
I came among these hills; when like a roe
I bounded o'er the mountains, by the sides
Of the deep rivers, and the lonely streams,

Wherever nature led: more like a man   70
Flying from something that he dreads than one
Who sought the thing he loved. For nature then
(The coarser pleasures of my boyish days,
And their glad animal movements all gone by)
To me was all in all.—I cannot paint
What then I was. The sounding cataract
Haunted me like a passion: the tall rock,
The mountain, and the deep and gloomy wood,
Their colours and their forms, were then to me
An appetite; a feeling and a love,   80
That had no need of a remoter charm,
By thought supplied, nor any interest
Unborrowed from the eye.—That time is past,
And all its aching joys are now no more,
And all its dizzy raptures. Not for this
Faint I, nor mourn nor murmur; other gifts
Have followed; for such loss, I would believe,
Abundant recompense. For I have learned
To look on nature, not as in the hour
Of thoughtless youth; but hearing oftentimes   90
The still, sad music of humanity,
Nor harsh nor grating, though of ample power
To chasten and subdue. And I have felt
A presence that disturbs me with the joy
Of elevated thoughts; a sense sublime
Of something far more deeply interfused,
Whose dwelling is the light of setting suns,
And the round ocean and the living air,
And the blue sky, and in the mind of man:
A motion and a spirit, that impels   100
All thinking things, all objects of all thought,
And rolls through all things. Therefore am I still
A lover of the meadows and the woods,
And mountains; and of all that we behold
From this green earth; of all the mighty world
Of eye, and ear,—both what they half create,
And what perceive; well pleased to recognize
In nature and the language of the sense
The anchor of my purest thoughts, the nurse,
The guide, the guardian of my heart, and soul   110
Of all my moral being.
                        Nor perchance,
If I were not thus taught, should I the more
Suffer my genial spirits to decay:

For thou art with me here upon the banks
Of this fair river; thou my dearest Friend,
My dear, dear Friend; and in thy voice I catch
The language of my former heart, and read
My former pleasures in the shooting lights
Of thy wild eyes. Oh! yet a little while
May I behold in thee what I was once,   120
My dear, dear Sister! and this prayer I make,
Knowing that Nature never did betray
The heart that loved her; 'tis her privilege,
Through all the years of this our life, to lead
From joy to joy: for she can so inform
The mind that is within us, so impress
With quietness and beauty, and so feed
With lofty thoughts, that neither evil tongues,
Rash judgments, nor the sneers of selfish men,
Nor greetings where no kindness is, nor all   130
The dreary intercourse of daily life,
Shall e'er prevail against us, or disturb
Our cheerful faith, that all which we behold
Is full of blessings. Therefore let the moon
Shine on thee in thy solitary walk;
And let the misty mountain-winds be free
To blow against thee: and, in after years,
When these wild ecstasies shall be matured
Into a sober pleasure; when thy mind
Shall be a mansion for all lovely forms,   140
Thy memory be as a dwelling-place
For all sweet sounds and harmonies; oh! then,
If solitude, or fear, or pain, or grief,
Should be thy portion, with what healing thoughts
Of tender joy wilt thou remember me,
And these my exhortations! Nor, perchance—
If I should be where I no more can hear
Thy voice, nor catch from thy wild eyes these gleams
Of past existence—wilt thou then forget
That on the banks of this delightful stream   150
We stood together; and that I, so long
A worshipper of Nature, hither came
Unwearied in that service: rather say
With warmer love—oh! with far deeper zeal
Of holier love. Nor wilt thou then forget
That after many wanderings, many years
Of absence, these steep woods and lofty cliffs,

And this green pastoral landscape, were to me
More dear, both for themselves and for thy sake!

from THE PRELUDE

Book V

   . . . One day, when from my lips a like complaint   50
Had fallen in presence of a studious friend,
He with a smile made answer, that in truth
'Twas going far to seek disquietude;
But on the front of his reproof confessed
That he himself had oftentimes given way   55
To kindred hauntings. Whereupon I told,
That once in the stillness of a summer's noon,
While I was seated in a rocky cave
By the seaside, perusing, so it chanced,
The famous history of the errant knight   60
Recorded by Cervantes, these same thoughts
Beset me, and to height unusual rose,
While listlessly I sate, and, having closed
The book, had turned my eyes toward the wide sea.
On poetry and geometric truth,   65
And their high privilege of lasting life,
From all internal injury exempt,
I mused upon these chiefly; and at length,
My senses yielding to the sultry air,
Sleep seized me, and I passed into a dream.   70
I saw before me stretched a boundless plain
Of sandy wilderness, all black and void,
And as I looked around, distress and fear
Came creeping over me, when at my side,
Close at my side, an uncouth shape appeared   75
Upon a dromedary, mounted high.
He seemed an Arab of the Bedouin tribes:
A lance he bore, and underneath one arm
A stone, and in the opposite hand a shell
Of a surpassing brightness. At the sight   80
Much I rejoiced, not doubting but a guide
Was present, one who with unerring skill
Would through the desert lead me; and while yet
I looked and looked, self-questioned what this freight
Which the newcomer carried through the waste   85
Could mean, the Arab told me that the stone
  (To give it in the language of the dream)

Was "Euclid's Elements"; and "This," said he,
"Is something of more worth"; and at the word
Stretched forth the shell, so beautiful in shape,   90
In color so resplendent, with command
That I should hold it to my ear. I did so,
And heard that instant in an unknown tongue,
Which yet I understood, articulate sounds,
A loud prophetic blast of harmony;   95
An Ode, in passion uttered, which foretold
Destruction to the children of the earth
By deluge, now at hand. No sooner ceased
The song, than the Arab with calm look declared
That all would come to pass of which the voice   100
Had given forewarning, and that he himself
Was going then to bury those two books:
The one that held acquaintance with the stars,
And wedded soul to soul in purest bond
Of reason, undisturbed by space or time;   105
The other that was a god, yea, many gods,
Had voices more than all the winds, with power
To exhilarate the spirit, and to soothe,
Through every clime, the heart of human kind.
While this was uttering, strange as it may seem,   110
I wondered not, although I plainly saw
The one to be a stone, the other a shell;
Nor doubted once but that they both were books,
Having a perfect faith in all that passed.
Far stronger, now, grew the desire I felt   115
To cleave unto this man; but when I prayed
To share his enterprise, he hurried on
Reckless of me: I followed, not unseen,
For oftentimes he cast a backward look,
Grasping his twofold treasure.—Lance in rest,   120
He rode, I keeping pace with him; and now
He, to my fancy, had become the knight
Whose tale Cervantes tells; yet not the knight,
But was an Arab of the desert too;
Of these was neither, and was both at once.   125
His countenance, meanwhile, grew more disturbed;
And, looking backwards when he looked, mine eyes
Saw, over half the wilderness diffused,
A bed of glittering light: I asked the cause:
"It is," said he, "the waters of the deep   130
Gathering upon us"; quickening then the pace
Of the unwieldy creature he bestrode,

He left me: I called after him aloud;
He heeded not; but, with his twofold charge
Still in his grasp, before me, full in view,   135
Went hurrying o'er the illimitable waste,
With the fleet waters of a drowning world
In chase of him; whereat I waked in terror,
And saw the sea before me, and the book,
In which I had been reading, at my side.   140

*   *   *

from PREFACE *to* LYRICAL BALLADS [1800]

. . . The principal object, then, proposed in these Poems was to choose incidents and situations from common life, and to relate or describe them throughout, as far as was possible, in a selection of language really used by men, and, at the same time, to throw over them a certain colouring of imagination, whereby ordinary things should be presented to the mind in an unusual aspect; and further, and above all, to make these incidents and situations interesting by tracing in them, truly though not ostentatiously, the primary laws of our nature: chiefly, as far as regards the manner in which we associate ideas in a state of excitement. Humble and rustic life was generally chosen, because, in that condition, the essential passions of the heart find a better soil in which they can attain their maturity, are less under restraint, and speak a plainer and more emphatic language; because in that condition of life our elementary feelings co-exist in a state of greater simplicity, and, consequently, may be more accurately contemplated, and more forcibly communicated; because the manners of rural life germinate from those elementary feelings, and, from the necessary character of rural occupations, are more easily comprehended, and are more durable; and, lastly, because in that condition the passions of men are incorporated with the beautiful and permanent forms of nature. The language, too, of these men has been adopted (purified indeed from what appear to be its real defects, from all lasting and rational causes of dislike or disgust), because such men hourly communicate with the best objects from which the best part of language is originally derived; and because, from their rank in society and the sameness and narrow circle of their intercourse, being less under the influence of social vanity, they convey their feelings and notions in simple and unelaborated expressions. Accordingly, such a language, arising out of repeated experience and regular feelings, is a more permanent, and a far more philosophical language, than that which is frequently substituted for it by Poets, who think that they are conferring honour upon themselves and their art in proportion as they separate themselves from the sympathies of men, and indulge in arbitrary and capricious habits of expression, in order to furnish food for fickle tastes, and fickle appetites, of their own creation.[1] . . .

. . . From such verses the Poems in these volumes will be found distinguished at least by one mark of difference, that each of them has a worthy *purpose.* Not that I always began to write with a distinct purpose formally conceived; but habits of meditation have, I trust, so prompted and regulated my feelings, that my descriptions of such objects as strongly excite those feelings will be found to carry along with them a *purpose.* If this opinion be erroneous, I can have little right to the name of a Poet. For all good poetry is the spontaneous overflow of powerful feelings: and though this be true, Poems to which any value can be attached were never produced on any variety of subjects but by a man who, being possessed of more than usual organic sensibility, had also thought long and deeply. For our continued influxes of feeling are modified and directed by our thoughts, which are indeed the representatives of all our past feelings; and as, by contemplating the relation of these general representatives to each other, we discover what is really important to men, so, by the repetition and continuance of this act, our feelings will be connected with important subjects, till at length, if we be originally possessed of much sensibility, such habits of mind will be produced that, by obeying blindly and mechanically the impulses of those habits, we shall describe objects, and utter sentiments, of such a nature, and in such connection with each other, that the understanding of the Reader must necessarily be in some degree enlightened, and his affections strengthened and purified.

It has been said that each of these Poems has a purpose. Another circumstance must be mentioned which distinguishes these Poems from the popular Poetry of the day; it is this, that the feeling therein developed gives importance to the action and situation, and not the action and situation to the feeling.

A sense of false modesty shall not prevent me from asserting that the Reader's attention is pointed to this mark of distinction, far less for the sake of these particular Poems than from the general importance of the subject. The subject is indeed important! For the human mind is capable of being excited without the application of gross and violent stimulants; and he must have a very faint perception of its beauty and dignity who does not know this, and who does not further know, that one being is elevated

---

[1] "It is worth while here to observe that the affecting parts of Chaucer are almost always expressed in language pure and universally intelligible even to this day." [Wordsworth's note.]

above another in proportion as he possesses this capability. It has therefore appeared to me, that to endeavour to produce or enlarge this capability is one of the best services in which, at any period, a Writer can be engaged; but this service, excellent at all times, is especially so at the present day. For a multitude of causes, unknown to former times, are now acting with a combined force to blunt the discriminating powers of the mind, and, unfitting it for all voluntary exertion, to reduce it to a state of almost savage torpor. The most effective of these causes are the great national events which are daily taking place, and the increasing accumulation of men in cities, where the uniformity of their occupations produces a craving for extraordinary incident, which the rapid communication of intelligence hourly gratifies. To this tendency of life and manners the literature and theatrical exhibitions of the country have conformed themselves. The invaluable works of our elder writers, I had almost said the works of Shakespeare and Milton, are driven into neglect by frantic novels, sickly and stupid German Tragedies, and deluges of idle and extravagant stories in verse.—When I think upon this degrading thirst after outrageous stimulation, I am almost ashamed to have spoken of the feeble endeavour made in these volumes to counteract it; and, reflecting upon the magnitude of the general evil, I should be oppressed with no dishonourable melancholy, had I not a deep impression of certain inherent and indestructible qualities of the human mind, and likewise of certain powers in the great and permanent objects that act upon it, which are equally inherent and indestructible; and were there not added to this impression a belief, that the time is approaching when the evil will be systematically opposed by men of greater powers, and with far more distinguished success. . . .

. . . Aristotle, I have been told, has said, that Poetry is the most philosophic of all writing: it is so: its object is truth, not individual and local, but general and operative; not standing upon external testimony, but carried alive into the heart by passion; truth which is its own testimony, which gives competence and confidence to the tribunal to which it appeals, and receives them from the same tribunal. Poetry is the image of man and nature. The obstacles which stand in the way of the fidelity of the Biographer and Historian, and of their consequent utility, are incalculably greater than those which are to be encountered by the Poet who comprehends the dignity of his art. The Poet writes under one restriction only, namely, the necessity of giving immediate pleasure to a human Being possessed of that information which may be expected from him, not as a lawyer, a physician, a mariner, an astronomer, or a natural philosopher, but as a Man. Except this one restriction, there is no object standing between the Poet and the image of things; between this, and the Biographer and Historian, there are a thousand.

Nor let this necessity of producing immediate pleasure be considered as a degradation of the Poet's art. It is far otherwise. It is an acknowledgment of the beauty of the universe, an acknowledgment the more sincere because not formal, but indirect; it is a task light and easy to him who looks at the world in the spirit of love: further, it is a homage paid to the native and naked dignity of man, to the grand elementary principle of pleasure, by which he knows, and feels, and lives, and moves. We have no sympathy but what is propagated by pleasure: I would not be misunderstood; but wherever we sympathise with pain, it will be found that the sympathy is produced and carried on by subtle combinations with pleasure. We have no knowledge, that is, no general principles drawn from the contemplation of particular facts, but what has been built up by pleasure, and exists in us by pleasure alone. The Man of science, the Chemist and Mathematician, whatever difficulties and disgusts they may have had to struggle with, know and feel this. However painful may be the objects with which the Anatomist's knowledge is connected, he feels that his knowledge is pleasure; and where he has no pleasure he has no knowledge. What then does the Poet? He considers man and the objects that surround him as acting and re-acting upon each other, so as to produce an infinite complexity of pain and pleasure; he considers man in his own nature and in his ordinary life as contemplating this with a certain quantity of immediate knowledge, with certain convictions, intuitions, and deductions, which from habit acquire the quality of intuitions; he considers him as looking upon this complex scene of ideas and sensations, and finding everywhere objects that immediately excite in him sympathies which, from the necessities of his nature, are accompanied by an overbalance of enjoyment.

To this knowledge which all men carry about with them, and to these sympathies in which, without any other discipline than that of our daily life, we are fitted to take delight, the Poet principally directs his attention. He considers man and nature as essentially adapted to each other, and the mind of man as naturally the mirror of the fairest and most interesting properties of nature. And thus the Poet, prompted by this feeling of pleasure, which accompanies him through the whole course of his studies, converses with general nature, with affections akin to those which, through labour and length of time, the Man of science has raised up in himself, by conversing with those particular parts of nature which

Preface to "Lyrical Ballads"

are the objects of his studies. The knowledge both of the Poet and the Man of science is pleasure; but the knowledge of the one cleaves to us as a necessary part of our existence, our natural and unalienable inheritance; the other is a personal and individual acquisition, slow to come to us, and by no habitual and direct sympathy connecting us with our fellow-beings. The Man of science seeks truth as a remote and unknown benefactor; he cherishes and loves it in his solitude: the Poet, singing a song in which all human beings join with him, rejoices in the presence of truth as our visible friend and hourly companion. Poetry is the breath and finer spirit of all knowledge; it is the impassioned expression which is in the countenance of all Science. Emphatically may it be said of the Poet, as Shakespeare hath said of man, "that he looks before and after." He is the rock of defence for human nature; an upholder and preserver, carrying everywhere with him relationship and love. In spite of difference of soil and climate, of language and manners, of laws and customs: in spite of things silently gone out of mind, and things violently destroyed; the Poet binds together by passion and knowledge the vast empire of human society, as it is spread over the whole earth, and over all time. The objects of the Poet's thoughts are everywhere; though the eyes and senses of man are, it is true, his favourite guides, yet he will follow wheresoever he can find an atmosphere of sensation in which to move his wings. Poetry is the first and last of all knowledge—it is as immortal as the heart of man. If the labours of Men of science should ever create any material revolution, direct or indirect, in our condition, and in the impressions which we habitually receive, the Poet will sleep then no more than at present; he will be ready to follow the steps of the Man of science, not only in those general indirect effects, but he will be at his side, carrying sensation into the midst of the objects of the science itself. The remotest discoveries of the Chemist, the Botanist, or Mineralogist, will be as proper objects of the Poet's art as any upon which it can be employed, if the time should ever come when these things shall be familiar to us, and the relations under which they are contemplated by the followers of these respective sciences shall be manifestly and palpably material to us as enjoying and suffering beings. If the time should ever come when what is now called science, thus familiarised to men, shall be ready to put on, as it were, a form of flesh and blood, the Poet will lend his divine spirit to aid the transfiguration, and will welcome the Being thus produced as a dear and genuine inmate of the household of man.—It is not, then, to be supposed that any one, who holds that sublime notion of Poetry which I have attempted to convey, will break in upon the sanctity and truth of

233

his pictures by transitory and accidental ornaments, and endeavour to excite admiration of himself by arts, the necessity of which must manifestly depend upon the assumed meanness of his subject.

What has been thus far said applies to Poetry in general; but especially to those parts of composition where the Poet speaks through the mouths of his characters; and upon this point it appears to authorise the conclusion that there are few persons of good sense who would not allow that the dramatic parts of composition are defective in proportion as they deviate from the real language of nature, and are coloured by a diction of the Poet's own, either peculiar to him as an individual Poet or belonging simply to Poets in general; to a body of men who, from the circumstance of their compositions being in metre, it is expected will employ a particular language.

It is not, then, in the dramatic parts of composition that we look for this distinction of language; but still it may be proper and necessary where the Poet speaks to us in his own person and character. To this I answer by referring the Reader to the description before given of a Poet. Among the qualities there enumerated as principally conducing to form a Poet, is implied nothing differing in kind from other men, but only in degree. The sum of what was said is, that the Poet is chiefly distinguished from other men by a greater promptness to think and feel without immediate external excitement, and a greater power in expressing such thoughts and feelings as are produced in him in that manner. But these passions and thoughts and feelings are the general passions and thoughts and feelings of men. And with what are they connected? Undoubtedly with our moral sentiments and animal sensations, and with the causes which excite these; with the operations of the elements, and the appearances of the visible universe; with storm and sunshine, with the revolutions of the seasons, with cold and heat, with loss of friends and kindred, with injuries and resentments, gratitude and hope, with fear and sorrow. These, and the like, are the sensations and objects which the Poet describes, as they are the sensations of other men and the objects which interest them. The Poet thinks and feels in the spirit of human passions. How, then, can his language differ in any material degree from that of all other men who feel vividly and see clearly? It might be *proved* that it is impossible. But supposing that this were not the case, the Poet might then be allowed to use a peculiar language when expressing his feelings for his own gratification, or that of men like himself. But Poets do not write for Poets alone, but for men. Unless, therefore, we are advocates for that admiration which subsists upon ignorance, and that pleasure which arises from hearing what we do not understand, the Poet must descend from this supposed height; and, in order to excite rational sympathy, he must express himself as other men express themselves. To this it may be added, that while he is only selecting from the real language of men, or, which amounts to the same thing, composing accurately in the spirit of such selection, he is treading upon safe ground, and we know what we are to expect from him. Our feelings are the same with respect to metre; for, as it may be proper to remind the Reader, the distinction of metre is regular and uniform, and not, like that which is produced by what is usually called POETIC DICTION, arbitrary, and subject to infinite caprices, upon which no calculation whatever can be made. In the one case, the Reader is utterly at the mercy of the Poet, respecting what imagery or diction he may choose to connect with the passion; whereas, in the other, the metre obeys certain laws, to which the Poet and Reader both willingly submit because they are certain, and because no interference is made by them with the passion but such as the concurring testimony of ages has shown to heighten and improve the pleasure which co-exists with it.

*   *   *

alfred tennyson

THE POET AND A DARWINIAN UNIVERSE

from IN MEMORIAM

1

I held it truth, with him[1] who sings
    To one clear harp in divers tones,
    That men may rise on stepping-stones
On their dead selves to higher things.

But who shall so forecast the years
    And find in loss a gain to match?
    Or reach a hand through time to catch
The far-off interest of tears?

Let Love clasp Grief lest both be drowned,
    Let darkness keep her raven gloss:
    Ah, sweeter to be drunk with loss,
To dance with death, to beat the ground,

Than that the victor Hours should scorn
    The long result of love, and boast,
    "Behold the man that loved and lost,
But all he was is overworn."

3

O Sorrow, cruel fellowship,
    O Priestess in the vaults of Death,
    O sweet and bitter in a breath,
What whispers from thy lying lip?

[1] *him:* Goethe.

236

"The stars," she whispers, "blindly run;
    A web is wov'n across the sky;
    From out waste places comes a cry,
And murmurs from the dying sun:

"And all the phantom, Nature, stands—
    With all the music in her tone,
    A hollow echo of my own,—
A hollow form with empty hands."

And shall I take a thing so blind,
    Embrace her as my natural good;
    Or crush her, like a vice of blood,
Upon the threshold of the mind?

6

One writes, that "Other friends remain,"
    That "Loss is common to the race"—
    And common is the commonplace,
And vacant chaff well meant for grain.

That loss is common would not make
    My own less bitter, rather more:
    Too common! Never morning wore
To evening, but some heart did break.

O father, wheresoe'er thou be,
    Who pledgest now thy gallant son;
    A shot, ere half thy draught be done,
Hath stilled the life that beat from thee.

O mother, praying God will save
    Thy sailor,—while thy head is bowed,
    His heavy-shotted hammock-shroud
Drops in his vast and wandering grave.

Ye know no more than I who wrought
    At that last hour to please him well;
    Who mused on all I had to tell,
And something written, something thought;

Expecting still his advent home;
    And ever met him on his way
    With wishes, thinking, "here to-day,"
Or "here to-morrow will he come."

O somewhere, meek, unconscious dove,
   That sittest ranging[2] golden hair;
   And glad to find thyself so fair,
Poor child, that waitest for thy love!

For now her father's chimney glows
   In expectation of a guest;
   And thinking "this will please him best,"
She takes a riband or a rose;

For he will see them on to-night;
   And with the thought her colour burns;
   And, having left the glass, she turns
Once more to set a ringlet right;

And, even when she turned, the curse
   Had fallen, and her future Lord
   Was drowned in passing through the ford,
Or killed in falling from his horse.

O what to her shall be the end?
   And what to me remains of good?
   To her, perpetual maidenhood,
And unto me no second friend.

7

Dark house,[3] by which once more I stand
   Here in the long unlovely street,
   Doors, where my heart was used to beat
So quickly, waiting for a hand,

A hand that can be clasped no more—
   Behold me, for I cannot sleep,
   And like a guilty thing I creep
At earliest morning to the door.

He is not here; but far away
   The noise of life begins again,
   And ghastly through the drizzling rain
On the bald street breaks the blank day.

[2] *ranging:* arranging.
[3] *Dark house,* where Hallam lived.

21

I sing to him that rests below,
    And, since the grasses round me wave,
    I take the grasses of the grave,
And make them pipes whereon to blow.

The traveller hears me now and then,
    And sometimes harshly will he speak:
    "This fellow would make weakness weak,
And melt the waxen hearts of men."

Another answers, "Let him be,
    He loves to make parade of pain,
    That with his piping he may gain
The praise that comes to constancy."

A third is wroth: "Is this an hour
    For private sorrow's barren song,
    When more and more the people throng
The chairs and thrones of civil power?

"A time to sicken and to swoon,
    When Science reaches forth her arms
    To feel from world to world, and charms
Her secret from the latest moon?"

Behold, ye speak an idle thing:
    Ye never knew the sacred dust:
    I do but sing because I must,
And pipe but as the linnets sing:

And one is glad; her note is gay,
    For now her little ones have ranged;
    And one is sad; her note is changed,
Because her brood is stolen away.

27

I envy not in any moods
    The captive void of noble rage,
    The linnet born within the cage,
That never knew the summer woods:

I envy not the beast that takes
    His license in the field of time,

Unfettered by the sense of crime,
To whom a conscience never wakes;

Nor, what may count itself as blest,
   The heart that never plighted troth
   But stagnates in the weeds of sloth;
Nor any want-begotten rest.

I hold it true, whate'er befall;
   I feel it, when I sorrow most;
   'Tis better to have loved and lost
Than never to have loved at all.

34

My own dim life should teach me this,
   That life shall live for evermore,
   Else earth is darkness at the core,
And dust and ashes all that is;

This round of green, this orb of flame,
   Fantastic beauty; such as lurks
   In some wild Poet, when he works
Without a conscience or an aim.

What then were God to such as I?
   'Twere hardly worth my while to choose
   Of things all mortal, or to use
A little patience ere I die;

'Twere best at once to sink to peace,
   Like birds the charming serpent draws,
   To drop head-foremost in the jaws
Of vacant darkness and to cease.

50

Be near me when my light is low,
   When the blood creeps, and the nerves prick
   And tingle; and the heart is sick,
And all the wheels of Being slow.

Be near me when the sensuous frame
   Is racked with pangs that conquer trust;
   And Time, a maniac scattering dust,
And Life, a Fury slinging flame.

Be near me when my faith is dry,
  And men the flies of latter spring,
  That lay their eggs, and sting and sing
And weave their petty cells and die.

Be near me when I fade away,
  To point the term of human strife,
  And on the low dark verge of life
The twilight of eternal day.

54

Oh yet we trust that somehow good
  Will be the final goal of ill,
  To pangs of nature, sins of will,
Defects of doubt, and taints of blood;

That nothing walks with aimless feet;
  That not one life shall be destroyed,
  Or cast as rubbish to the void,
When God hath made the pile complete;

That not a worm is cloven in vain;
  That not a moth with vain desire
  Is shrivelled in a fruitless fire,
Or but subserves another's gain.

Behold, we know not anything;
  I can but trust that good shall fall
  At last—far off—at last, to all,
And every winter change to spring.

So runs my dream: but what am I?
  An infant crying in the night:
  An infant crying for the light:
And with no language but a cry.

55

The wish, that of the living whole
  No life may fail beyond the grave,
  Derives it not from what we have
The likest God within the soul?

Are God and Nature then at strife,
  That Nature lends such evil dreams?

ALFRED TENNYSON

So careful of the type she seems,
So careless of the single life;

That I, considering everywhere
  Her secret meaning in her deeds,
  And finding that of fifty seeds
She often brings but one to bear,

I falter where I firmly trod,
  And falling with my weight of cares
  Upon the great world's altar-stairs
That slope through darkness up to God,

I stretch lame hands of faith, and grope,
  And gather dust and chaff, and call
  To what I feel is Lord of all,
And faintly trust the larger hope.

56

"So careful of the type?" but no.
  From scarpèd cliff and quarried stone
  She⁴ cries, "A thousand types are gone:
I care for nothing, all shall go.

"Thou makest thine appeal to me:
  I bring to life, I bring to death:
  The spirit does but mean the breath:
I know no more." And he, shall he,

Man, her last work, who seemed so fair,
  Such splendid purpose in his eyes,
  Who rolled the psalm to wintry skies,
Who built him fanes of fruitless prayer,

Who trusted God was love indeed
  And love Creation's final law—
  Though Nature, red in tooth and claw
With ravine, shrieked against his creed—

Who loved, who suffered countless ills,
  Who battled for the True, the Just,
  Be blown about the desert dust,
Or sealed within the iron hills?

⁴ *She:* Nature.

242

No more? A monster then, a dream,
    A discord. Dragons of the prime,[5]
    That tear each other in their slime,
Were mellow music matched with him.

O life as futile, then, as frail!
    O for thy voice to soothe and bless!
    What hope of answer, or redress?
Behind the veil, behind the veil.

72

Risest thou thus, dim dawn, again,
    And howlest, issuing out of night,
    With blasts that blow the poplar white,
And lash with storm the streaming pane?

Day, when my crowned estate begun
    To pine in that reverse of doom,
    Which sickened every living bloom,
And blurred the splendour of the sun;

Who usherest in the dolorous hour
    With thy quick tears that make the rose
    Pull sideways, and the daisy close
Her crimson fringes to the shower;

Who might'st have heaved a windless flame
    Up the deep East, or, whispering, played
    A chequer-work of beam and shade
Along the hills, yet looked the same.

As wan, as chill, as wild as now;
    Day, marked as with some hideous crime,
    When the dark hand struck down through time,
And cancelled nature's best: but thou,

Lift as thou may'st thy burthened brows
    Through clouds that drench the morning star,
    And whirl the ungarnered sheaf afar,
And sow the sky with flying boughs,

And up thy vault with roaring sound
    Climb thy thick noon, disastrous day;

---

[5] *Dragons . . . prime:* prehistoric dinosaurs.

Touch thy dull goal of joyless gray,
And hide thy shame beneath the ground.

85

This truth came borne with bier and pall,
    I felt it, when I sorrowed most,
    'Tis better to have loved and lost,
Than never to have loved at all——

O true in word, and tried in deed,
    Demanding, so to bring relief
    To this which is our common grief,
What kind of life is that I lead;

And whether trust in things above
    Be dimmed of sorrow, or sustained;
    And whether love for him have drained
My capabilities of love;

Your words have virtue such as draws
    A faithful answer from the breast,
    Through light reproaches, half exprest,
And loyal unto kindly laws.

My blood an even tenor kept,
    Till on mine ear this message falls,
    That in Vienna's fatal walls
God's finger touched him, and he slept.

*   *   *

I woo your love: I count it crime
    To mourn for any overmuch;
    I, the divided half of such
A friendship as had mastered Time;

Which masters Time indeed, and is
    Eternal, separate from fears:
    The all-assuming months and years
Can take no part away from this:

But Summer on the steaming floods,
    And Spring that swells the narrow brooks,
    And Autumn, with a noise of rooks,
That gather in the waning woods,

244

And every pulse of wind and wave
  Recalls, in change of light or gloom,
  My old affection of the tomb,
And my prime passion in the grave:

My old affection of the tomb,
  A part of stillness, yearns to speak:
  "Arise, and get thee forth and seek
A friendship for the years to come.

"I watch thee from the quiet shore;
  Thy spirit up to mine can reach;
  But in dear words of human speech
We two communicate no more."

And I, "Can clouds of nature stain
  The starry clearness of the free?
  How is it? Canst thou feel for me
Some painless sympathy with pain?"

And lightly does the whisper fall;
  " 'Tis hard for thee to fathom this;
  I triumph in conclusive bliss,
And that serene result of all."

So hold I commerce with the dead;
  Or so methinks the dead would say;
  Or so shall grief with symbols play
And pining life be fancy-fed.

❖   ❖   ❖

95

By night we linger'd on the lawn,
  For underfoot the herb was dry;
  And genial warmth; and o'er the sky
The silvery haze of summer drawn;

And calm that let the tapers burn
  Unwavering: not a cricket chirr'd;
  The brook alone far-off was heard,
And on the board the fluttering urn.

And bats went round in fragrant skies,
  And wheel'd or lit the filmy shapes

That haunt the dusk, with ermine capes
And woolly breasts and beaded eyes;

While now we sang old songs that peal'd
   From knoll to knoll, where, couch'd at ease,
   The white kine glimmer'd, and the trees
Laid their dark arms about the field.

But when those others, one by one,
   Withdrew themselves from me and night,
   And in the house light after light
Went out, and I was all alone,

A hunger seized my heart; I read
   Of that glad year which once had been,
   In those fallen leaves which kept their green,
The noble letters of the dead.

And strangely on the silence broke
   The silent-speaking words, and strange
   Was love's dumb cry defying change
To test his worth; and strangely spoke

The faith, the vigor, bold to dwell
   On doubts that drive the coward back,
   And keen thro' wordy snares to track
Suggestion to her inmost cell.

So word by word, and line by line,
   The dead man touch'd me from the past,
   And all at once it seem'd at last
The living soul was flash'd on mine,

And mine in this was wound, and whirl'd
   About empyreal heights of thought,
   And came on that which is, and caught
The deep pulsations of the world,

Æonian music measuring out
   The steps of Time—the shocks of Chance—
   The blows of Death. At length my trance
Was cancell'd, stricken thro' with doubt.

Vague words! but ah, how hard to frame
   In matter-moulded forms of speech,

Or even for intellect to reach
Thro' memory that which I became;

Till now the doubtful dusk reveal'd
   The knolls once more where, couch'd at ease,
   The white kine glimmer'd, and the trees
Laid their dark arms about the field;

And suck'd from out the distant gloom
   A breeze began to tremble o'er
   The large leaves of the sycamore,
And fluctuate all the still perfume,

And gathering freshlier overhead,
   Rock'd the full-foliaged elms, and swung
   The heavy-folded rose, and flung
The lilies to and fro, and said,

"The dawn, the dawn," and died away;
   And East and West, without a breath,
   Mixt their dim lights, like life and death,
To broaden into boundless day.

96

You say, but with no touch of scorn,
   Sweet-hearted, you, whose light-blue eyes
   Are tender over drowning flies,
You tell me, doubt is Devil-born.

I know not: one indeed I knew
   In many a subtle question versed,
   Who touched a jarring lyre at first,
But ever strove to make it true:

Perplext in faith, but pure in deeds,
   At last he beat his music out.
   There lives more faith in honest doubt,
Believe me, than in half the creeds.

124

That which we dare invoke to bless;
   Our dearest faith; our ghastliest doubt;
   He, They, One, All; within, without;
The Power in darkness whom we guess;

I found Him not in world or sun,
    Or eagle's wing, or insect's eye;
    Nor through the questions men may try,
The petty cobwebs we have spun:

If e'er when faith had fall'n asleep,
    I heard a voice "believe no more"
    And heard an ever-breaking shore
That tumbled in the Godless deep;

A warmth within the breast would melt
    The freezing reason's colder part,
    And like a man in wrath the heart
Stood up and answered "I have felt."

No, like a child in doubt and fear:
    But that blind clamour made me wise;
    Then was I as a child that cries,
But, crying, knows his father near;

And what I am beheld again
    What is, and no man understands;
    And out of darkness came the hands
That reach through nature, moulding men.

       ❈   ❈   ❈

from THE PROLOGUE

    . . . A soul shall draw from out the vast
And strike his being into bounds,

And, moved through life of lower phase,
    Result in man, be born and think,
    And act and love, a closer link
Betwixt us and the crowning race

Of those that, eye to eye, shall look
    On knowledge; under whose command
    Is Earth and Earth's, and in their hand
Is Nature like an open book;

No longer half-akin to brute,
    For all we thought and loved and did,
    And hoped, and suffered, is but seed
Of what in them is flower and fruit;

Whereof the man, that with me trod
  This planet, was a noble type
  Appearing ere the times were ripe,
That friend of mine who lives in God,

That God, which ever lives and loves,
  One God, one law, one element,
  And one far-off divine event,
To which the whole creation moves.

AN AMERICAN ROMANTIC
AND PSYCHOLOGICAL REALITY

ANNABEL LEE

It was many and many a year ago,
   In a kingdom by the sea,
That a maiden there lived whom you may know
   By the name of Annabel Lee:
And this maiden she lived with no other thought   5
   Than to love and be loved by me.

She was a child and *I* was a child,
   In this kingdom by the sea;
But we loved with a love that was more than love—
   I and my Annabel Lee—   10
With a love that the wingèd seraphs of heaven
   Coveted her and me.

And this was the reason that, long ago,
   In this kingdom by the sea,
A wind blew out of a cloud, chilling   15
   My beautiful Annabel Lee—
So that her highborn kinsmen came
   And bore her away from me,
To shut her up in a sepulchre
   In this kingdom by the sea.   20

The angels, not half so happy in Heaven,
   Went envying her and me:—
Yes, that was the reason (as all men know,

250

In this kingdom by the sea)
That the wind came out of the cloud by night   25
   Chilling and killing my Annabel Lee.

But our love it was stronger by far than the love
   Of those who were older than we—
   Of many far wiser than we—
And neither the angels in Heaven above,   30
   Nor the demons down under the sea,
Can ever dissever my soul from the soul
   Of the beautiful Annabel Lee:—

For the moon never beams, without bringing me
      dreams
Of the beautiful Annabel Lee;   35
And the stars never rise, but I feel the bright eyes
   Of the beautiful Annabel Lee;
And so, all the night-tide, I lie down by the side
Of my darling, my darling, my life and my bride
   In her sepulchre there by the sea—   40
   In her tomb by the sounding sea.

THE CITY IN THE SEA

Lo! Death has reared himself a throne
In a strange city lying alone
Far down within the dim West,
Where the good and the bad and the worst and the best
Have gone to their eternal rest.
There shrines and palaces and towers
(Time-eaten towers that tremble not!)
Resemble nothing that is ours.
Around, by lifting winds forgot,
Resignedly beneath the sky   10
The melancholy waters lie.

No rays from the holy heaven come down
On the long night-time of that town;
But light from out the lurid sea
Streams up the turrets silently—
Gleams up the pinnacles far and free—
Up domes—up spires—up kingly halls—
Up fanes—up Babylon-like walls—
Up shadowy long-forgotten bowers
Of sculptured ivy and stone flowers—   20
Up many and many a marvellous shrine

251

.

Whose wreathéd friezes intertwine
The viol, the violet, and the vine.

Resignedly beneath the sky
The melancholy waters lie.
So blend the turrets and shadows there
That all seem pendulous in air,
While from a proud tower in the town
Death looks gigantically down.

There open fanes and gaping graves
Yawn level with the luminous waves;
But not the riches there that lie
In each idol's diamond eye—
Not the gaily-jewelled dead
Tempt the waters from their bed;
For no ripples curl, alas!
Along that wilderness of glass—
No swellings tell that winds may be
Upon some far-off happier sea—
No heavings hint that winds have been
On seas less hideously serene.

But lo, a stir is in the air!
The wave—there is a movement there!
As if the towers had thrust aside,
In slightly sinking, the dull tide—
As if their tops had feebly given
A void within the filmy Heaven.
The waves have now a redder glow—
The hours are breathing faint and low—
And when, amid no earthly moans,
Down, down that town shall settle hence,
Hell, rising from a thousand thrones,
Shall do it reverence.

EUREKA

AN ESSAY ON THE MATERIAL AND SPIRITUAL UNIVERSE

(To the few who love me and whom I love—to those who feel rather than to those who think—to the dreamers and those who put faith in dreams as in the only realities—I offer this Book of Truths, not in its character of Truth-Teller, but for the Beauty that abounds in its Truth—constituting it true. To these

I present the composition as an Art-Product alone—let us say as a Romance; or, if I be not urging too lofty a claim, as a Poem.

What I here propound is true—therefore it cannot die:—or if by any means it be now trodden down so that it die, it will "rise again to the Life Everlasting."

Nevertheless, it is as a Poem only that I wish this work to be judged after I am dead.—E. A. P.)

* * *

. . . I have already alluded to that absolute *reciprocity of adaptation* which is the idiosyncrasy of the divine Art—stamping it divine. Up to this point of our reflection, we have been regarding the electrical influence as a something by dint of whose repulsion alone Matter is enabled to exist in that state of diffusion demanded for the fulfilment of its purposes:—so far, in a word, we have been considering the influence in question as ordained for Matter's sake to subserve the objects of matter. With a perfectly legitimate reciprocity, we are now permitted to look at Matter as created *solely for the sake of this influence*—solely to serve the objects of this spiritual Ether. Through the aid—by the means—through the agency of matter, and by dint of its heterogeneity—is this Ether manifested—is *Spirit individualised*. It is merely in the development of this Ether, through heterogeneity, that particular masses of Matter become animate—sensitive—and in the ratio of their heterogeneity;—some reaching a degree of sensitiveness involving what we call *Thought*, and thus attaining Conscious Intelligence.

In this view, we are enabled to perceive Matter as a Means not as an End. Its purposes are thus seen to have been comprehended in its diffusion; and with the return into Unity these purposes cease. The absolutely consolidated globe of globes would be *objectless*—therefore not for a moment could it continue to exist. Matter, created for an end, would unquestionably, on fulfilment of that end, be Matter no longer. Let us endeavour to understand that it would disappear, and that God would remain all in all.

. . . When, on fulfilment of its purposes, then, Matter shall have returned into its original condition of *One*—a condition which presupposes the expulsion of the separative ether, whose province and whose capacity are limited to keeping the atoms apart until that great day when, this ether being no longer needed, the overwhelming pressure of the finally collective Attraction shall at length just sufficiently predominate and expel it:—when, I say, Matter, finally expelling the Ether, shall have returned into absolute Unity—it will then (to speak paradoxically for the moment) be Matter without Attraction and without Repulsion—in other words,

Matter without Matter—in other words, again, *Matter no more.*
In sinking into Unity, it will sink at once into that Nothingness
which, to all Finite Perception, Unity must be—into that Material
Nihility from which alone we can conceive it to have been evoked
—to have been *created* by the Volition of God.

I repeat, then, let us endeavour to comprehend that the final
globe of globes will instantaneously disappear, and that God will
remain all in all.

But are we here to pause? Not so. On the Universal agglomera-
tion and dissolution, we can readily conceive that a new and perhaps totally different series of conditions may ensue—another
creation and irradiation, returning into itself—another action and
reaction of the Divine Will. Guiding our imagination by that omniprevalent law of laws, the law of periodicity, are we not, indeed,
more than justified in entertaining a belief—let us say, rather, in
indulging a hope—that the processes we have here ventured to
contemplate will be renewed for ever, and for ever, and for ever;
a novel Universe swelling into existence, and then subsiding into
nothingness, at every throb of the Heart Divine?

And now—this Heart Divine—what *is* it? *It is our own.*

Let not the merely seeming irreverence of this idea frighten our
souls from that cool exercise of consciousness—from that deep
tranquillity of self-inspection—through which alone we can hope
to attain the presence of this, the most sublime of truths, and look
it leisurely in the face.

The *phenomena* on which our conclusions must at this point
depend are merely spiritual shadows, but not the less thoroughly
substantial.

We walk about, amid the destinies of our world-existence, encompassed by dim but ever present *Memories* of a Destiny more
vast—very distant in the by-gone time, and infinitely awful.

We live out a Youth peculiarly haunted by such dreams; yet
never mistaking them for dreams. As Memories we *know* them.
During our Youth the distinction is too clear to deceive us even
for a moment.

So long as this Youth endures, the feeling *that we exist* is the
most natural of all feelings. We understand it *thoroughly.* That
there was a period at which we did *not* exist—or that it might so
have happened that we never had existed at all—are the considerations, indeed, which *during this youth* we find difficulty in understanding. Why we should *not* exist is, *up to the epoch of our Manhood,* of all queries the most unanswerable. Existence—self-exist-
ence—existence from all Time and to all Eternity—seems, up to
the epoch of Manhood, a normal and unquestionable condition:—
seems, because it is.

But now comes the period at which a conventional World-Reason awakens us from the truth of our dream. Doubt, Surprise, and Incomprehensibility arrive at the same moment. They say:—"You live, and the time was when you lived not. You have been created. An Intelligence exists greater than your own; and it is only through this Intelligence you live at all." These things we struggle to comprehend and cannot—*cannot*, because these things, being untrue, are thus, of necessity, incomprehensible.

No thinking being lives who, at some luminous point of his life of thought, has not felt himself lost amid the surges of futile efforts at understanding or believing that anything exists *greater than his own soul*. The utter impossibility of any one soul feeling itself inferior to another; the intense, overwhelming dissatisfaction and rebellion at the thought;—these, with the omniprevalent aspirations at perfection, are but the spiritual, coincident with the material, struggles towards the original Unity—are, to my mind at least, a species of proof far surpassing what Man terms demonstration, that no one soul *is* inferior to another—that nothing is, or can be, superior to any one soul—that each soul is, in part, its own God—its own Creator:—in a word, that God—the material *and* spiritual God—*now* exists solely in the diffused Matter and Spirit of the Universe; and that the regathering of this diffused Matter and Spirit will be but the reconstitution of the *purely* Spiritual and Individual God.

In this view, and in this view alone, we comprehend the riddles of Divine Injustice—of Inexorable Fate. In this view alone the existence of Evil becomes intelligible; but in this view it becomes more—it becomes endurable. Our souls no longer rebel at a *Sorrow* which we ourselves have imposed upon ourselves, in furtherance of our own purposes—with a view—if even with a futile view—to the extension of our own *Joy*.

I have spoken of *Memories* that haunt us during our youth. They sometimes pursue us even in our Manhood:—assume gradually less and less indefinite shapes:—now and then speak to us with low voices, saying:

"There was an epoch in the Night of Time when a still-existent Being existed—one of an absolutely infinite number of similar Beings that people the absolutely infinite domains of the absolutely infinite space. It was not and is not in the power of this Being—any more than it is in your own—to extend, by actual increase, the joy of his Existence; but just as it *is* in your power to expand or to concentrate your pleasures (the absolute amount of happiness remaining always the same) so did and does a similar capability appertain to this divine being, who thus passes his Eternity in perpetual variation of Concentrated Self and almost Infinite Self-Diffu-

EDGAR ALLAN POE

sion. What you call The Universe is but his present expansive
existence. He now feels his life through an infinity of imperfect
pleasures—the partial and pain-intertangled pleasures of those
inconceivably numerous things which you designate as his creatures, but which are really but infinite individualisations of Himself. All these creatures—*all*—those which you term animate, as
well as those to whom you deny life for no better reason than that
you do not behold it in operation—*all* these creatures have, in a
greater or less degree, a capacity for pleasure and for pain:—*but
the general sum of their sensations is precisely that amount of
Happiness which appertains by right to the Divine Being when
concentrated within Himself.* These creatures are all, too, more or
less conscious Intelligences; conscious, first, of a proper identity;
conscious, secondly, and by faint indeterminate glimpses, of an
identity with the Divine Being of whom we speak—of an identity
with God. Of the two classes of consciousness, fancy that the former
will grow weaker, the latter stronger, during the long succession
of ages which must elapse before these myriads of individual Intelligences become blended—when the bright stars become blended
—into One. Think that the sense of individual identity will be
gradually merged in the general consciousness—that Man, for example, ceasing imperceptibly to feel himself Man, will at length
attain that awfully triumphant epoch when he shall recognize his
existence as that of Jehovah. In the meantime bear in mind that
all is Life—Life—Life within Life—the less within the greater,
and all within the *Spirit Divine.*"

nathaniel hawthorne

AN ANALYSIS OF A SCIENTIST'S MORALITY

["The Birthmark"; from *Mosses from an Old Manse* (1846).] In the latter part of the last century there lived a man of science, an eminent proficient in every branch of natural philosophy, who not long before our story opens had made experience of a spiritual affinity more attractive than any chemical one. He had left his laboratory to the care of an assistant, cleared his fine countenance from the furnace smoke, washed the stain of acids from his fingers, and persuaded a beautiful woman to become his wife. In those days, when the comparatively recent discovery of electricity and other kindred mysteries of Nature seemed to open paths into the region of miracle, it was not unusual for the love of science to rival the love of woman in its depth and absorbing energy. The higher intellect, the imagination, the spirit, and even the heart might all find their congenial aliment in pursuits which, as some of their ardent votaries believed, would ascend from one step of powerful intelligence to another, until the philosopher should lay his hand on the secret of creative force and perhaps make new worlds for himself. We know not whether Aylmer possessed this degree of faith in man's ultimate control over Nature. He had devoted himself, however, too unreservedly to scientific studies ever to be weaned from them by any second passion. His love for his young wife might prove the stronger of the two; but it could only be by intertwining itself with his love of science and uniting the strength of the latter to his own.

Such a union accordingly took place, and was attended with truly remarkable consequences and a deeply impressive moral. One day, very soon after their marriage, Aylmer sat gazing at his wife with a trouble in his countenance that grew stronger until he spoke.

"Georgiana," said he, "has it never occurred to you that the mark upon your cheek might be removed?"

"No, indeed," said she, smiling; but, perceiving the seriousness of his manner, she blushed deeply. "To tell you the truth, it has been so often called a charm that I was simple enough to imagine it might be so."

"Ah, upon another face perhaps it might," replied her husband; "but never on yours. No, dearest Georgiana, you came so nearly perfect from the hand of Nature that this slightest possible defect, which we hesitate whether to term a defect or a beauty, shocks me, as being the visible mark of earthly imperfection."

"Shocks you, my husband!" cried Georgiana, deeply hurt; at first reddening with momentary anger, but then bursting into tears. "Then why did you take me from my mother's side? You cannot love what shocks you!"

To explain this conversation, it must be mentioned that in the centre of Georgiana's left cheek there was a singular mark, deeply interwoven, as it were, with the texture and substance of her face. In the usual state of her complexion—a healthy though delicate bloom—the mark wore a tint of deeper crimson, which imperfectly defined its shape amid the surrounding rosiness. When she blushed it gradually became more indistinct, and finally vanished amid the triumphant rush of blood that bathed the whole cheek with its brilliant glow. But if any shifting motion caused her to turn pale there was the mark again, a crimson stain upon the snow, in what Aylmer sometimes deemed an almost fearful distinctness. Its shape bore not a little similarity to the human hand, though of the smallest pygmy size. Georgiana's lovers were wont to say that some fairy at her birth hour had laid her tiny hand upon the infant's cheek, and left this impress there in token of the magic endowments that were to give her such sway over all hearts. Many a desperate swain would have risked life for the privilege of pressing his lips to the mysterious hand. It must not be concealed, however, that the impression wrought by this fairy sign manual varied exceedingly according to the difference of temperament in the beholders. Some fastidious persons—but they were exclusively of her own sex—affirmed that the bloody hand, as they chose to call it, quite destroyed the effect of Georgiana's beauty and rendered her countenance even hideous. But it would be as reasonable to say that one of those small blue stains which sometimes occur in the purest statuary marble would convert the Eve of Powers[1] to a monster Masculine observers, if the birthmark did not heighten their admiration, contented themselves with wishing it away, that the

---

[1] A famous statue by the American sculptor Hiram Powers (1805-73).

world might possess one living specimen of ideal loveliness without the semblance of a flaw. After his marriage,—for he thought
little or nothing of the matter before,—Aylmer discovered that
this was the case with himself.

Had she been less beautiful,—if Envy's self could have found
aught else to sneer at,—he might have felt his affection heightened
by the prettiness of this mimic hand, now vaguely portrayed, now
lost, now stealing forth again and glimmering to and fro with
every pulse of emotion that throbbed within her heart; but, seeing
her otherwise so perfect, he found this one defect grow more and
more intolerable with every moment of their united lives. It was
the fatal flaw of humanity which Nature, in one shape or another,
stamps ineffaceably on all her productions, either to imply that they
are temporary and finite, or that their perfection must be wrought
by toil and pain. The crimson hand expressed the ineludible gripe
in which mortality clutches the highest and purest of earthly
mould, degrading them into kindred with the lowest, and even
with the very brutes, like whom their visible frames return to dust.
In this manner, selecting it as the symbol of his wife's liability to
sin, sorrow, decay, and death, Aylmer's sombre imagination was
not long in rendering the birthmark a frightful object, causing
him more trouble and horror than ever Georgiana's beauty,
whether of soul or sense, had given him delight.

At all the seasons which should have been their happiest he
invariably, and without intending it, nay, in spite of a purpose to
the contrary, reverted to this one disastrous topic. Trifling as it at
first appeared, it so connected itself with innumerable trains of
thought and modes of feeling that it became the central point of
all. With the morning twilight Aylmer opened his eyes upon his
wife's face and recognized the symbol of imperfection; and when
they sat together at the evening hearth his eyes wandered stealth-
ily to her cheek, and beheld, flickering with the blaze of the wood
fire, the spectral hand that wrote mortality where he would fain
have worshipped. Georgiana soon learned to shudder at his gaze. It
needed but a glance with the peculiar expression that his face often
wore to change the roses of her cheek into a deathlike paleness,
amid which the crimson hand was brought strongly out, like a bass
relief of ruby on the whitest marble.

Late one night, when the lights were growing dim so as hardly
to betray the stain on the poor wife's cheek, she herself, for the
first time, voluntarily took up the subject.

"Do you remember, my dear Aylmer," said she, with a feeble
attempt at a smile, "have you any recollection, of a dream last
night about this odious hand?"

"None! none whatever!" replied Aylmer, starting; but then he added, in a dry, cold tone, affected for the sake of concealing the real depth of his emotion, "I might well dream of it; for, before I fell asleep, it had taken a pretty firm hold of my fancy."

"And you did dream of it?" continued Georgiana, hastily; for she dreaded lest a gush of tears should interrupt what she had to say. "A terrible dream! I wonder that you can forget it. Is it possible to forget this one expression?—'It is in her heart now; we must have it out!' Reflect, my husband; for by all means I would have you recall that dream."

The mind is in a sad state when Sleep, the all-involving, cannot confine her spectres within the dim region of her sway, but suffers them to break forth, affrighting this actual life with secrets that perchance belong to a deeper one. Aylmer now remembered his dream. He had fancied himself with his servant Aminadab, attempting an operation for the removal of the birthmark; but the deeper went the knife, the deeper sank the hand, until at length its tiny grasp appeared to have caught hold of Georgiana's heart; whence, however, her husband was inexorably resolved to cut or wrench it away.

When the dream had shaped itself perfectly in his memory Aylmer sat in his wife's presence with a guilty feeling. Truth often finds its way to the mind close muffled in robes of sleep, and then speaks with uncompromising directness of matters in regard to which we practise an unconscious self-deception during our waking moments. Until now he had not been aware of the tyrannizing influence acquired by one idea over his mind, and of the lengths which he might find in his heart to go for the sake of giving himself peace.

"Aylmer," resumed Georgiana, solemnly, "I know not what may be the cost to both of us to rid me of this fatal birthmark. Perhaps its removal may cause cureless deformity; or it may be the stain goes as deep as life itself. Again: do we know that there is a possibility, on any terms, of unclasping the firm gripe of this little hand which was laid upon me before I came into the world?"

"Dearest Georgiana, I have spent much thought upon the subject," hastily interrupted Aylmer. "I am convinced of the perfect practicability of its removal."

"If there be the remotest possibility of it," continued Georgiana, "let the attempt be made, at whatever risk. Danger is nothing to me; for life, while this hateful mark makes me the object of your horror and disgust,—life is a burden which I would fling down with joy. Either remove this dreadful hand, or take my wretched life! You have deep science. All the world bears witness of it. You have achieved great wonders. Cannot you remove this little, little mark, which I cover with the tips of two small fingers? Is this beyond your power, for the sake of your own peace, and to save your poor wife from madness?"

"Noblest, dearest, tenderest wife," cried Aylmer, rapturously, "doubt not my power. I have already given this matter the deepest thought—thought which might almost have enlightened me to create a being less perfect than yourself. Georgiana, you have led me deeper than ever into the heart of science. I feel myself fully competent to render this dear cheek as faultless as its fellow; and then, most beloved, what will be my triumph when I shall have corrected what Nature left imperfect in her fairest work! Even Pygmalion, when his sculptured woman assumed life, felt not greater ecstasy than mine will be."

"It is resolved, then," said Georgiana, faintly smiling. "And, Aylmer, spare me not, though you should find the birthmark take refuge in my heart at last."

Her husband tenderly kissed her cheek—her right cheek—not that which bore the impress of the crimson hand.

The next day Aylmer apprised his wife of a plan that he had formed whereby he might have opportunity for the intense thought and constant watchfulness which the proposed operation would require; while Georgiana, likewise, would enjoy the perfect repose essential to its success. They were to seclude themselves in the extensive apartments occupied by Aylmer as a laboratory, and where, during his toilsome youth, he had made discoveries in the elemental powers of Nature that had roused the admiration of all the learned societies in Europe. Seated calmly in this laboratory, the pale philosopher had investigated the secrets of the highest cloud region and of the profoundest mines; he had satisfied himself of the causes that kindled and kept alive the fires of the volcano; and had explained the mystery of fountains, and how it is that they gush forth, some so bright and pure, and others with such rich medicinal virtues from the dark bosom of the earth. Here, too, at an earlier period, he had studied the wonders of the human frame, and attempted to fathom the very process by which Nature assimilates all her precious influences from earth and air, and from the spiritual world, to create and foster man, her masterpiece. The latter pursuit, however, Aylmer had long laid aside in unwilling recognition of the truth—against which all seekers sooner or later stumble—that our great creative Mother, while she amuses us with apparently working in the broadest sunshine, is yet severely careful to keep her own secrets, and, in spite of her pretended openness, shows us nothing but results. She permits us, indeed, to mar, but seldom to mend, and, like a jealous patentee, on no account to make. Now, however, Aylmer resumed these half-forgotten investigations; not, of course, with such hopes or wishes as first suggested them; but because they involved much physiological truth and lay in the path of his proposed scheme for the treatment of Georgiana.

As he led her over the threshold of the laboratory, Georgiana was cold and tremulous. Aylmer looked cheerfully into her face, with intent to reassure her, but was so startled with the intense glow of the birthmark upon the whiteness of her cheek that he could not restrain a strong convulsive shudder. His wife fainted.

"Aminadab! Aminadab!" shouted Aylmer, stamping violently on the floor.

Forthwith there issued from an inner apartment a man of low stature, but bulky frame, with shaggy hair hanging about his visage, which was grimed with the vapors of the furnace. This personage had been Aylmer's underworker during his whole scientific career, and was admirably fitted for that office by his great mechanical readiness, and the skill with which, while incapable of comprehending a single principle, he executed all the details of his master's experiments. With his vast strength, his shaggy hair, his smoky aspect, and the indescribable earthiness that incrusted him, he seemed to represent man's physical nature; while Aylmer's slender figure, and pale, intellectual face, were no less apt a type of the spiritual element.

"Throw open the door of the boudoir, Aminadab," said Aylmer, "and burn a pastil."

"Yes, master," answered Aminadab, looking intently at the lifeless form of Georgiana; and then he muttered to himself, "If she were my wife, I'd never part with that birthmark."

When Georgiana recovered consciousness she found herself breathing an atmosphere of penetrating fragrance, the gentle potency of which had recalled her from her deathlike faintness. The scene around her looked like enchantment. Aylmer had converted those smoky, dingy, sombre rooms, where he had spent his brightest years in recondite pursuits, into a series of beautiful apartments not unfit to be the secluded abode of a lovely woman. The walls were hung with gorgeous curtains, which imparted the combination of grandeur and grace that no other species of adornment can achieve; and, as they fell from the ceiling to the floor, their rich and ponderous folds, concealing all angles and straight lines, appeared to shut in the scene from infinite space. For aught Georgiana knew, it might be a pavilion among the clouds. And Aylmer, excluding the sunshine, which would have interfered with his chemical processes, had supplied its place with perfumed lamps, emitting flames of various hue, but all uniting in a soft, impurpled radiance. He now knelt by his wife's side, watching her earnestly, but without alarm;

for he was confident in his science, and felt that he could draw a magic circle round her within which no evil might intrude.

"Where am I? Ah, I remember," said Georgiana, faintly; and she placed her hand over her cheek to hide the terrible mark from her husband's eyes.

"Fear not, dearest!" exclaimed he. "Do not shrink from me! Believe me, Georgiana, I even rejoice in this single imperfection, since it will be such a rapture to remove it."

"O, spare me!" sadly replied his wife. "Pray do not look at it again. I never can forget that convulsive shudder."

In order to soothe Georgiana, and, as it were, to release her mind from the burden of actual things, Aylmer now put in practice some of the light and playful secrets which science had taught him among its profounder lore. Airy figures, absolutely bodiless ideas, and forms of unsubstantial beauty came and danced before her, imprinting their momentary footsteps on beams of light. Though she had some indistinct idea of the method of these optical phenomena, still the illusion was almost perfect enough to warrant the belief that her husband possessed sway over the spiritual world. Then again, when she felt a wish to look forth from her seclusion, immediately, as if her thoughts were answered, the procession of external existence flitted across a screen. The scenery and the figures of actual life were perfectly represented, but with that bewitching yet indescribable difference which always makes a picture, an image, or a shadow so much more attractive than the original. When wearied of this, Aylmer bade her cast her eyes upon a vessel containing a quantity of earth. She did so, with little interest at first; but was soon startled to perceive the germ of a plant shooting upward from the soil. Then came the slender stalk; the leaves gradually unfolded themselves; and amid them was a perfect and lovely flower.

"It is magical!" cried Georgiana. "I dare not touch it."

"Nay, pluck it," answered Aylmer,—"pluck it, and inhale its brief perfume while you may. The flower will wither in a few moments and leave nothing save its brown seed vessels; but thence may be perpetuated a race as ephemeral as itself."

But Georgiana had no sooner touched the flower than the whole plant suffered a blight, its leaves turning coal-black as if by the agency of fire.

"There was too powerful a stimulus," said Aylmer, thoughtfully.

To make up for this abortive experiment, he proposed to take her portrait by a scientific process of his own invention. It was to be effected by rays of light striking upon a polished plate of metal. Georgiana assented; but, on looking at the result, was affrighted to find the features of the portrait blurred and indefinable; while the minute figure of a hand appeared where the cheek should have been. Aylmer snatched the metallic plate and threw it into a jar of corrosive acid.

Soon, however, he forgot these mortifying failures. In the intervals of study and chemical experiment he came to her flushed and exhausted, but seemed invigorated by her presence, and spoke in glowing language of the resources of his art. He gave a history of the long dynasty of the alchemists, who spent so many ages in quest of the universal solvent by which the golden principle might be elicited from all things vile and base. Aylmer appeared to believe that, by the plainest scientific logic, it was altogether within the limits of possibility to discover this long-sought medium; "but," he added, "a philosopher who should go deep enough to acquire the power would attain too lofty a wisdom to stoop to the exercise of it." Not less singular were his opinions in regard to the elixir vitae. He more than intimated that it was at his option to concoct a liquid that should prolong life for years, perhaps interminably; but that it would produce a discord in Nature which all the world, and chiefly the quaffer of the immortal nostrum, would find cause to curse.

"Aylmer, are you in earnest?" asked Georgiana, looking at him with amazement and fear. "It is terrible to possess such power, or even to dream of possessing it."

"O, do not tremble, my love," said her husband. "I would not wrong either you or myself by working such inharmonious effects upon our lives; but I would have you consider how trifling, in comparison, is the skill requisite to remove this little hand."

At the mention of the birthmark, Georgiana, as usual, shrank as if a red-hot iron had touched her cheek.

Again Aylmer applied himself to his labors. She could hear his voice in the distant furnace room giving directions to Aminadab, whose harsh, uncouth, misshapen tones were audible in response, more like the grunt or growl of a brute than human speech. After hours of absence, Aylmer reappeared and proposed that she should now examine his cabinet of chemical products and natural treasures of the earth. Among the former he showed her a small vial, in which, he remarked, was contained a gentle yet most powerful fragrance, capable of impregnating all the breezes that blow across a kingdom. They were of inestimable value, the contents of that little vial; and, as he said so, he threw some of the perfume into the air and filled the room with piercing and invigorating delight.

"And what is this?" asked Georgiana, pointing to a small crystal globe containing a gold-colored liquid. "It is so beautiful to the eye that I could imagine it the elixir of life."

"In one sense it is," replied Aylmer; "or rather, the elixir of immortality. It is the most precious poison that ever was concocted in this world. By its aid I could apportion the life-time of any mortal at whom you might point your finger. The strength of the dose would determine whether he were to linger out years, or drop dead in the midst of a breath. No king on his guarded throne could keep his life if I, in my private station, should deem that the welfare of millions justified me in depriving him of it."

"Why do you keep such a terrific drug?" inquired Georgiana in horror.

"Do not mistrust me, dearest," said her husband, smiling; "its virtuous potency is yet greater than its harmful one. But see! here is a powerful cosmetic. With a few drops of this in a vase of water, freckles may be washed away as easily as the hands are cleansed. A stronger infusion would take the blood out of the cheek, and leave the rosiest beauty a pale ghost."

"Is it with this lotion that you intend to bathe my cheek?" asked Georgiana, anxiously.

"O, no," hastily replied her husband; "this is merely superficial. Your case demands a remedy that shall go deeper."

In his interviews with Georgiana, Aylmer generally made minute inquiries as to her sensations, and whether the confinement of the rooms and the temperature of the atmosphere agreed with her. These questions had such a particular drift that Georgiana began to conjecture that she was already subjected to certain physical influences, either breathed in with the fragrant air or taken with her food. She fancied likewise, but it might be altogether fancy, that there was a stirring up of her system—a strange, indefinite sensation creeping through her veins, and tingling, half painfully, half pleasurably, at her heart. Still, whenever she dared to look into the mirror, there she beheld herself pale as a white rose and with the crimson birthmark stamped upon her cheek. Not even Aylmer now hated it so much as she.

To dispel the tedium of the hours which her husband found it necessary to devote to the processes of combination and analysis, Georgiana turned over the volumes of his scientific library. In many dark old tomes she met with chapters full of romance and poetry. They were the works of the philosophers of the middle ages, such as Albertus Magnus, Cornelius Agrippa, Paracelsus, and the famous friar who created the prophetic Brazen Head.[2] All these antique

---

[2] Medieval scholastics who delved in science. The *famous friar* is Roger Bacon (1214?-1294), who was reputed to have been interested in magic and to have created a bronze head that could see into the past and the future. The story of Roger Bacon and his bronze head was dramatized in *The Honourable History of Friar Bacon and Friar Bungay*, a play by Robert Greene (1558-1592).

naturalists stood in advance of their centuries, yet were imbued with some of their credulity, and therefore were believed, and perhaps imagined themselves to have acquired from the investigation of Nature a power above Nature, and from physics a sway over the spiritual world. Hardly less curious and imaginative were the early volumes of the Transactions of the Royal Society,[3] in which the members, knowing little of the limits of natural possibility, were continually recording wonders or proposing methods whereby wonders might be wrought.

But to Georgiana, the most engrossing volume was a large folio from her husband's own hand, in which he had recorded every experiment of his scientific career, its original aim, the methods adopted for its development, and its final success or failure, with the circumstances to which either event was attributable. The book, in truth, was both the history and emblem of his ardent, ambitious, imaginative, yet practical and laborious life. He handled physical details as if there were nothing beyond them; yet spiritualized them all and redeemed himself from materialism by his strong and eager aspiration towards the infinite. In his grasp the veriest clod of earth assumed a soul. Georgiana, as she read, reverenced Aylmer and loved him more profoundly than ever, but with a less entire dependence on his judgment than heretofore. Much as he had accomplished, she could not but observe that his most splendid successes were almost invariably failures, if compared with the ideal at which he aimed. His brightest diamonds were the merest pebbles, and felt to be so by himself, in comparison with the inestimable gems which lay hidden beyond his reach. The volume, rich with achievements that had won renown for its author, was yet as melancholy a record as ever mortal hand had penned. It was the sad confession and continual exemplification of the shortcomings of the composite man, the spirit burdened with clay and working in matter, and of the despair that assails the higher nature at finding itself so miserably thwarted by the earthly part. Perhaps every man of genius, in whatever sphere, might recognize the image of his own experience in Aylmer's journal.

So deeply did these reflections affect Georgiana that she laid her face upon the open volume and burst into tears. In this situation she was found by her husband.

"It is dangerous to read in a sorcerer's books," said he with a smile, though his countenance was uneasy and displeased. "Georgiana, there are pages in that volume which I can scarcely glance over and keep my senses. Take heed lest it prove detrimental to you."

[3] English scientific organization founded in 1662.

"It has made me worship you more than ever," said she.

"Ah, wait for this one success," rejoined he, "then worship me if you will. I shall deem myself hardly unworthy of it. But come, I have sought you for the luxury of your voice. Sing to me, dearest."

So she poured out the liquid music of her voice to quench the thirst of his spirit. He then took his leave with a boyish exuberance of gayety, assuring her that her seclusion would endure but a little longer, and that the result was already certain. Scarcely had he departed when Georgiana felt irresistibly impelled to follow him. She had forgotten to inform Aylmer of a symptom which for two or three hours past had begun to excite her attention. It was a sensation in the fatal birthmark, not painful, but which induced a restlessness throughout her system. Hastening after her husband, she intruded for the first time into the laboratory.

The first thing that struck her eye was the furnace, that hot and feverish worker, with the intense glow of its fire, which by the quantities of soot clustered above it seemed to have been burning for ages. There was a distilling apparatus in full operation. Around the room were retorts, tubes, cylinders, crucibles, and other apparatus of chemical research. An electrical machine stood ready for immediate use. The atmosphere felt oppressively close, and was tainted with gaseous odors which had been tormented forth by the processes of science. The severe and homely simplicity of the apartment, with its naked walls and brick pavement, looked strange, accustomed as Georgiana had become to the fantastic elegance of her boudoir. But what chiefly, indeed almost solely, drew her attention, was the aspect of Aylmer himself.

He was pale as death, anxious and absorbed, and hung over the furnace as if it depended upon his utmost watchfulness whether the liquid which it was distilling should be the draught of immortal happiness or misery. How different from the sanguine and joyous mien that he had assumed for Georgiana's encouragement!

"Carefully now, Aminadab; carefully, thou human machine; carefully, thou man of clay," muttered Aylmer, more to himself than his assistant. "Now, if there be a thought too much or too little, it is all over."

"Ho! ho!" mumbled Aminadab. "Look, master! look!"

Aylmer raised his eyes hastily, and at first reddened, then grew paler than ever, on beholding Georgiana. He rushed towards her and seized her arm with a gripe that left the print of his fingers upon it.

"Why do you come hither? Have you no trust in your husband?" cried he, impetuously. "Would you throw the blight of that fatal birthmark over my labors? It is not well done. Go, prying woman! go!"

"Nay, Aylmer," said Georgiana with the firmness of which she possessed no stinted endowment, "it is not you that have a right to complain. You mistrust your wife; you have concealed the anxiety with which you watch the development of this experiment. Think not so unworthily of me, my husband. Tell me all the risk we run, and fear not that I shall shrink; for my share in it is far less than your own."

"No, no, Georgiana!" said Aylmer, impatiently; "it must not be."

"I submit," replied she, calmly. "And, Aylmer, I shall quaff whatever draught you bring me; but it will be on the same principle that would induce me to take a dose of poison if offered by your hand."

"My noble wife," said Aylmer, deeply moved, "I knew not the height and depth of your nature until now. Nothing shall be concealed. Know, then, that this crimson hand, superficial as it seems, has clutched its grasp into your being with a strength of which I had no previous conception. I have already administered agents powerful enough to do aught except to change your entire physical system. Only one thing remains to be tried. If that fail us we are ruined."

"Why did you hesitate to tell me this?" asked she.

"Because, Georgiana," said Aylmer, in a low voice, "there is danger."

"Danger? There is but one danger—that this horrible stigma shall be left upon my cheek!" cried Georgiana. "Remove it, remove it, whatever be the cost, or we shall both go mad!"

"Heaven knows your words are too true," said Aylmer, sadly. "And now, dearest, return to your boudoir. In a little while all will be tested."

He conducted her back and took leave of her with a solemn tenderness which spoke far more than his words how much was now at stake. After his departure Georgiana became rapt in musings. She considered the character of Aylmer and did it completer justice than at any previous moment. Her heart exulted, while it trembled, at his honorable love—so pure and lofty that it would accept nothing less than perfection nor miserably make itself contented with an earthlier nature than he had dreamed of. She felt how much more precious was such a sentiment than that meaner kind which would have borne with the imperfection for her sake, and have been guilty of treason to holy love by degrading its perfect idea to the level of the actual; and with her whole spirit she prayed that, for a single moment, she might satisfy his highest and deepest conception. Longer than one moment she well knew it could not be; for his spirit was ever on the march, ever ascending, and each instant required something that was beyond the scope of the instant before.

The sound of her husband's footsteps aroused her. He bore a crystal goblet containing a liquor colorless as water, but bright enough to be the draught of immortality. Aylmer was pale; but it seemed rather the consequence of a highly-wrought state of mind and tension of spirit than of fear or doubt.

"The concoction of the draught has been perfect," said he, in answer to Georgiana's look. "Unless all my science have deceived me, it cannot fail."

"Save on your account, my dearest Aylmer," observed his wife, "I might wish to put off this birthmark of mortality by relinquishing mortality itself in preference to any other mode. Life is but a sad possession to those who have attained precisely the degree of moral advancement at which I stand. Were I weaker and blinder, it might be happiness. Were I stronger, it might be endured hopefully. But, being what I find myself, methinks I am of all mortals the most fit to die."

"You are fit for heaven without tasting death!" replied her husband. "But why do we speak of dying? The draught cannot fail. Behold its effect upon this plant."

On the window seat there stood a geranium diseased with yellow blotches which had overspread all its leaves. Aylmer poured a small quantity of the liquid upon the soil in which it grew. In a little time, when the roots of the plant had taken up the moisture, the unsightly blotches began to be extinguished in a living verdure.

"There needed no proof," said Georgiana, quietly. "Give me the goblet. I joyfully stake all upon your word."

"Drink, then, thou lofty creature!" exclaimed Aylmer, with fervid admiration. "There is no taint of imperfection on thy spirit. Thy sensible frame, too, shall soon be all perfect."

She quaffed the liquid and returned the goblet to his hand.

"It is grateful," said she, with a placid smile. "Methinks it is like water from a heavenly fountain; for it contains I know not what of unobtrusive fragrance and deliciousness. It allays a feverish thirst that had parched me for many days. Now, dearest, let me sleep. My earthly senses are closing over my spirit like the leaves around the heart of a rose at sunset."

She spoke the last words with a gentle reluctance, as if it required almost more energy than she could command to pronounce the faint and lingering syllables. Scarcely had they loitered through her lips ere she was lost in slumber. Aylmer sat by her side, watching her aspect with the emotions proper to a man the whole value of whose existence was involved in the process now to be tested.

Mingled with this mood, however, was the philosophic investigation characteristic of the man of science. Not the minutest symptom escaped him. A heightened flush of the cheek, a slight irregularity of breath, a quiver of the eyelid, a hardly perceptible tremor through the frame,—such were the details which, as the moments passed, he wrote down in his folio volume. Intense thought had set its stamp upon every previous page of that volume; but the thoughts of years were all concentrated upon the last.

While thus employed, he failed not to gaze often at the fatal hand, and not without a shudder. Yet once, by a strange and unaccountable impulse, he pressed it with his lips. His spirit recoiled, however, in the very act; and Georgiana, out of the midst of her deep sleep, moved uneasily and murmured as if in remonstrance. Again Aylmer resumed his watch. Nor was it without avail. The crimson hand, which at first had been strongly visible upon the marble paleness of Georgiana's cheek, now grew more faintly outlined. She remained not less pale than ever; but the birthmark, with every breath that came and went lost somewhat of its former distinctness. Its presence had been awful; its departure was more awful still. Watch the stain of the rainbow fading out of the sky, and you will know how that mysterious symbol passed away.

"By Heaven! it is well nigh gone!" said Aylmer to himself, in almost irrepressible ecstasy. "I can scarcely trace it now. Success! success! And now it is like the faintest rose color. The lightest flush of blood across her cheek would overcome it. But she is so pale!"

He drew aside the window curtain and suffered the light of natural day to fall into the room and rest upon her cheek. At the same time he heard a gross, hoarse chuckle, which he had long known as his servant Aminadab's expression of delight.

"Ah, clod! ah, earthly mass!" cried Aylmer, laughing in a sort of frenzy, "you have served me well! Matter and spirit—earth and heaven—have both done their part in this! Laugh, thing of the senses! You have earned the right to laugh."

These exclamations broke Georgiana's sleep. She slowly unclosed her eyes and gazed into the mirror which her husband had arranged for that purpose. A faint smile flitted over her lips when she recognized how barely perceptible was now that crimson hand which had once blazed forth with such disastrous brilliancy as to scare away all their happiness. But then her eyes sought Aylmer's face with a trouble and anxiety that he could by no means account for.

"My poor Aylmer!" murmured she.

"Poor? Nay, richest, happiest, most favored!" exclaimed he. "My peerless bride, it is successful! You are perfect!"

"My poor Aylmer," she repeated, with a more than human tenderness, "you have aimed loftily; you have done nobly. Do not repent that, with so high and pure a feeling, you have rejected the best the earth could offer. Aylmer, dearest Aylmer, I am dying!"

Alas! it was too true! The fatal hand had grappled with the mystery of life, and was the bond by which an angelic spirit kept itself in union with a mortal frame. As the last crimson tint of the birthmark—that sole token of human imperfection—faded from her cheek, the parting breath of the now perfect woman passed into the atmosphere, and her soul, lingering a moment near her husband, took its heavenward flight. Then a hoarse, chuckling laugh was heard again! Thus ever does the gross fatality of earth exult in its invariable triumph over the immortal essence which, in this dim sphere of half development, demands the completeness of a higher state. Yet, had Aylmer reached a profounder wisdom, he need not thus have flung away the happiness which would have woven his mortal life of the selfsame texture with the celestial. The momentary circumstance was too strong for him; he failed to look beyond the shadowy scope of time, and, living once for all in eternity, to find the perfect future in the present.

271

walt whitman

DEMOCRACY IN AN EXPANDING UNIVERSE

GRAND IS THE SEEN

Grand is the seen, the light, to me—grand are the sky and stars,
Grand is the earth, and grand are lasting time and space,
And grand their laws, so multiform, puzzling, evolutionary;
But grander far the unseen soul of me, comprehending, endowing
    all those,
Lighting the light, the sky and stars, delving the earth, sailing the
    sea,
(What were all those, indeed, without thee, unseen soul? of what
    amount without thee?)
More evolutionary, vast puzzling, O my soul!
More multiform far—more lasting thou than they.

ON THE BEACH AT NIGHT ALONE

On the beach at night alone,
As the old mother sways her to and fro singing her husky song,
As I watch the bright stars shining, I think a thought of the clef of
    the universes and of the future.

A vast similitude interlocks all,
All spheres, grown, ungrown, small, large, suns, moons, planets,
All distances of place however wide,
All distances of time, all inanimate forms,
All souls, all living bodies though they be ever so different, or in
    different worlds,
All gaseous, watery, vegetable, mineral processes, the fishes, the
    brutes,
All nations, colors, barbarisms, civilizations, languages,

All identities that have existed or may exist on this globe, or any
    globe,
All lives and deaths, all of the past, present, future,
This vast similitude spans them, and always has spann'd,
And shall forever span them and compactly hold and enclose them.

mark twain

AN AMERICAN SATIRE
ON SCIENCE-WORSHIP

["Some Learned Fables, for Good Old Boys and Girls"; from *Sketches, New and Old* (1875).] *Part First—How the Animals of the Wood Sent Out a Scientific Expedition.* Once the creatures of the forest held a great convention and appointed a commission consisting of the most illustrious scientists among them to go forth, clear beyond the forest and out into the unknown and unexplored world, to verify the truth of the matters already taught in their schools and colleges and also to make discoveries. It was the most imposing enterprise of the kind the nation had ever embarked in. True, the government had once sent Dr. Bull Frog, with a picked crew, to hunt for a northwesterly passage through the swamp to a right-hand corner of the wood, and had since sent out many expeditions to hunt for Dr. Bull Frog; but they never could find him, and so government finally gave him up and ennobled his mother to show its gratitude for the services her son had rendered to science. And once government sent Sir Grass Hopper to hunt for the sources of the rill that emptied into the swamp; and afterward sent out many expeditions to hunt for Sir Grass, and at last they were successful—they found his body, but if he had discovered the sources meantime, he did not let on. So government acted handsomely by deceased, and many envied his funeral.

But these expeditions were trifles compared with the present one; for this one comprised among its servants the very greatest among the learned; and besides it was to go to the utterly unvisited regions believed to lie beyond the mighty forest—as we have remarked before. How the members were banqueted, and glorified, and talked about! Everywhere that one of them showed himself, straightway there was a crowd to gape and stare at him.

Finally they set off, and it was a sight to see the long procession of dryland Tortoises heavily laden with savants, scientific instruments, Glow-Worms and Fire-Flies for signal service, provisions, Ants and Tumble-Bugs to fetch and carry and delve, Spiders to carry the surveying chain and do other engineering duty, and so forth and so on; and after the Tortoises came another long train of ironclads—stately and spacious Mud Turtles for marine transportation service; and from every Tortoise and every Turtle flaunted a flaming gladiolus or other splendid banner; at the head of the column a great band of Bumble-Bees, Mosquitoes, Katy-Dids, and Crickets discoursed martial music; and the entire train was under the escort and protection of twelve picked regiments of the Army Worm.

At the end of three weeks the expedition emerged from the forest and looked upon the great Unknown World. Their eyes were greeted with an impressive spectacle. A vast level plain stretched before them, watered by a sinuous stream; and beyond there towered up against the sky a long and lofty barrier of some kind, they did not know what. The Tumble-Bug said he believed it was simply land tilted up on its edge, because he knew he could see trees on it. But Professor Snail and the others said:

"You are hired to dig, sir—that is all. We need your muscle, not your brains. When we want your opinion on scientific matters, we will hasten to let you know. Your coolness is intolerable, too—loafing about here meddling with august matters of learning, when the other laborers are pitching camp. Go along and help handle the baggage."

The Tumble-Bug turned on his heel uncrushed, unabashed, observing to himself, "If it isn't land tilted up, let me die the death of the unrighteous."

Professor Bull Frog (nephew of the late explorer) said he believed the ridge was the wall that inclosed the earth. He continued:

"Our fathers have left us much learning, but they had not traveled far, and so we may count this a noble new discovery. We are safe for renown now, even though our labors began and ended with this single achievement. I wonder what this wall is built of? Can it be fungus? Fungus is an honorable good thing to build a wall of."

Professor Snail adjusted his field-glass and examined the rampart critically. Finally he said:

"The fact that it is not diaphanous convinces me that it is a dense vapor formed by the calorification of ascending moisture dephlogisticated by refraction. A few endiometrical experiments would confirm this, but it is not necessary. The thing is obvious."

So he shut up his glass and went into his shell to make a note of the discovery of the world's end, and the nature of it.

"Profound mind!" said Professor Angle-Worm to Professor Field-Mouse; "profound mind! nothing can long remain a mystery to that august brain."

Night drew on apace, the sentinel crickets were posted, the Glow-Worm and Fire-Fly lamps were lighted, and the camp sank to silence and sleep. After breakfast in the morning, the expedition moved on. About noon a great avenue was reached, which had in it two endless parallel bars of some kind of hard black substance, raised the height of the tallest Bull Frog above the general level. The scientists climbed up on these and examined and tested them in various ways. They walked along them for a great distance, but found no end and no break in them. They could arrive at no decision. There was nothing in the records of science that mentioned anything of this kind. But at last the bald and venerable geographer, Professor Mud Turtle, a person who, born poor, and of a drudging low family, had, by his own native force raised himself to the headship of the geographers of his generation, said:

"My friends, we have indeed made a discovery here. We have found in a palpable, compact, and imperishable state what the wisest of our fathers always regarded as a mere thing of the imagination. Humble yourselves, my friends, for we stand in a majestic presence. These are parallels of latitude!"

Every heart and every head was bowed, so awful, so sublime was the magnitude of the discovery. Many shed tears.

The camp was pitched and the rest of the day given up to writing voluminous accounts of the marvel, and correcting astronomical tables to fit it. Toward midnight a demoniacal shriek was heard, then a clattering and rumbling noise, and the next instant a vast terrific eye shot by, with a long tail attached, and disappeared in the gloom, still uttering triumphant shrieks.

The poor camp laborers were stricken to the heart with fright, and stampeded for the high grass in a body. But not the scientists. They had no superstitions. They calmly proceeded to exchange theories. The ancient geographer's opinion was asked. He went into his shell and deliberated long and profoundly. When he came out at last, they all knew by his worshiping countenance that he brought light. Said he:

"Give thanks for this stupendous thing which we have been permitted to witness. It is the Vernal Equinox!"

There were shoutings and great rejoicings.

"But," said the Angle-Worm, uncoiling after reflection, "this is dead summer-time."

"Very well," said the Turtle, "we are far from our region; the season differs with the difference of time between the two points."

"Ah, true. True enough. But it is night. How should the sun pass in the night?"

"In these distant regions he doubtless passes always in the night at this hour."

"Yes, doubtless that is true. But it being night, how is it that we could see him?"

"It is a great mystery. I grant that. But I am persuaded that the humidity of the atmosphere in these remote regions is such that particles of daylight adhere to the disk and it was by aid of these that we were enabled to see the sun in the dark."

This was deemed satisfactory, and due entry was made of the decision.

But about this moment those dreadful shriekings were heard again; again the rumbling and thundering came speeding up out of the night; and once more a flaming great eye flashed by and lost itself in the gloom and distance.

The camp laborers gave themselves up for lost. The savants were sorely perplexed. Here was a marvel hard to account for. They thought and they talked, they talked and they thought. Finally the learned and aged Lord Grand-Daddy-Longlegs, who had been sitting in deep study, with his slender limbs crossed and his stemmy arms folded, said:

"Deliver your opinions, brethren, and then I will tell my thought —for I think I have solved this problem."

"So be it, good your lordship," piped the weak treble of the wrinkled and withered Professor Woodlouse, "for we shall hear from your lordship's lips naught but wisdom." (Here the speaker threw in a mess of trite, threadbare, exasperating quotations from the ancient poets and philosophers, delivering them with unction in the sounding grandeurs of the original tongues, they being from the Mastodon, the Dodo, and other dead languages.) "Perhaps I ought not to presume to meddle with matters pertaining to astronomy at all, in such a presence as this, I who have made it the business of my life to delve only among the riches of the extinct languages and unearth the opulence of their ancient lore; but still, as unacquainted as I am with the noble science of astronomy, I beg with deference and humility to suggest that inasmuch as the last of these wonderful apparitions proceeded in exactly the opposite direction from that pursued by the first, which you decide to be the Vernal Equinox, and greatly resembled it in all particulars, is it not possible, nay certain, that this last is the *Autumnal* Equi——"

"O-o-o!" "O-o-o! go to bed! go to bed!" with annoyed derision from everybody. So the poor old Woodlouse retreated out of sight, consumed with shame.

277

Further discussion followed, and then the united voice of the commission begged Lord Longlegs to speak. He said:

"Fellow-scientists, it is my belief that we have witnessed a thing which has occurred in perfection but once before in the knowledge of created beings. It is a phenomenon of inconceivable importance and interest, view it as one may, but its interest to us is vastly heightened by an added knowledge of its nature which no scholar has heretofore possessed or even suspected. This great marvel which we have just witnessed, fellow-savants (it almost takes my breath away), is nothing less than the transit of Venus!"

Every scholar sprang to his feet pale with astonishment. Then ensued tears, handshakings, frenzied embraces, and the most extravagant jubilations of every sort. But by and by, as emotion began to retire within bounds, and reflection to return to the front, the accomplished Chief Inspector Lizard observed:

"But how is this? Venus should traverse the sun's surface, not the earth's."

The arrow went home. It carried sorrow to the breast of every apostle of learning there, for none could deny that this was a formidable criticism. But tranquilly the venerable Duke crossed his limbs behind his ears and said:

"My friend has touched the marrow of our mighty discovery. Yes—all that have lived before us thought a transit of Venus consisted of a flight across the sun's face; they thought it, they maintained it, they honestly believed it, simple hearts, and were justified in it by the limitations of their knowledge; but to us has been granted the inestimable boon of proving that the transit occurs across the earth's face, *for we have* SEEN *it!*"

The assembled wisdom sat in speechless adoration of this imperial intellect. All doubts had instantly departed, like night before the lightning.

The Tumble-Bug had just intruded, unnoticed. He now came reeling forward among the scholars, familiarly slapping first one and then another on the shoulder, saying "nice ('ic!) nice old boy!" and smiling a smile of elaborate content. Arrived at a good position for speaking, he put his left arm akimbo with his knuckles planted in his hip just under the edge of his cut-away coat, bent his right leg, placing his toe on the ground and resting his heel with easy grace against his left shin, puffed out his aldermanic stomach, opened his lips, leaned his right elbow on Inspector Lizard's shoulder, and——

But the shoulder was indignantly withdrawn and the hard-handed son of toil went to earth. He floundered a bit, but came up smiling, arranged his attitude with the same careful detail as before, only choosing Professor Dogtick's shoulder for a support, opened his lips and——

Went to earth again. He presently scrambled up once more, still smiling, made a loose effort to brush the dust off his coat and legs, but a smart pass of his hand missed entirely, and the force of the unchecked impulse slewed him suddenly around, twisted his legs together, and projected him, limber and sprawling, into the lap of the Lord Longlegs. Two or three scholars sprang forward, flung the low creature head over heels into a corner, and reinstated the patrician, smoothing his ruffled dignity with many soothing and regretful speeches. Professor Bull Frog roared out:

"No more of this, sirrah Tumble-Bug! Say your say and then get you about your business with speed! Quick what is your errand? Come—move off a trifle; you smell like a stable; what have you been at?"

"Please ('ic!) please your worship I chanced to light upon a find. But no m (*e-uck!*) matter 'bout that. There's b ('ic!) been another find which—beg pardon, your honors, what was that th ('ic!) thing that ripped by here first?"

"It was the Vernal Equinox."

"Inf ('ic!) fernal equinox. 'At's all right. D ('ic!) Dunno *him*. What's other one?"

"The transit of Venus."

"G ('ic!) Got me again. No matter. Las' one dropped something."

"Ah, indeed! Good luck! Good news! Quick—what is it?"

"M ('ic!) Mosey out 'n' see. It'll pay."

No more votes were taken for four-and-twenty hours. Then the following entry was made:

"The commission went in a body to view the find. It was found to consist of a hard, smooth, huge object with a rounded summit surmounted by a short upright projection resembling a section of a cabbage stalk divided transversely. This projection was not solid, but was a hollow cylinder plugged with a soft woody substance unknown to our region—that is, it had been so plugged, but unfortunately this obstruction had been heedlessly removed by Norway Rat, Chief of the Sappers and Miners, before our arrival. The vast object before us, so mysteriously conveyed from the glittering domains of space, was found to be hollow and nearly filled with a pungent liquid of a brownish hue, like rainwater that has stood for some time. And such a spectacle as met our view! Norway Rat was perched upon the summit engaged in thrusting his tail into the cylindrical projection, drawing it out dripping, permitting the struggling multitude of laborers to suck the end of it, then straightway reinserting it and delivering the fluid to the mob as before. Evidently this liquor had strangely potent qualities; for all that partook of it were immediately exalted with great and pleasurable emotions, and went staggering about singing ribald songs, embracing, fighting, dancing, discharging irruptions of profanity, and defying all authority. Around us struggled a massed and uncontrolled mob—uncontrolled and likewise uncontrollable, for the whole army, down to the very sentinels, were mad like the rest, by reason of the drink. We were seized upon by these reckless creatures, and within the hour we, even we, were undistinguishable from the rest—the demoralization was complete and universal. In time the camp wore itself out with its orgies and sank into a stolid and pitiable stupor, in whose mysterious bonds rank was forgotten and strange bedfellows made, our eyes, at the resurrection, being blasted and our souls petrified with the incredible spectacle of that intolerable stinking scavenger, the Tumble-Bug, and the illustrious patrician my Lord Grand Daddy, Duke of Longlegs, lying soundly steeped in sleep, and clasped lovingly in each other's arms, the like whereof hath not been seen in all the ages that tradition compasseth, and doubtless none shall ever in this world find faith to master the belief of it save only we that have beheld the damnable and unholy vision. Thus inscrutable be the ways of God, whose will be done!

"This day, by order, did the engineer-in-chief, Herr Spider, rig the necessary tackle for the overturning of the vast reservoir, and so its calamitous contents were discharged in a torrent upon the thirsty earth, which drank it up, and now there is no more danger, we reserving but a few drops for experiment and scrutiny, and to exhibit to the king and subsequently preserve among the wonders of the museum. What this liquid is has been determined. It is without question that fierce and most destructive fluid called lightning. It was wrested, in its container, from its storehouse in the clouds, by the resistless might of the flying planet, and hurled at our feet as she sped by. An interesting discovery here results. Which is, that lightning, kept to itself, is quiescent; it is the assaulting contact of the thunderbolt that releases it from captivity, ignites its awful fires, and so produces an instantaneous combustion and explosion which spread disaster and desolation far and wide in the earth."

After another day devoted to rest and recovery, the expedition proceeded upon its way. Some days later it went into camp in a pleasant part of the plain, and the savants sallied forth to see what they might find. Their reward was at hand. Professor Bull Frog discovered a strange tree, and called his comrades. They inspected it with profound interest. It was very tall and straight, and wholly devoid of bark, limbs, or foliage. By triangulation Lord Longlegs determined its altitude; Herr Spider measured its circumference at the base and computed the circumference at its top by a mathematical demonstration based upon the warrant furnished by the uniform degree of its taper upward. It was considered a very extraordinary find; and since it was a tree of a hitherto unknown species, Professor Woodlouse gave it a name of a learned sound, being none other than that of Professor Bull Frog translated into the ancient Mastodon language, for it had always been the custom with discoverers to perpetuate their names and honor themselves by this sort of connection with their discoveries.

Now Professor Field-Mouse having placed his sensitive ear to the tree, detected a rich, harmonious sound issuing from it. This surprising thing was tested and enjoyed by each scholar in turn, and great was the gladness and astonishment of all. Professor Woodlouse was requested to add to and extend the tree's name so as to make it suggest the musical quality it possessed—which he did, furnishing the addition *Anthem Singer,* done into the Mastodon tongue.

By this time Professor Snail was making some telescopic inspections. He discovered a great number of these trees, extending in a single rank, with wide intervals between, as far as his instrument would carry, both southward and northward. He also presently discovered that all these trees were bound together, near their tops, by fourteen great ropes, one above another, which ropes were continuous, from tree to tree, as far as his vision could reach. This was surprising. Chief Engineer Spider ran aloft and soon reported that these ropes were simply a web hung there by some colossal member of his own species, for he could see its prey dangling here and there from the strands, in the shape of mighty shreds and rags that had a woven look about their texture and were no doubt the discarded skins of prodigious insects which had been caught and eaten. And then he ran along one of the ropes to make a closer inspection, but felt a smart sudden burn on the soles of his feet, accompanied by a paralyzing shock, wherefore he let go and swung himself to the earth by a thread of his own spinning, and advised all to hurry at once to camp, lest the monster should appear and get as much interested in the savants as they were in him and his works. So they departed with speed, making notes about the gigantic web as they went. And that evening the naturalist of the expedition built a beautiful model of the colossal spider, having no need to see it in order to do this, because he had picked up a fragment of its vertebræ by the tree, and so knew exactly what the creature looked like and what its habits and its preferences were by this simple evidence alone. He built it with a tail, teeth, fourteen legs, and a snout, and said it ate grass, cattle, pebbles, and dirt with equal enthusiasm.

This animal was regarded as a very precious addition to science. It was hoped a dead one might be found to stuff. Professor Wood-louse thought that he and his brother scholars, by lying hid and being quiet, might maybe catch a live one. He was advised to try it. Which was all the attention that was paid to his suggestion. The conference ended with the naming the monster after the naturalist, since he, after God, had created it.

"And improved it, mayhap," muttered the Tumble-Bug, who was intruding again, according to his idle custom and his unappeasable curiosity.

Part Second—How the Animals of the Wood Completed Their Scientific Labors. A week later the expedition camped in the midst of a collection of wonderful curiosities. These were a sort of vast caverns of stone that rose singly and in bunches out of the plain by the side of the river which they had first seen when they emerged from the forest. These caverns stood in long, straight rows on opposite sides of broad aisles that were bordered with single ranks of trees. The summit of each cavern sloped sharply both ways. Several horizontal rows of great square holes, obstructed by a thin, shiny, transparent substance, pierced the frontage of each cavern. Inside were caverns within caverns; and one might ascend and visit these minor compartments by means of curious winding ways consisting of continuous regular terraces raised one above an-other. There were many huge, shapeless objects in each compart-ment which were considered to have been living creatures at one time, though now the thin brown skin was shrunken and loose, and rattled when disturbed. Spiders were here in great number, and their cobwebs, stretched in all directions and wreathing the great skinny dead together, were a pleasant spectacle, since they inspired with life and wholesome cheer a scene which would otherwise have brought to the mind only a sense of forsakenness and desola-tion. Information was sought of these spiders, but in vain. They were of a different nationality from those with the expedition, and their language seemed but a musical, meaningless jargon. They were a timid, gentle race, but ignorant, and heathenish worshipers of unknown gods. The expedition detailed a great detachment of missionaries to teach them the true religion, and in a week's time a precious work had been wrought among those darkened creatures, not three families being by that time at peace with each other or having a settled belief in any system of religion whatever. This encouraged the expedition to establish a colony of missionaries there permanently, that the work of grace might go on.

But let us not outrun our narrative. After close examination of the fronts of the caverns, and much thinking and exchanging of theories, the scientists determined the nature of these singular formations. They said that each belonged mainly to the Old Red Sandstone period; that the cavern fronts rose in innumerable and wonderfully regular strata high in the air, each stratum about five frog-spans thick, and that in the present discovery lay an over-powering refutation of all received geology; for between every two layers of Old Red Sandstone reposed a thin layer of decomposed limestone; so instead of there having been but one Old Red Sand-stone period there had certainly been not less than a hundred and seventy-five! And by the same token it was plain that there had also been a hundred and seventy-five floodings of the earth and deposit-ings of limestone strata! The unavoidable deduction from which pair of facts was the overwhelming truth that the world, instead of being only two hundred thousand years old, was older by millions upon millions of years! And there was another curious thing: every stratum of Old Red Sandstone was pierced and divided at mathe-matically regular intervals by vertical strata of limestone. Up-shoot-ings of igneous rock through fractures in water formations were common; but here was the first instance where water-formed rock had been so projected. It was a great and noble discovery, and its value to science was considered to be inestimable.

A critical examination of some of the lower strata demonstrated the presence of fossil ants and tumble-bugs (the latter accompanied by their peculiar goods), and with high gratification the fact was enrolled upon the scientific record; for this was proof that these vulgar laborers belonged to the first and lowest orders of created beings, though at the same time there was something repulsive in the reflection that the perfect and exquisite creature of the modern uppermost order owed its origin to such ignominious beings through the mysterious laws of Development of Species.

The Tumble-Bug, overhearing this discussion, said he was will-ing that the parvenus of these new times should find what comfort they might in their wise-drawn theories, since as far as he was con-cerned he was content to be of the old first families and proud to point back to his place among the old original aristocracy of the land.

"Enjoy your mushroom dignity, stinking of the varnish of yester-day's veneering, since you like it," said he; "suffice it for the Tum-ble-Bugs that they come of a race that rolled their fragrant spheres down the solemn aisles of antiquity, and left their imperishable works embalmed in the Old Red Sandstone to proclaim it to the wasting centuries as they file along the highway of Time!"

"Oh, take a walk!" said the chief of the expedition, with derision.

The summer passed, and winter approached. In and about many of the caverns were what seemed to be inscriptions. Most of the scientists said they were inscriptions, a few said they were not. The chief philologist, Professor Woodlouse, maintained that they were writings, done in a character utterly unknown to scholars, and in a language equally unknown. He had early ordered his artists and draftsmen to make facsimiles of all that were discovered; and had set himself about finding the key to the hidden tongue. In this work he had followed the method which had always been used by decipherers previously. That is to say, he placed a number of copies of inscriptions before him and studied them both collectively and in detail. To begin with, he placed the following copies together:

THE AMERICAN HOTEL.
THE SHADES.
BOATS FOR HIRE CHEAP.
BILLIARDS.
THE A1 BARBER SHOP.
KEEP OFF THE GRASS.
COTTAGES FOR RENT DURING THE WATERING SEASON.
FOR SALE CHEAP.
FOR SALE CHEAP.
MEALS AT ALL HOURS.
NO SMOKING.
UNION PRAYER MEETING, 4 P.M.
THE WATERSIDE JOURNAL.
TELEGRAPH OFFICE.
TRY BRANDRETH'S PILLS.
FOR SALE CHEAP.
FOR SALE CHEAP.

At first it seemed to the professor that this was a sign-language, and that each word was represented by a distinct sign; further examination convinced him that it was a written language, and that every letter of its alphabet was represented by a character of its own; and finally he decided that it was a language which conveyed itself partly by letters, and partly by signs or hieroglyphics. This conclusion was forced upon him by the discovery of several specimens of the following nature:

He observed that certain inscriptions were met with in greater frequency than others. Such as "FOR SALE CHEAP"; "BILLIARDS"; "S. T.—1860—X"; "KENO"; "ALE ON DRAUGHT." Naturally, then, these must be religious maxims. But this idea was cast aside by and by, as the mystery of the strange alphabet began to clear itself. In time, the professor was enabled to translate several of the inscriptions with considerable plausibility, though not to the perfect satisfaction of all the scholars. Still, he made constant and encouraging progress.

Finally a cavern was discovered with these inscriptions upon it:

WATERSIDE MUSEUM
Open at All Hours.
Admission 50 cents.
WONDERFUL COLLECTION OF WAXWORKS, ANCIENT FOSSILS, ETC.

Professor Woodlouse affirmed that the word "Museum" was equivalent to the phrase *"lumgath molo,"* or "Burial Place." Upon entering, the scientists were well astonished. But what they saw may be best conveyed in the language of their own official report:

"Erect in a row, were a sort of rigid great figures which struck us instantly as belonging to the long extinct species of reptile called MAN, described in our ancient records. This was a peculiarly gratifying discovery, because of late times it has become fashionable to regard this creature as a myth and a superstition, a work of the inventive imaginations of our remote ancestors. But here, indeed, was Man, perfectly preserved, in a fossil state. And this was his burial place, as already ascertained by the inscription. And now it began to be suspected that the caverns we had been inspecting had been his ancient haunts in that old time that he roamed the earth —for upon the breast of each of these tall fossils was an inscription in the character heretofore noticed. One read, 'CAPTAIN KIDD THE PIRATE'; another, 'QUEEN VICTORIA'; another, 'ABE LINCOLN'; another, 'GEORGE WASHINGTON,' etc.

"With feverish interest we called for our ancient scientific records to discover if perchance the description of Man there set down would tally with the fossils before us. Professor Woodlouse read it aloud in its quaint and musty phraseology, to wit:

" 'In ye time of our fathers Man still walked ye earth, as by tradition we know. It was a creature of exceeding great size, being compassed about with a loose skin, sometimes of one color, sometimes of many, the which it was able to cast at will; which being done, the hind legs were discovered to be armed with short claws like to a mole's but broader, and ye forelegs with fingers of a curious slimness and a length much more prodigious than a frog's, armed also with broad talons for scratching in ye earth for its food. It had a sort of feathers upon its head such as hath a rat, but longer, and a beak suitable for seeking its food by ye smell thereof. When it was stirred with happiness, it leaked water from its eyes; and when it suffered or was sad, it manifested it with a horrible hellish

285

cackling clamor that was exceeding dreadful to hear and made one long that it might rend itself and perish, and so end its troubles. Two Mans being together, they uttered noises at each other like this: "Haw-haw-haw—dam good, dam good," together with other sounds of more or less likeness to these, wherefore yᵉ poets conceived that they talked, but poets be always ready to catch at any frantic folly, God he knows. Sometimes this creature goeth about with a long stick yᵉ which it putteth to its face and bloweth fire and smoke through yᵉ same with a sudden and most damnable bruit and noise that doth fright its prey to death, and so seizeth it in its talons and walketh away to its habitat, consumed with a most fierce and devilish joy.'

"Now was the description set forth by our ancestors wonderfully indorsed and confirmed by the fossils before us, as shall be seen. The specimen marked 'Captain Kidd' was examined in detail. Upon its head and part of its face was a sort of fur like that upon the tail of a horse. With great labor its loose skin was removed, whereupon its body was discovered to be of a polished white texture, thoroughly petrified. The straw it had eaten, so many ages gone by, was still in its body, undigested—and even in its legs.

"Surrounding these fossils were objects that would mean nothing to the ignorant, but to the eye of science they were a revelation. They laid bare the secrets of dead ages. These musty Memorials told us when Man lived, and what were his habits. For here, side by side with Man, were the evidences that he had lived in the earliest ages of creation, the companion of the other low orders of life that belonged to that forgotten time. Here was the fossil nautilus that sailed the primeval seas; here was the skeleton of the mastodon, the ichthyosaurus, the cave-bear, the prodigious elk. Here, also, were the charred bones of some of these extinct animals and of the young of Man's own species, split lengthwise, showing that to his taste the marrow was a toothsome luxury. It was plain that Man had robbed those bones of their contents, since no tooth-mark of any beast was upon them—albeit the Tumble-Bug intruded the remark that 'no beast could mark a bone with its teeth, anyway.' Here were proofs that Man had vague, groveling notions of art; for this fact was conveyed by certain things marked with the untranslatable words, 'FLINT HATCHETS, KNIVES, ARROW-HEADS, AND BONE ORNAMENTS OF PRIMEVAL MAN.' Some of these seemed to be rude weapons chipped out of flint, and in a secret place was found some more in process of construction, with this untranslatable legend, on a thin, flimsy material, lying by:

" 'Jones, if you don't want to be discharged from the Musseum, make the next primeaveal weppons more careful—you couldn't even fool one of these sleapy old syentiffic grannys from the Coledge

*with the last ones. And mind you the animles you carved on some
of the Bone Ornaments is a blame sight too good for any primeaveal
man that was ever fooled—Varnum, Manager.'*

"Back of the burial place was a mass of ashes, showing that
Man always had a feast at a funeral—else why the ashes in such a
place; and showing, also, that he believed in God and the immortality of the soul—else why these solemn ceremonies?

"To sum up. We believe that Man had a written language. We
know that he indeed existed at one time, and is not a myth; also,
that he was the companion of the cave-bear, the mastodon, and
other extinct species; that he cooked and ate them and likewise the
young of his own kind; also, that he bore rude weapons, and knew
something of art; that he imagined he had a soul, and pleased
himself with the fancy that it was immortal. But let us not laugh;
there may be creatures in existence to whom we and our vanities
and profundities may seem as ludicrous."

Part Third. Near the margin of the great river the scientists
presently found a huge, shapely stone, with this inscription:

*"In 1847, in the spring, the river overflowed its banks and cov-
ered the whole township. The depth was from two to six feet.
More than 900 head of cattle were lost, and many homes destroyed.
The Mayor ordered this memorial to be erected to perpetuate the
event. God spare us the repetition of it!"*

With infinite trouble, Professor Woodlouse succeeded in making
a translation of this inscription, which was sent home, and straightway an enormous excitement was created about it. It confirmed,
in a remarkable way, certain treasured traditions of the ancients.
The translation was slightly marred by one or two untranslatable
words, but these did not impair the general clearness of the meaning. It is here presented:

*"One thousand eight hundred and forty-seven years ago, the
(fires?) descended and consumed the whole city. Only some nine
hundred souls were saved, all others destroyed. The (king?) commanded this stone to be set up to . . . (untranslatable) . . .
prevent the repetition of it."*

This was the first successful and satisfactory translation that had
been made of the mysterious character left behind him by extinct
man, and it gave Professor Woodlouse such reputation that at once
every seat of learning in his native land conferred a degree of the
most illustrious grade upon him, and it was believed that if he
had been a soldier and had turned his splendid talents to the ex-
termination of a remote tribe of reptiles, the king would have ennobled him and made him rich. And this, too, was the origin of
that school of scientists called Manologists, whose specialty is the

287

deciphering of the ancient records of the extinct bird termed Man. (For it is now decided that Man was a bird and not a reptile.) But Professor Woodlouse began and remained chief of these, for it was granted that no translations were ever so free from error as his. Others made mistakes—he seemed incapable of it. Many a memorial of the lost race was afterward found, but none ever attained to the renown and veneration achieved by the "Mayoritish Stone"—it being so called from the word "Mayor" in it, which, being translated "King," "Mayoritish Stone" was but another way of saying "King Stone."

Another time the expedition made a great "find." It was a vast round flattish mass, ten frog-spans in diameter and five or six high. Professor Snail put on his spectacles and examined it all around, and then climbed up and inspected the top. He said:

"The result of my perlustration and perscontation of this isoperimetrical protuberance is a belief that it is one of those rare and wonderful creations left by the Mound Builders. The fact that this one is lamellibranchiate in its formation, simply adds to its interest as being possibly of a different kind from any we read of in the records of science, but yet in no manner marring its authenticity. Let the megalophonous grasshopper sound a blast and summon hither the perfunctory and circumforaneous Tumble-Bug, to the end that excavations may be made and learning gather new treasures."

Not a Tumble-Bug could be found on duty, so the Mound was excavated by a working party of Ants. Nothing was discovered. This would have been a great disappointment, had not the venerable Longlegs explained the matter. He said:

"It is now plain to me that the mysterious and forgotten race of Mound Builders did not always erect these edifices as mausoleums, else in this case, as in all previous cases, their skeletons would be found here, along with the rude implements which the creatures used in life. Is not this manifest?"

"True! true!" from everybody.

"Then we have made a discovery of peculiar value here; a discovery which greatly extends our knowledge of this creature in place of diminishing it; a discovery which will add luster to the achievements of this expedition and win for us the commendations of scholars everywhere. For the absence of the customary relics here means nothing less than this: The Mound Builder, instead of being the ignorant, savage reptile we have been taught to consider him, was a creature of cultivation and high intelligence, capable of not only appreciating worthy achievements of the great and noble of his species, but of commemorating them. Fellow-scholars, this stately Mound is not a sepulcher, it is a monument!"

A profound impression was produced by this.

But it was interrupted by rude and derisive laughter—and the Tumble-Bug appeared.

"A monument!" quoth he. "A monument set up by a Mound Builder! Aye, so it is! So it is, indeed, to the shrewd keen eye of science; but to an ignorant poor devil who has never seen a college, it is not a Monument, strictly speaking, but is yet a most rich and noble property; and with your worship's good permission I will proceed to manufacture it into spheres of exceeding grace and——"

The Tumble-Bug was driven away with stripes, and the draftsmen of the expedition were set to making views of the Monument from different standpoints, while Professor Woodlouse, in a frenzy of scientific zeal, traveled all over it and all around it hoping to find an inscription. But if there had ever been one, it had decayed or been removed by some vandal as a relic.

The views having been completed, it was now considered safe to load the precious Monument itself upon the backs of four of the largest Tortoises and send it home to the king's museum, which was done; and when it arrived it was received with enormous *éclat* and escorted to its future abiding-place by thousands of enthusiastic citizens, King Bullfrog XVI. himself attending and condescending to sit enthroned upon it throughout the progress.

The growing rigor of the weather was now admonishing the scientists to close their labors for the present, so they made preparations to journey homeward. But even their last day among the Caverns bore fruit; for one of the scholars found in an out-of-the-way corner of the Museum or "Burial Place" a most strange and extraordinary thing. It was nothing less than a double Man-Bird lashed together breast to breast by a natural ligament, and labeled with the untranslatable words, *"Siamese Twins."* The official report concerning this thing closed thus:

"Wherefore it appears that there were in old times two distinct species of this majestic fowl, the one being single and the other double. Nature has a reason for all things. It is plain to the eye of science that the Double-Man originally inhabited a region where dangers abounded; hence he was paired together to the end that while one part slept the other might watch; and likewise that, danger being discovered, there might always be a double instead of a single power to oppose it. All honor to the mystery-dispelling eye of godlike Science!"

And near the Double Man-Bird was found what was plainly an ancient record of his, marked upon numberless sheets of a thin white substance and bound together. Almost the first glance that Professor Woodlouse threw into it revealed this following sentence, which he instantly translated and laid before the scientists, in a tremble, and it uplifted every soul there with exultation and astonishment:

"In truth it is believed by many that the lower animals reason and talk together."

When the great official report of the expedition appeared, the above sentence bore this comment:

"Then there are lower animals than Man! This remarkable passage can mean nothing else. Man himself is extinct, but *they* may still exist. What can they be? Where do they inhabit? One's enthusiasm bursts all bounds in the contemplation of the brilliant field of discovery and investigation here thrown open to science. We close our labors with the humble prayer that your Majesty will immediately appoint a commission and command it to rest not nor spare expense until the search for this hitherto unsuspected race of the creatures of God shall be crowned with success."

The expedition then journeyed homeward after its long absence and its faithful endeavors, and was received with a mighty ovation by the whole grateful country. There were vulgar, ignorant carpers, of course, as there always are and always will be; and naturally one of these was the obscene Tumble-Bug. He said that all he had learned by his travels was that science only needed a spoonful of supposition to build a mountain of demonstrated fact out of; and that for the future he meant to be content with the knowledge that nature had made free to all creatures and not go prying into the august secrets of the Deity.

robert frost

A MODERN POET'S SKEPTICISM
TOWARD FAITH AND SCIENCE

ASTROMETAPHYSICAL

Lord, I have loved your sky,
Be it said against or for me,
Have loved it clear and high,
Or low and stormy;
Till I have reeled and stumbled
From looking up too much,
And fallen and been humbled
To wear a crutch.
My love for every Heaven
O'er which you, Lord have lorded,
From number One to Seven
Should be rewarded.
It may not give me hope
That when I am translated
My scalp will in the cope
Be constellated.
But if that seems to tend
To my undue renown,
At least it ought to send
Me up, not down.

SKEPTIC

Far star that tickles for me my sensitive plate
And fries a couple of ebon atoms white,

I don't believe I believe a thing you state.
I put no faith in the seeming facts of light.
I don't believe I believe you're the last in space,
I don't believe you're anywhere near the last,
I don't believe what makes you red in the face
Is after explosion going away so fast.
The universe may or may not be very immense.
As a matter of fact there are times when I am apt
To feel it close in tight against my sense
Like a caul in which I was born and still am wrapped.

WHY WAIT FOR SCIENCE

Sarcastic Science she would like to know,
In her complacent ministry of fear,
How we propose to get away from here
When she has made things so we have to go
Or be wiped out. Will she be asked to show
Us how by rocket we may hope to steer
To some star off there say a half light-year
Through temperature of absolute zeró?
Why wait for Science to supply the how
When any amateur can tell it now?
The way to go away should be the same
As fifty million years ago we came—
If anyone remembers how that was.
I have a theory, but it hardly does.

SITTING BY A BUSH IN BROAD SUNLIGHT

When I spread out my hand here today,
I catch no more than a ray
To feel of between thumb and fingers;
No lasting effect of it lingers.
There was one time and only the one
When dust really took in the sun;
And from that one intake of fire
All creatures still warmly suspire.
And if men have watched a long time
And never seen sun-smitten slime
Again come to life and crawl off,
We must not be too ready to scoff.
God once declared he was true
And then took the veil and withdrew,
And remember how final a hush
Then descended of old on the bush.

God once spoke to people by name.
The sun once imparted its flame.
One impulse persists as our breath;
The other persists as our faith.

THE ARMFUL

For every parcel I stoop down to seize,
I lose some other off my arms and knees,
And the whole pile is slipping, bottles, buns,
Extremes too hard to comprehend at once,
Yet nothing I should care to leave behind.
With all I have to hold with, hand and mind
And heart, if need be, I will do my best
To keep their building balanced at my breast.
I crouch down to prevent them as they fall;
Then sit down in the middle of them all.
I had to drop the armful in the road
And try to stack them in a better load.

RIDERS

The surest thing there is is we are riders,
And though none too successful at it, guiders,
Through everything presented, land and tide
And now the very air, of what we ride.
What is this talked-of mystery of birth
But being mounted bareback on the earth?
We can just see the infant up astride,
His small fist buried in the bushy hide.
There is our wildest mount—a headless horse.
But though it runs unbridled off its course,
And all our blandishments would seem defied,
We have ideas yet that we haven't tried.

THE BEAR

The bear puts both arms around the tree above her
And draws it down as if it were a lover
And its choke cherries lips to kiss good-by,
Then lets it snap back upright in the sky.
Her next step rocks a boulder on the wall
(She's making her cross-country in the fall).
Her great weight creaks the barbed-wire in its staples
As she flings over and off down through the maples,
Leaving on one wire tooth a lock of hair.

293

Such is the uncaged progress of the bear.
The world has room to make a bear feel free;
The universe seems cramped to you and me.
Man acts more like the poor bear in a cage
That all day fights a nervous inward rage,
His mood rejecting all his mind suggests.
He paces back and forth and never rests
The toe-nail click and shuffle of his feet,
The telescope at one end of his beat,
And at the other end the microscope,
Two instruments of nearly equal hope,
And in conjunction giving quite a spread.
Or if he rests from scientific tread,
'Tis only to sit back and sway his head
Through ninety odd degrees of arc, it seems,
Between two metaphysical extremes.
He sits back on his fundamental butt
With lifted snout and eyes (if any) shut,
(He almost looks religious but he's not),
And back and forth he sways from cheek to cheek,
At one extreme agreeing with one Greek,
At the other agreeing with another Greek
Which may be thought, but only so to speak.
A baggy figure, equally pathetic
When sedentary and when peripatetic.

INNATE HELIUM

Religious faith is a most filling vapor.
It swirls occluded in us under tight
Compression to uplift us out of weight—
As in those buoyant bird bones thin as paper,
To give them still more buoyancy in flight.
Some gas like helium must be innate.

Study Aids

ANALYSIS AND DISCUSSION

HUXLEY

1. Huxley asserts that "an exclusively scientific training will bring about a mental twist as surely as an exclusively literary training." If this be so, why does he endorse the Scientific College?

2. The Humanists fail to appreciate a "scientific criticism of life," Mr. Huxley notes, "not because they are too full of the spirit of the ancient Greek, but because they lack it." Explain.

ARNOLD

1. How does Arnold's concept of *literature* differ from that imputed to him by Huxley?

2. Discuss the difference between "instrument-knowledge" and the kind of knowledge imparted by literature. To what human faculties does literature address itself that "instrument-knowledge" does not?

3. In Arnold's terms, could classical literature, with its grotesque conceptions of the physical universe, fit into the context of modern science?

LARRABEE

1. In what ways does Larrabee show science to be the modern "faith"?

2. In what ways may it be claimed that scientists, as individuals and as a social group, have failed their obligations to the human community? In what ways have their failures been metaphysical? Why do these failures generate an attitude that Larrabee calls "anti-science"?

MACLEISH

1. Why, according to Macleish, should poetry be taught?

2. What are the dangers, according to the author, for a civilization that claims to "know the world through its abstractions"?

3. What significant point does Macleish draw from the ancient Chinese practice of testing civil service candidates in poetry?

SNOW

1. F. R. Leavis, in his now famous article entitled *The Two Cultures?* in *The Spectator,* March 9, 1962, said of Snow's essay that it "exhibited an utter lack of intellectual distinction and an embarrassing vulgarity of style." Snow's phrasing in *The Two Cultures,* Leavis stated, "emerges spontaneously from the cultural world to which Snow belongs and it registers uncritically (hence the self-evident force it has for him) its assumptions and attitudes and ignorances." Leavis asserted that Snow is an undisciplined thinker whose very success mirrors the degeneration

of intellectual culture in our time. Implicit in this assertion is his idea that language is the highest and most precise expression of man. Any writer, scientist or artist, reveals his depth of understanding by the kind of language he uses, by the degree of precision, and the amount of cliché present. Attempt a thorough language analysis of Snow's essay. Can you find clichés? For example, what does Snow mean by "culture"; by "anthropological"; by "tragedy"? Does he ever explain the meaning or function of "science"? How does he propose to bring the "two cultures" together?

2. Trace the logical development of Snow's essay. Is the logical development of an idea ultimately dependent on the precision of the language used to express it? To what extent does Snow's idea have a validity outside his expression of it?

BUSH

1. Explain the harmony of science and faith during the Medieval period and Renaissance. How was superstition explained according to this harmonious relationship? How were supernatural phenomena explained according to this harmony?

2. Why was the Aristotelian-Ptolemaic system of the universe more reassuring and appealing to Renaissance man than was the Copernican system?

WILLEY ON MILTON

1. How do the aims and methods of science differ from those of metaphysics? In what way, therefore, did Galileo "differ" from Aquinas?

2. How did Galileo's principle of inertia conflict with and help dispense with the scholastic theory of corruptibility and incorruptibility in the heavens?

3. Milton begins by stating that his epic poem will "justify the ways of God to man"; that is, it will show how a divine order exists beyond the limited comprehension of man. In what ways are Satan's self-justifications in direct opposition to the stated aims of the poem? For example, according to Satan, what should be the center of power in the universe?

4. The scientific phenomena in Book VI are explained to Adam as part of a vast ordered universe in which Adam has an honored and prominent place as a human being. What would be Adam's role in such a universe as compared with the role Satan assigns for himself?

5. Elaborate on Willey's statement that Milton "could draw images and fables which were not only 'poetic' but also 'true.'" How is this another way of saying that Milton was able to synthesize literature and science in *Paradise Lost?*

NICOLSON ON KEPLER, HARVEY, AND DONNE

1. How did "The Circle of Perfection," from the middle ages to the seventeenth century, unify science, philosophy, and morality?

2. In what way does Kepler stand midway between the medieval and modern attitude toward science and its quest for knowledge? In what way does Harvey come closer to the modern attitude toward knowl-

edge than to the medieval? Where does Gilbert stand according to the two attitudes?

3. In what ways are Harvey and Gilbert considered as mechanists? In what ways are they "modern scientists"?

4. Does Donne come to a real reconciliation of the new findings of science and orthodox Christianity in *An Anatomy of the World?* Explain.

CRUM ON BLAKE, POPE, AND SWIFT

1. Illustrate from Blake's poetry and Crum's essay how scientific knowledge differed for Blake from poetic knowledge?

2. From Crum's essay and from an analysis of "Introduction to Songs of Experience," what do you think Blake felt about the role of the poet in society?

3. Many of Pope's lines have a familiar ring because they have been often quoted—sometimes as apt phrases in support of dubious conclusions. One of the most frequently quoted phrases is the line—"Whatever is, is right." Considering this line in light of the Pope selections as a whole, what seems to be a proper interpretation of it?

4. Swift's narrator Gulliver, describing fantastic events in a matter-of-fact tone, makes us see these events as extremely ridiculous. Analyze two or three incidents to explain how their ridiculousness amounts to a serious criticism of some form of human behavior. To what extent is science or an aspect of science being criticised through ridicule?

5. Compare the attitudes of Pope and Swift toward science in *An Essay on Man* and "A Voyage to Laputa." Do Swift's criticisms of science reflect a basic philosophical disagreement with Pope?

DE SELINCOURT

1. Could you attribute the doubt and conflict in Matthew Arnold's essay "Science and Literature" to the ideas of Darwin and Lyell?

2. In what way did Tennyson's interest in and knowledge of science, especially natural science, eventually lead him to reject science as the source of ultimate truth? How does he compare to Donne in this respect? To Milton?

3. What, according to De Selincourt, should be the implications of Darwinism for twentieth century literature?

EVANS ON WORDSWORTH

1. Evans says that Whitehead (a philosopher of science) was unhappy with Wordsworth's phrase (from "The Tables Turned")—"We murder to dissect." How might the implications of this phrase be taken as hostile to science?

2. Evans' comment on the phrase "We murder to dissect" is that its meaning or "mood is clear if the poem is read as a whole." What does the poem say about detailed and exact, or "scientific" knowledge as opposed to other kinds of knowledge?

3. Of all the sciences, why did mathematics particularly attract Wordsworth?

4. Wordsworth, unlike Blake, believed that science and art are

not irreconcilable or antipathetic. How does Wordsworth propose to synthesize science and art in the *Preface to Lyrical Ballads* and the selection in this anthology from *The Prelude?*

5. In the poems "The Tables Turned" and "Tintern Abbey," what relationship is implied between man and the natural world around him?

BUCKLEY ON TENNYSON

1. How are the concepts of order, continuity, and aesthetics in Tennyson's poetry related to his concept of God?

2. How is Tennyson's attitude towards science related to his concept of God? How did he react to the position of men like William Paley (*Natural Theology*, 1802), who saw the design of God in the adaptations of animal organs to function and to environment?

3. Compare Tennyson's attitudes towards science and art to Blake's and Wordsworth's.

DAVIDSON ON POE

1. From an examination of *Eureka,* what evidence can you find for Davidson's statements about Poe's methods of reasoning? To what extent is Poe's method inductive? To what extent is it the deductive method of science?

2. In his critical essay, *The Philosophy of Composition,* Poe suggests the psychological role that horror plays in his aesthetics and philosophy:

"Regarding, then, Beauty, as my province, my next question referred to the *tone* of its highest manifestation—and all experience has shown that this tone is one of *sadness.* Beauty of whatever kind, in its supreme development, invariably excites the sensitive soul to tears. Melancholy is thus the most legitimate of all the poetical tones.".

Through what elements of "Annabel Lee" has Poe exploited psychological insights in order to develop a sense of "Beauty." For example, how does the fairy-tale background evoke a sense of beauty as well as horror? How does Poe prepare the reader for the climax of horror at the end of the poem?

3. Compare Poe's method of unifying science and art with Wordsworth's. To what extent do they both use psychological insights to unify science and art? If they both use psychology for this purpose, why is the element of "horror" more prominent in Poe than in Wordsworth?

4. Compare Poe's attitude toward science as a religion with Hawthorne's as treated in Heilman's essay.

HEILMAN ON HAWTHORNE

1. Heilman shows that Aylmer is the scientist who tries for an impossible perfection and fails. Is it necessary to believe that this failing of Aylmer's is exclusively a scientific failing? What evidence can you find to prove that Aylmer's is a more general human failing? To what extent might Hawthorne feel these failings are shared by an ambitious artist?

2. Heilman interprets "The Birthmark" through a detailed analysis. He shows how Hawthorne uses carefully chosen words to evoke images

and emotions that direct the reader, emotionally as well as intellectually, to certain conclusions. Attempt a detailed analysis of your own on "The Birthmark." For example, what does the birthmark symbolize for Aylmer? How does Hawthorne invite the reader to enlarge the meaning of the birthmark beyond Aylmer's concept of it?

TWAIN

1. Wordsworth claimed that the creative writer would be able to give science "a form of flesh and blood"; that is, make the implications of scientific concepts real and vivid in human terms. To what extent has Twain done this? What has Twain done with the scientific discovery that various species on earth have become extinct, while others have evolved to a "higher" level? To what extent does Twain's tale build a lesson in humility from the scientific theory of evolution?

2. How does Twain use humor, ridicule, and satire to build his lesson in humility?

3. Davidson describes Twain's "naturalism" as a belief that "man is . . . lodged in a universe of evil." How does the tale illustrate Twain's belief in an inescapable evil built into the scheme of the universe?

WHITMAN

1. Davidson, while describing Poe's difficulty in reconciling fact and feeling, mentions Whitman's approach to the same difficulty:

"There were several possible solutions to the fear that there is an un-bridgeable gap between mind and reality, between art and world. One was to posit that the human mind is somehow, mysteriously even, a part of the universal mind. On this point Whitman fixed all his thought and his poetic career." (244-5)

Consider "On the Beach at Night" in light of this statement. How does the poem connect the scientific reality of the stars with the emotion present in the watchers and in the speaker of the poem? Does the connection in any way justify the statement that Whitman has made the human mind "a part of the universal mind"?

2. According to Crum's analysis, Blake felt that a description that is merely "scientific" and mechanically factual represents only a small part of reality as perceived by the human mind. To what extent do Whitman's descriptions reveal meanings beyond the merely factual level?

WAGGONER ON FROST

1. How is Frost's philosophy related to his attitude towards science?

2. From Frost's poetry, can you discover his concept of faith? In what ways is this faith a religious faith?

3. What is the conflict between religious faith and science in Frost's poetry?

4. What is the function of humor in Frost's poetry?

301

THEME TOPICS

1. From an examination of Ulysses' speech in *Troilus and Cressida*, describe Shakespeare's concept of harmony in the universe.

2. How does Shakespeare reveal a growing skepticism toward medieval concepts of harmony in his great plays? Examine *Julius Caesar, Hamlet, King Lear, The Tempest,* or *Antony and Cleopatra.* Can you find his skepticism allied to the new discoveries in science?

3. Show from the play *Doctor Faustus* that Marlow illustrates "a disturbed orthodoxy just on the eve of the new scientific developments."

4. Show the influence of Kepler's astronomy on Milton in *Paradise Lost.* (Consult especially J. H. Adamson's brief essay, "Kepler and Milton," in *Modern Language Notes,* December 1959).

5. Show the influence of Galileo's discoveries on Milton. Why did Milton describe a Ptolemaic system of the universe in *Paradise Lost* when he knew of Copernicus' discoveries and knew that they had been validated by Galileo? (Consult especially Marjorie Hope Nicolson's *Science and Imagination,* Chapter IV, "Milton and the Telescope.")

6. Show how the discovery of the telescope and the microscope influenced the literary imagination in the 17th and 18th centuries. (Consult especially Marjorie Hope Nicolson's *Science and Imagination,* Chapters I, VI.)

7. What was the influence of Newtonian physics on Voltaire and Diderot? (Consult the chapter on the French Enlightenment in Crum's book, *Scientific Thought in Poetry,* the chapter following that reprinted in this collection.)

8. In *Candide,* how does Voltaire—through irony and satire directed at the character of Pangloss—show the implications of Newtonian physics for man? Can you find any evidence in the book that Voltaire was himself bound by belief in Newtonian physics?

9. Read "The Age of Reason" by Thomas Paine and Franklin's "Autobiography." If they were both influenced by Newtonian physics, to what extent were they influenced by different facets of it?

10. Make a further examination of Blake's sense of the division between science and art in *The Four Zoas* and in *Jerusalem.*

11. Examine Newton's religious views in the *Principia* and compare them to Blake's.

12. To what extent is Wordsworth's attitude toward science different in his first version of *The Prelude* (1805) from that in his final form in 1850? Can you find biographical detail to illuminate the differences?

13. Trace scientific imagery in Shelley's "Ode to the West Wind." Does

Shelley put "flesh and blood" on science as Wordsworth (in *Preface to Lyrical Ballads*) says it is the poet's duty to do?

14. Describe the cosmos that Shelley presents in *Prometheus Unbound.* To what extent is Shelley describing the structure of the physical world? To what extent is he describing the structure of the social world?

15. Describe Tennyson's attitude toward poetry in "The Lotus Eaters," "The Palace of Art," and "The Lady of Shallot." Why is Tennyson dissatisfied with poetry in these poems?

16. What is the relationship between science and political action in Tennyson's "Maud," "Locksley Hall," and "Locksley Hall Sixty Years After"?

17. In Poe's only novel, *Arthur Gordon Pym,* the same plot incident is repeated in different circumstances and with increasingly morbid implications. How does this repetition lead to an understanding of the end of the book? How does it reveal as its basic theme what Edward H. Davidson calls "the cheating deceptiveness of reality"?

18. To what extent do Poe's deductive, scientific attitudes toward art in "The Philosophy of Composition" contradict his attitudes toward science and art in *Eureka?*

19. To what extent do the narrators in "The Fall of the House of Usher" and "Ligeia" confuse fantasy with reality? What evidence can you find to show that this fantasy symbolizes the interior state of the narrator's mind?

20. Compare Hawthorne's treatment of the scientist in "The Birthmark," "Dr. Heiddegger's Experiment," "Rappaccini's Daughter." Compare also the character of Chillingworth in *The Scarlet Letter.*

21. Compare Hawthorne's treatment of the artist in "The Artist of the Beautiful," *The Marble Faun,* and *The Blithedale Romance.* What potential salvation does the artist possess?

22. Compare Whitman's *Preface to Leaves of Grass* (1855) with Wordsworth's *Preface to Lyrical Ballads* (1802). To what extent did they agree on the value of science to the poet?

23. Compare the attitudes towards science of Whitman and Emerson. How did the philosophical tenets that Emerson held prevent him from embracing science and technology with the lack of restraint that Whitman showed?

24. How does Twain apply Darwinism to society in *Pudd'n Head Wilson?* To what extent is the ironic reversal of the white and negro boys in society due to a social caste system as rigid as the evolutionary system?

25. Trace the influence of Darwinism in Hardy's *Jude the Obscure, Return of the Native,* or Samuel Butler's *The Way of All Flesh.*

26. By citing evidence from the early, middle, and later poetry, show how Frost, like Emerson, "tried to soften the fall from Christian supernaturalism to scientific naturalism."

27. In the *Education of Henry Adams,* read the chapter "The Dynamo and the Virgin." Explain the symbolism of the dynamo, the cross, and the virgin.

28. Describe Dreiser's concept of social Darwinism in *Sister Carrie*. How does Drieser trace the evolution of Carrie through dramatic props such as clothes and places of residence? How does the insect and flower imagery reveal his concept of social Darwinism?

29. Consider how T. S. Eliot in *The Four Quartets* has assimilated orthodox Christianity with modern science. To what extent has Einstein's theory of relativity enabled him to synthesize the two?

30. Trace Eliot's struggle with a faith in God from *The Wasteland,* and *Ash Wednesday* through the *Four Quartets.* What influence did science have on his initial loss of faith? What role did science play in his renewed faith?

31. What new freedoms does James Joyce feel science has allowed the artist of modern times in *Portrait of the Artist?* To what extent does Joyce reconcile empirical science with classical thought in *Portrait of the Artist?*

BIBLIOGRAPHIES

THE TWO CULTURES—ARTICLES

Barzun, Jacques, "The Ivory Tab" from *Teacher in America*, Little, Brown, 1944.

Blicksberg, C.D., "Literature and Science: a Study in Conflict," *Science Monthly*, 59: 467-72, December 1944.

Burroughs, John, "Science and Literature" from *Indoor Studies*, Houghton Mifflin; reprinted in Gardner's *Great Essays in Science*.

Grimaldi, William, S.J., "Science or Literature as a New Humanism," *Catholic World*, September 1962.

Halford, Ralph S., "Sculptors, Scabblers, Scientists and Satellites" *Columbia University Forum*, Vol. I, No. 2, Spring 1958; reprinted in Obler's *Mirrors of Man*.

Krutch, Joseph Wood, "The Colloid and the Crystal" from *The Best of Two Worlds*, 1950; reprinted in Gardner's *Great Essays in Science* (paperback).

Plank, R., "Lighter Than Air, but Heavy as Hate; an Essay in Space Travel" (in fiction), *Partisan Review*, 24: 106-16, Winter 1957.

Salomon, Louis B., "How Impractical Are the Humanities?" *American Association of University Professors Bulletin*, Vol. 41, No. 2, Spring 1955; reprinted in Obler's *Mirrors of Man*.

Santayana, George, "Understanding, Imagination, and Mysticism" from *Interpretations of Poetry and Religion*, Scribners.

Walton, M. and Weiss, T., "Science and Poetry: a Symposium," *Review of Metaphysics* (Dec. 1961), Vol. 15, 236-255.

Wolfle, D., "Science in the Liberal Arts" *American Scholar*, 28: 203-9, Spring 1959.

THE TWO CULTURES—COMPLETE WORKS

Bronowski, J., *Science and Human Values*, New York: Harper, 1959.

Bryan, W. L., *Wars of Families of Minds*, New Haven: Yale University Press, 1940.

Hook, Sidney, ed., *Determinism and Freedom in the Age of Modern Science*, New York: Collier, 1961.

Jeffares, Alexander, *Language, Literature, and Science*, Cambridge: Leeds University Press, 1959.

Standen, Anthony, *Science Is a Sacred Cow*, E. P. Dutton, 1950.

Zirkle, Conway, *Evolution, Marxian Biology, and the Social Scene*, Philadelphia: University of Pennsylvania Press, 1959.

READINGS IN SCIENCE—ARTICLES

Butterfield, Herbert, "The Scientific Revolution" (On the interaction of science and technology from the Renaissance to the present), *Scientific American* (Sept. 1960), Vol. 203, No. 3, 173-192.

STUDY AIDS

Christianson, John, "The Celestial Palace of Tycho Brahe" (On an island near Copenhagen the great astronomer built a fantastic observatory), *Scientific American* (Feb. 1961), Vol. 204, No. 2, 118-130 (Illus.).

Coulson, Charles A., "The Age of the Universe," by permission of the author; reprinted in Kane and Peters, *Writing Prose,* Oxford U. P., 1959.

Darwin, Charles, *Origin of the Species;* "Conclusion" and "The Survival of the Fittest."

Dingle, Herbert, "Copernicus and the Planet" from *The History of Science, Origins and Results of the Scientific Revolution, a Symposium,* 1951.

Eddington, Arthur S., *The Nature of the Physical World,* Cambridge University Press, 1928.

Eiseley, Loren C., "Is Man Here to Stay?," *Scientific American,* Vol. 183, No. 5, November 1950.

Gamow, George, "Galaxies in Flight" from *Scientific American Reader,* Simon and Schuster, 1953.

Hoyle, Fred, "The Origin of the Earth and the Planets" from *The Nature of the Universe,* Harper and Brothers, 1950.

Meserve, Walter J., "Man as Scientist," *The American Scientist,* Vol. 47, No. 3, June 1959, 222-232; reprinted in Obler's *Mirrors of Man.*

Oppenheimer, J. Robert, "Physics in the Contemporary World" from Dr. J. Robert Oppenheimer and the A. D. Little Lecture Committee; reprinted in Gardner's *Great Essays in Science.*

Quine, W. V., "Paradox" (self-contradictory statements can strike at the foundations of logic or mathematics), *Scientific American,* (April 1962), Vol. 206, No. 4, 84-99.

Shapely, Harlow, "Some Music from the Spheres," *American Scholar,* Vol. 82, No. 2, Spring 1959.

Simpson, G. G., "Reappraisals; Lamarck, Darwin, and Butler: Three Approaches to Evolution," *American Scholar,* 30: 238-49, Spring 1961.

Stehling, Kurt R., "Time Dilation in Space Travel," *Space Aeronautics* (May 1959).

Sullivan, J. W. N., "The Reason for Science" from *The Limitations of Science,* Viking, 1933.

Whipple, Fred, "The Dust Cloud Hypothesis" from *Scientific American Reader,* Simon and Schuster, 1953.

READINGS IN SCIENCE—COMPLETE WORKS

Andrade, E. N., da C., *Sir Isaac Newton: His Life and Work,* Garden City: Doubleday.

Barnett, Lincoln, *The Universe of Doctor Einstein.*

Burtt, E. A., *The Metaphysical Foundations of Modern Physical Science* (Rev. ed., 1932) New York: Humanities Press, 1932.

Butterfield, Herbert, *The Origin of Modern Science 1300-1800,* (new ed.) New York: Macmillan, 1961.

Caspar, Max, *Kepler,* New York: Collier, 1962.

Crombie, A. C., *Medieval and Early Modern Science,* 2 Vols. (rev. ed.) Garden City: Doubleday, 1959.

Dampier, William C., and Margaret Dampier, *Readings in the Literature of Science*, New York: Harpers, 1959.

Downs, Robert B., *Books That Changed the World*, New York: Mentor.

Fermi, Laura and Gilberto Bernandini, *Galileo and the Scientific Revolution*, New York: Basic Books, 1961.

Frank, Philipp, *Modern Science and Its Philosophy*, New York: Collier, 1961.

Koestler, Arthur, *The Watershed: A Biography of Johannes Kepler*, Garden City: Doubleday.

Landau, L. D., and G. B. Rumer, *What is Relativity?*, New York: Basic Books, 1959.

Mason, Stephen F., *A History of the Sciences* (rev. ed.), New York: Colliers, 1962.

Neugebauer, O., *The Exact Sciences in Antiquity*, (2nd ed., 1957), New York: Harper, 1962.

Pachter, Henry M., *Paracelsus: Magic Into Science*, New York: Collier, 1961.

Palter, Robert M., ed., *Toward Modern Science;* Vol. I (Studies in Ancient and Medieval Science); Vol. II (Renaissance Science and the Transition to Modern Science), New York: Noonday Press, 1961.

Pledge, H. T., *Science Since 1500*, New York: Harper, 1959.

Russell, John, *Science and Metaphysics*, New York: Sheed and Ward, 1958.

Sarton, George, *Ancient Science and Modern Civilization*, New York: Harper, 1959.

Santillana, Georgio de, *The Crime of Galileo*, Chicago: University of Chicago Press, 1955.

Simpson, George Gaylord, *Charles Darwin's Autobiography*, intro. by G. G. Simpson, New York: Collier.

Smith, Vincent E., *The General Science of Nature*, Milwaukee, 1958. Thomas Aquinas' general physical theory.

Weisheipl, James A., *The Development of Physical Theory in the Middle Ages*, New York: Sheed and Ward, 1959.

Wolf, A., *A History of Science, Technology, and Philosophy in the 16th and 17 Centuries*, 2 Vol., New York: Harper, 1959.

Wolf, A., *A History of Science, Technology, and Philosophy in the 18th Century*, 2 Vols. New York: Harper, 1961.

INTERRELATION OF SCIENCE AND LITERATURE—ARTICLES

Clark, H. H. "The Influence of Science on American Ideas 1775-1809," *Transcription of the Wisconsin Academy of Science, Arts, and Letters*, XXXV (1943), 305-349.

Hill, H. L. Jr., "Mark Twain's Brace of Brief Lectures on Science" (with text), *New England Quarterly*, 34: 228-39, June 1961.

Hirsch, W., "Image of the Scientist in Science Fiction: a Content Analysis" (bibliog., illus.), *American Journal of Sociology*, 63: 506-12, March 1958.

Hoagland, Clayton, "The Universe of Eureka: A Comparison of the

Theories of Eddington and Poe," *Southern Literary Messenger*, I (May, 1939), 307-313.

Hornberger, Theodore, "The Effect of the New Science on the Thought of Jonathan Edwards," *American Literature*, 9: 196-207, May 1937.

Hornberger, Theodore, "Puritanism and Science: The Relationship Revealed in the Writing of John Cotton," *New England Quarterly* (Summer, 1937).

Hornberger, Theodore, "Science and the New World," *Catalogue* of the Huntington Library, 1937, pp. 3-18.

International Federation for Modern Languages and Literatures, (subtitle: *Literature and Science*), Proceedings of the Sixth Triennial Congress, Oxford: Basil Blackwell, 1954. Note articles by Temple, Briggs, Johnson, Parker, Legge, David and Peacock; especially note articles by Dingle, Crombie, Shackleton, and Pettit.

Jones, A. E. Jr., "Darwinism and Its Relationship to Realism and Naturalism in American Fiction 1860-1890," *Drew University Bulletin*, 38: 1-21, December 1950.

Lowenberg, B. J. "The Controversy over Evolution in New England 1859-1873," *New England Quarterly*, VIII (December, 1935) 555-561.

Pearson, Norman, "The American Poet in Relation to Science," *American Quarterly*, 1:116-26, Summer 1949.

Ringe, D. A., "William Cullen Bryant and the Science of Geology," *American Literature*, 26: 507-14, January 1955.

Scott, F. S., "Seventh Sphere: a Note on Troilus and Criseyde" (method of Chaucer's day to number the sphere's outwards from the earth), bibliog., *Modern Language Review*, 51: 2-5, January 1956.

Simpson, H. C., "The Vogue of Science in English Literature 1600-1800," *Univ. of Toronto Quarterly*, 2: 143-67, 1933.

Wasserman, E. R., "Dryden's Epistle to Charleton," *Journal of English and German Philology*, 55: 201-12, April 1956.

Weaver, Warren, "Lewis Carroll: Mathematician," *Scientific American*, Vol. 194, No. 4 (April 1956).

Wilson, W. G., "Francis Thompson's Outlook on Science," *Contemporary Review*, 192: 263-6, November 1957.

INTERRELATION OF SCIENCE AND LITERATURE
—COMPLETE WORKS

Beaver, Joseph, *Walt Whitman, Poet of Science*, Columbia University Press, 1951.

Buchanan, Scott, *Poetry and Mathematics*, New York: The John Day Company, 1929.

Bush, Douglas, *Science and English Poetry: a Historical Sketch 1590-1950*, Oxford University Press, 1950.

Cassidy, Harold G., *The Sciences and the Arts: a New Alliance*, Harper and Brothers, 1962.

Crum, Ralph, *Scientific Thought in Poetry*, Columbia University Press, 1931.

Day-Lewis, Cecil, *The Poet's Way of Knowledge*, Cambridge: Cambridge University Press, 1957.

Dowden, Edward, *Studies in Literature 1789-1877,* (Chapter 3) London; Paul, Trench, 1882, 1909.

Drachman, Julian, *Studies in the Literature of Natural Science,* New York: Macmillan, 1930.

Dudley, Fred Adair, *et al. The Relations of Literature and Science: A Selected Bibliography 1930-1949,* Pullman: State College of Washington, 1949.

Eastman, Max, *The Literary Mind: Its Place in an Age of Science,* New York: Scribners, 1931.

Evans, B. Ifor, *Literature and Science,* Humanities Press.

Foerster, Norman, *The American Scholar: A Study in "Litterae Inhumaniores."* Chapel Hill: University of North Carolina Press, 1929.

Grabo, Carl, *A Newton Among Poets: Shelley's Use of Science in Prometheus Unbound,* Chapel Hill: University of North Carolina Press, 1930.

Henkin, Leo, *Darwinism in the English Novel 1860-1910,* New York: Corporate Press, 1940.

Johnson, Francis, *Astronomical Thought in Renaissance England: A Study of English Scientific Writings from 1500-1645.* Baltimore: Johns Hopkins Press, 1937.

Levy, Hyman and Spalding, Helen, *Literature for an Age of Science,* London: Methuen, 1952.

Libby, Margaret, *The Attitude of Voltaire to Magic and the Sciences,* London: King, 1935.

Mohr, Jennie, *A Study of Popular Books on the Physical Sciences,* New York: Columbia University (thesis), 1942.

Nicolson, Majorie Hope, *The Breaking of the Circle,* Columbia University Press, Revised, 1960.

Nicolson, Marjorie Hope, *Newton Demands the Muse,* Princeton: Princeton University Press, 1946.

Nicolson, Marjorie, *Science and the Imagination,* Cornell University Press (Great Seal Books).

O'Brien, E. J. H., *The Dance of the Machines:* the American Short Story and the Industrial Age, New York: Macanday, 1929.

Pollack, T. C., *The Nature of Literature: Its Relation to Science, Language and Human Experience,* Princeton: Princeton University Press, 1942.

Rhys, H. H., ed., *Seventeenth Century Science and the Arts,* Princeton University Press, 1961.

Richards, I. A., *Science and Poetry.*

Roberts, Michael, *The Modern Mind,* London: Faber, 1937.

Sewell, Elizabeth, *The Orphic Voice: Poetry and Natural History,* New Haven: Yale University Press, 1960.

Stevenson, Lionel, *Darwin Among the Poets,* Chicago: University of Chicago Press, 1932.

Tate, Allen, *On the Limits of Poetry.*

Todd, Ruthven, *Tracks in the Snow: Studies in English Science and Art,* New York: Scribners, 1947.

Waggoner, Hyatt Howe, *The Heel of Elohim: Science and Its Values in Modern American Poetry,* University of Oklahoma Press, 1950.

STUDY AIDS

Willey, Basil, *The Seventeenth Century Background,* Garden City: Doubleday, 1953.

Wood, Herbert G., *Thought, Life, and Time as Reflected in Science and Poetry,* Cambridge: Cambridge University Press, 1957.

ANTHOLOGIES

Gardner, Martin, ed., *Great Essays in Science,* Pocketbooks Inc., 1957.

Hampshire, Stuart, *The Age of Reason: The 17th Century Philosophers,* New York: Mentor, 1956.

McColley, Grant, *Literature and Science: An Anthology from English and American Literature, 1600-1900,* Chicago: Packard, 1940.

Obler, Paul C., ed., *Mirrors of Man,* American Book Company (New York), 1962.

Satin, Joseph, ed., *Ideas in Context,* Houghton Mifflin, 1958.

Santillana, Georgio de, *The Age of Adventure: The Renaissance Philosophers,* New York: Mentor, 1956.